Helping Children Cope with Separation and Loss

CLAUDIA JEWETT JARRATT

**REVISED
EDITION**

THE HARVARD COMMON PRESS

BOSTON, MASSACHUSETTS

*To the Giver of Health,
who provides for the return
of love, hope, joy, and meaning;
to Fran, whose dying began it all;
and to Bob, just because.*

❧

The Harvard Common Press
535 Albany Street
Boston, Massachusetts 02118

Printed in the United States of America.

Library of Congress Cataloging in Publication Data

Jarratt, Claudia Jewett, 1939–
    Helping children cope with separation and loss / Claudia
Jewett Jarratt. — [Rev. ed.]
        p. cm.
    Includes bibliographical references and index.
    ISBN 1-55832-052-0 (cloth). — ISBN 1-55832-051-2 (paper).
    1. Grief in children. 2. Separation (Psychology) in
children. 3. Loss (Psychology) in children. 4. Children—
Counseling of.
    I. Title.
    BF723.G75J48   1994
    155.9'37'083—dc20   93-33178
                                                          CIP

Interior design by Joyce C. Weston
Cover design by Paul Bacon

10   9   8   7   6   5

CONTENTS

CONTENTS

5
Responding to Problems of Self-Esteem and Control   143
Understanding and easing displacement reaction • Responding to scarcity behaviors • Reducing shame • Reworking self-blame • Helping children understand their personal histories • Understanding and working with control issues

6
Looking Back, Letting Go, and Moving On   199
Reviewing, reworking, and releasing • Ending the work

INTRODUCTION: WHO THIS
BOOK IS FOR

❧

Any adult who is involved with children, whether caregiver or professional, may need at some point to help a grieving child. Census statistics document that over a quarter of all children in this country under the age of eighteen live with only one of their parents (Rawlings 1993). Almost every child will experience the death of a significant other—pet, friend, or relative. In an average-size school, a child will die about every three to four years, affecting the lives of the child's friends, schoolmates, teachers, and family (Linn 1980, 13).

Parents are particularly likely to be anxious when their children experience separation and loss, especially if they themselves are devastated by grief and pain. At school, teachers and other personnel must find ways to cope with children whose behavior and performance suffer drastic changes following loss. Doctors and nurses need to be alert to the physiological connections between grief and physical changes such as hyperactivity, serious lethargy, increased susceptibility to colds and flu. Therapists, ministers, social workers, and other counselors all need techniques to help children understand and accept what has happened as well as to guide caregivers as to how best to respond appropriately to grieving children. Close neighbors, relatives, or friends of the family often want to help; they, too, need to understand better how to support a child during a time of grief.

Children's immediate reactions to loss and their responses to the challenges that follow it are striking: fears for personal survival;

separation anxiety; impaired ability to make emotional attachments; sadness, anger, guilt, shame, depression, and despair; problems with control issues; diminished developmental energy; loss of
self-esteem; ongoing pessimism and feelings of futility are all normal in grieving children. Many believe that childhood bereavement and the consequent changes within children and their social
and familial circles can create severe emotional and behavioral
challenges that last well into adult life. Growing evidence links
childhood loss with depression, alcoholism, anxiety, and suicidal
tendencies in adolescence and adulthood.

Clearly, adults who care about children can benefit from learning how to recognize and work with grief. But partly because of the
paucity of training in grief work with children, even professionals
may not understand that much of the difficult behavior the child
displays can be directly connected to grief or that appropriate support can help the child replace troubling behaviors with more constructive expressions of inner turmoil. Many children are denied
help after a loss because those around them discount the severity
of its effect on them. Or they receive help only at the beginning of
the grief process, leaving them to meet the subsequent challenges
alone. Sometimes children themselves are reluctant to talk to their
caregivers about a shared loss for fear of creating more pain. It is no
wonder that children are sometimes called "the forgotten
mourners."

Even when a child is given good support over a long period of
time, it appears that losses and separations may leave vulnerabili-
ties that can be retriggered by new developmental tasks, new relationships or achievements, or any of the changes that come to people in the course of their lives. Loss is a cumulative experience;
unless the child is helped to resolve a major loss, even trivial subsequent losses are likely to provoke intense stresses and reactions.
Still, research finds that children who are given high-quality care
by available family members during the mourning period or who
are effectively helped by alternate caregivers or other helpers experience less distress and perhaps fewer long-lasting repercussions
(Garmezy 1983).

Until the first edition of this book, there were almost no guidelines to follow nor methods advanced as to how to help children manage grief constructively. This book presents practical advice for those concerned with helping children through the recovery process. It identifies specific behaviors one can expect in a child who has suffered a loss, showing when and how these behaviors may arise, discussing those that may immediately follow a loss and those that may appear or recur years later, and offering clear suggestions on how concerned adults might best respond. The original techniques and descriptions of simple props that were the mainstay of the first edition of this book have been expanded as an outgrowth of my continuing work as a child and family therapist. The theoretical underpinnings that helped previous readers clarify what to look for and how to respond have been refined and enlarged as well. Parents, primary caregivers, and other helping adults—therapists, school counselors, teachers, day-care providers, doctors, nurses, ministers, friends, or relatives—will find plentiful descriptions of practical methods for helping children through the strong feelings, difficult behavior, and confusion that follow a loss.

Because the first problem is usually how to tell the child about the loss, the book begins with a general discussion of how to convey the news and support the child, followed by a chapter offering suggestions on how to tell children about specific losses. The next chapter traces the normal progression of grief, and chapters 4 and 5 discuss ways to help children who appear stuck at various points in the grief process to work through their problems. The final chapter deals with letting go and moving on. Examples and dialogues taken from a wide variety of situations are used to demonstrate how children can be supported as they weather the challenges and stress of acute grief, move through the subsequent adjustments and reactions, and become more able to get on with a healthy, functional life.

We assume a crucial task when we seek to help mourning children. Our success depends on our willingness to offer support during a troubled and baffling time. The methods this book describes can make this task clearer and easier. The challenge is great, but the rewards are greater, for these methods offer the promise of health and full, rich lives for the children you know and care about.

TELLING CHILDREN
ABOUT LOSS

❦

1

Greg has spent summers with his grandma and grandpa since he was quite young. He and his grandpa have always been very close, sharing jokes, rooting for rival baseball teams, and going fishing together as often as possible. Just as school is ending for the year, Greg's grandfather dies of a sudden heart attack. Greg must be told. His stricken parents not only must help their son come to grips with the death of his beloved grandfather but must also deal with the funeral arrangements and quickly make other plans for the summer.

Lisa Disaro stands at her bedroom window, listening to the muted sounds of her children at play outside, as tears stream down her cheeks. Though she and their father have struggled to work things out, they have decided that one of them must leave. Lisa feels overwhelmed and vulnerable. Her children must be told but the telling seems unbearable. She wishes time would just stop.

Gwenn Pettiway placed Tabor, who has lived with a series of caretakers, in the Tucker's foster home two years ago. Though the family has tried their best to work things out with this angry, difficult child, they feel as if they are getting nowhere. They have talked again and again about their increasing frustration about the lack of change in Tabor's behavior and their worry that this placement is having a negative effect on their other children. Eventually they call to ask Gwenn to begin looking for another home for Tabor. They express two concerns: will Gwenn be responsible for telling the child that she has to move again, and can she advise them on what to expect and how they should respond?

A neighbor stops Robert as he returns home from work. "Did you hear what happened to the Johnsons? Some drunk hit them. Jackie's dead; Kendra is still in surgery." "Dear God," Robert thinks. "It could have been Caroline." He braces himself as he moves quickly to his door, wondering what he will say to his family.

The first and foremost concern of adults in these situations is likely to be how they can best soften the pain and shock of the news they must tell. They may wonder what the children can bear to know and how much they should be told. How much can children understand about such matters? When should a child be told about a loss? Who should do the telling?

Because children's sorrow often evokes deep memories and triggers strong feelings in the adults who care about them, it is not unusual for them to wonder whether it might be better not to tell the children at all or to wish that they could avoid having to talk with the children about the loss. Sometimes adults skip past the difficult areas quickly, rushing through the hard facts to focus on anticipated benefits: "Now you'll have a new family with more people to love you." "Your mother and I will be happier, and I will be able to spend more time with you because we'll have the whole weekend together." "Your grammy was really sick for a long time. It's better this way." The truth is, however, that the child may not feel it is better for him or her. Such approaches may make the telling easier for adults, but they are likely to leave children feeling confused, misunderstood, and reluctant to risk trying to talk out and resolve their upset, either because they are afraid they will irritate their caregivers or because they have decided that such conversations will prove pointless.

Adults may also try to protect children from hurt and pain by deciding to keep things as normal and pleasant as possible. Too often, those around a child facing loss act (and encourage others to act) as if nothing out of the ordinary has happened, hoping to minimize the impact of the loss. Adults may fear that a child is too young or too fragile to handle direct information. Unfortunately, such choices join family members in a conspiracy of silence that deprives children of the right to express and resolve their own grief and concerns or to check out their own observations.

John Bowlby, whose work on separation and attachment laid much of the foundation for understanding how children experience and respond to loss, believes that a child can resolve losses appropriately when:

1. The child has enjoyed a reasonably secure relationship with the person who is leaving (or is gone).
2. The child receives prompt, accurate information about what has happened and is allowed to ask all sorts of questions, which adults answer as honestly as possible, acknowledging that they do not know the answer if that is the case.
3. The child is allowed to participate in the family grieving, both publicly and privately.
4. The child has easy access to a trusted parent or other adult who can be relied upon for comfort and a continuing relationship.

WHO SHOULD TELL THE NEWS?

Because all children appear to harbor some degree of fundamental and primitive terror that something catastrophic might happen to their caregivers and that without their caregivers' protection and care they themselves might die, it is best if the news comes from the adults to whom a child feels closest—whether parents, foster parents, or other caregivers. Access to someone with whom the child shares an ongoing history of trustworthiness, concern, and involvement is an important buffer during crisis or change and reassures the child that he or she is not alone, that there are other people available to provide protection and vital caretaking.

If the loss entails the departure of a parent (whether because of a new job assignment, parental separation, serious illness, or incarceration), it is best for both parents to tell the news together, so that the child has the chance to understand that everyone is involved in what is happening and that, regardless of the change, they are still a family. If the loss is the result of parental conflict (separation or divorce), it is particularly important for each parent to take special care to avoid influencing the child's reactions and to do whatever is necessary to reduce the likelihood that the child will feel caught in the middle of a parental conflict that requires choosing a side. If it is impossible for parents to tell the child together, then they should each talk to the child as soon as can be arranged. Whatever the situation, when parents share the news, whether separately or together, they should both make it clear that their love and positive concern for the child have not diminished and that the child is not the cause of the family change.

WHEN SHOULD I TELL THE CHILD?

The best way to help children face significant changes or losses is to let them know what is happening as soon as the loss, separation, or change seems definite. When parents try to delay telling the news, they often underestimate how sensitive children are to parental preoccupation and tension. Telling a child about an impending loss not only prevents the distress and anxiety that may build as the child increasingly wonders what is wrong but also allows the child to begin to prepare for what lies ahead rather than being caught off guard. The child has a chance to start getting used to the idea, to raise questions and concerns, to participate in the adjustments parents are making, to play and replay the separation experience as a way of integrating the changes that will occur, to practice coping skills before they must be called into action, to begin to grieve. Talking about the change can promote the awareness that, though the adjustments may be hard, the child can manage both the grief and the loss: what has happened is not so awful that it cannot be faced and talked about.

There can be problems with direct prompt approaches. Imagine a mother who has only the brief time it will take someone to bring her children home from school to prepare herself to tell them that their father has suddenly died. Reeling with her own shock and bereavement, it is understandable that she might wish to postpone talking to them, to avoid seeing them, or at least to discourage their expressions of distress. It would be better, however, for her to remember that she need not hide her own pain and strong reactions as long as she makes it clear that the children are not expected to solve her problems or make her feel better. Her children will be most able to believe this if they know which adult friends and relatives will be helping her, since this is most likely to reassure them that their mother is in competent, caring, grown-up hands. If the mother subsequently joins a loss group or seeks counseling, it might be helpful for the children to be invited to meet the therapist or pastor or group leader so that they can get direct reassurance that the helper understands how important the parent is and that the helper will be available as long as help is needed.

WHAT SHOULD I DO FIRST?

Sometimes when we are responsible for helping a child with the initial impact of a loss, we feel anxious about where to begin. One way is to begin with the adult reality. "The doctors say that Mommy is very sick and that she may not be able to get well and come home to us. They think that she may die." A social worker who needs to move a child to another caregiver might say, "Your foster mom and dad are getting pretty old. They have trouble doing the things that they want to be able to do for you. We all think that it's time to get a different mom and dad to help you grow up and to take care of you." When a loss is sudden, sometimes it is impossible to prepare the child. If the loss comes with no forewarning, the facts should be conveyed in as straightforward a way as possible: "Mom and I have been having some grown-up troubles lately. We have tried to work them out together. We didn't want you to worry so we have been pretending that everything was all right. But now we can't keep our troubles with each other a secret any more." Or, "Today when your sister was riding her bike, she had an accident and died." Or a social worker might explain, "Your mom has been having a lot of grown-up worries lately. She needs time to figure out how to take care of herself and take care of you. She will be going [to the hospital, to a counselor, for help with a drug or abuse problem], and she needs us to find someone else for you to live with while she is figuring things out."

Adults may find that when they try to prepare a child for a forthcoming loss, the child may discount the information, refusing to accept that the loss will actually happen: Maybe Daddy will change his mind, the child thinks. Maybe their sibling will get better. It is not unusual for a child to believe the news only when the event has actually occurred, and even then the child may cling to a conviction that the separation will be short-lived. Some may react quite matter-of-factly and then begin to cry later, perhaps at bedtime, begging to be told again. Others casually resume their play, apparently untouched. Children may be unwilling to listen; they may urgently try to change the subject, drown the news out with chatter or noise, cover their ears, or even fall asleep. Or they may be too overwhelmed to listen and shut down or glaze over. Adults are often dismayed and confused when they try to figure out what the child has actually heard.

The more directly the knowledge of loss is conveyed, the less chance children have to become confused, to deny the truth, or to blame themselves for what is happening, which helps them become more ready to begin the internal readjustments needed to come to grips with loss. Children normally take in what they can understand or are ready to understand; what is too much or beyond them is likely to be come up later when they are older or more emotionally ready to accept it. It doesn't matter where helpers start or if they remember everything the first or second or third time. The information shared with the child does not have to be perfect. It can be corrected, expanded, rediscussed, and reapproached as adults clarify their own thinking or rethink what they have said and how they have said it. Often children will lead the way, showing what they need and when. Listen to their questions, and let them serve as guide to what the child might be thinking or needing to hear. For example, listen for emphatic all-or-nothing statements that often contain hidden questions: "You hate me!" ("Do you love me?") "Daddy never cared what happened to me!" ("Did he leave because he didn't care about me?") Be sure to follow up on statements that suggest underlying confusion. "Ryan's parents were having trouble over money, and then his father got a raise and now everything's OK," your child might say to you. "It wasn't just money that was the problem between me and Daddy," you need to point out and go on to explain the situation again, clearly.

If the child doesn't give you clear cues, initiate conversations, or ask questions about the separation or loss, then follow your instincts and bring things up when it seems appropriate to you. There are many good books for children of different ages that can help children express their own feelings and help you open up a supportive discussion. Such books also help children feel that they are not the only ones to have to struggle with these kinds of challenges. A visit with the children's librarian at your local library can be enormously helpful, and many loss-support groups have good bibliographies that will help you find books appropriate to the type of loss your child is dealing with.

Besides being approachable and frank, another important thing is to let the child know that you care and are concerned about what has happened; that you want to do your best to help; that you are willing to listen without judging how the child thinks, feels, and needs; that the child may take his or her own time reacting and adjusting to what has happened.

Understanding How Children Think

It is a little easier to tell children about loss if one understands that children take in, think about, and absorb information differently from adults and that the way they process it changes as they get older. Something that might make perfect sense to a nine-year-old could leave a five-year-old lost and confused. Devising ways to talk about things in a style tailored to a particular child's capacity for understanding may avoid significant troubles later.

Magical Thinking: The earliest stage of understanding and processing observations and discussions appears to be firmly in place in most children by about eighteen months and remains until they are around seven. Because children in this stage tend to personalize everything and believe that their own thoughts, or wishes, or actions are responsible for whatever happens to them (and to other people), their thought process is often called "magical thinking." Children at this stage typically focus primarily on the *you* part of any message. For example, an adopted child told, "Your parents couldn't take care of you," may understand this as "There was something so bad or unlovable about *me* that even my own parents couldn't manage or tolerate it." This particular misunderstanding could be avoided or eased by changing the wording, simply eliminating the word *you* and saying, "Your parents couldn't take care of *any* child at that time." (If you find it difficult to imagine how a child might react "magically" to the news you have to tell, try to remember an incident from your own childhood when you had a similar sense of unlimited power and responsibility. Many adults are familiar with the children's rhyme, "Step on a crack, break your mother's back," which is a prime example of magical thinking. Some may remember believing it, maybe taking anxious care to step over the cracks rather than to risk jeopardizing a parent. Later, some may have experimented with tentatively stepping on those same cracks and then checking to be sure that the parent was fine, that the magic hadn't worked. Still later, some of us may have discharged angry feelings by stomping deliberately and gleefully on every crack: No longer truly convinced of our power to make bad things happen, we could safely vent our frustrations or our wish to get even.)

In addition to the sense that everything happens to or because of them, children in this cognitive stage have limited life experience, so they are likely to connect unrelated things together causally. The helping adult must be very careful to avoid using euphemisms or figures of speech, especially in the case of a death. "We lost Grandpa" is all too easily absorbed by the child as literal information ("Where did you lose him, and why aren't you looking for him?"). "She has gone to her eternal rest" can make a child terrified to go to sleep at night. Remarks such as "the good die young" invite a child to link good behavior with death and accordingly to act as bad as possible. One family shared a story about a five-year-old who suddenly developed an acute fear of closets. Not only would the child not go near them, he became hysterical if his

mother did. It turned out that it wasn't the dark, or monsters hid-
ing inside, or the fear of being trapped that bothered him. Instead,
his fear stemmed from having heard that someone "came out of
the closet" and had AIDS. His reasoning convinced him that anyone who went into a closet might catch the disease, and he was
not about to take any chances.

In this stage, children also lack the ability accurately to discrimi-
nate reality from fantasy, which can compound their confusion.
The child at this age sees the world as a place of magical endings
where everyone lives happily ever after or where death and violence are casual, reversible events. The cartoons so popular with
this age group reinforce this misunderstanding. Characters are
seemingly annihilated only to reappear again and again. Sometimes children this age react quite casually to news of someone's
death because they are waiting for the person to stop "playing
dead."

Magical thinking diminishes as we grow older, but the ability or
tendency to fall back into it may never leave any of us completely.
Wishful or stricken, we may catch ourselves (and others) attribut-
ing the power to change our lives to external circumstances: "If
only I had a different job [spouse, living arrangement], my life
would be fine." "When I lose weight, I will be happier." "What if I
found a different doctor? There must be someone who knows what
to do."

The most important things to say to children who suffer a loss
at this stage are:

1. Someone [name who, preferably] will take care of you. [If it is
    not going to be you, continue . . .] It will not be me, but I will
    stay with you until [name] is here to keep you safe.
2. It was not your fault. It was not because you were bad in any
    way or because you were unlovable. There is nothing you could
    have done, or can do, to make things different.
3. It is OK for you to know about what happened, to think about
    it, and to figure it out.
4. You can have your own feelings about what has happened. You
    may feel differently from other people, even those you live

9

with. No one has the right to tell you what you feel or what you should feel.

5. You can take as much time as you need to figure things out and to have your feelings. You do not have to rush or pretend that you don't think or feel as you do.

If you don't feel comfortable giving any one of these messages, then you would probably be wise to arrange for the child to get this support from a helper who can give these permission statements objectively.

Concrete Thinking: Children move increasingly from magical to concrete thinking somewhere around age six, and concrete thinking remains their primary way of processing what they are told until they are eleven or twelve or older. In this stage, children think in absolutes such as good/bad, always/never, either/or. As they try to understand what they hear, they break down sentences into individual words, which they then translate into individual pictures. This can lead to misunderstandings even when an adult has tried to be clear and straightforward. (A Funky Winkerbean cartoon illustrates: "News bulletin: Today three armed men held up the First National Bank. Police are wondering how they could lift such a heavy building. Probably the fact that they had three arms helped.")

During this stage, there is little if any ability to deal with subtleties, ambiguities, or euphemisms. Adults must be careful not to lay land mines that may cause worries later. Think of an adopted child who has been told that money troubles caused his birth parents to give him up. Guess how that child might react to the news that a new caregiver had been laid off or fired. It is wise to remember that children grasp information most accurately and clearly when you frame what you have to tell them in terms of the senses. For example, "If you had been at court today, you would have seen the grown-ups arguing about what really happened. Then after everyone said what they thought, you would have heard the judge tell your Mama. . . ." Asking yourself, "If I made what I am saying into a literal picture, one word at a time, where might the child become

confused?" can help you avoid making statements that are mis-
leading if taken absolutely literally. It may help to note how frequently adult thought patterns and speech revert to concrete
thinking, especially in times of stress. The always/never, good/bad
scorekeeping can often be observed in situations that involve as-
signing blame, dealing with moral or religious issues, or wrangling
about politics, and it often shows up in domestic disagreements:
"You always expect me to pick up after you." "What do you mean?
I'm always happy to help." "Well, for one thing, you never wash
the dishes." "And what about you? Three times this week I've had
to remind you to put things back where they belong."

It is important to remember that, just as adults under stress may
revert to concrete thinking, so children under stress often regress
to earlier thought processes and patterns or mix different types of
thinking. Consequently, even if a child's age suggests that he or
she is in the concrete thinking stage, care should be taken to heed
the guidelines appropriate for magical thinking as well.

Helping Children Trust Themselves

Because young children get their understanding of life primarily
through their senses, tying news to a sensory or physical connection often helps them grasp it. Such an approach can also reinforce
their trust in their own powers of observation. So talk with children
about what they might have seen or heard: "When you heard us
fighting, you may have wondered what was happening and felt
worried and scared." "Today when Aunt Ruth came to get you at
school, did you guess that something bad had happened?" Beginning this way also encourages the child to think, "I am the sort of
person who can figure out what is happening." Corroborating
what the child has noticed sends one more reassuring signal that
the child is a thinking person, able to make sense of the world
and therefore able to understand significant happenings. In fact,
acknowledging that they have been aware of the adult actions or
situations that led up to the loss may help reassure them that it was
not their fault.

In some families, children are discouraged from observing, commenting on, or questioning what is going on with adults, especially

their parents. Such children may now need assurance that it is all right for them to have noticed that things were not going well. Consequently, when talking about a loss, you should deliberately relax any unwritten rules that children should not be "nosy" about the affairs of their elders and encourage your children to voice their questions and to confirm their own observations about what has been going on in the family. Remember: when a child suffers a loss, very little about what has happened is none of the child's business. A significant separation or loss definitely *is* the child's business and needs to be explained as thoroughly as possible to help avoid serious repercussions later. If the questions are too personal to handle or if the separation hinges on sexual or financial matters inappropriate for discussion with children, you might say, "That's an OK question, but I feel private about the answer, and I really don't want to talk about it."

WHAT CAN I DO TO MAKE ADJUSTMENT EASIER?

Helping Children Say Good-bye

After the news of the upcoming loss or change has been introduced and explored, children need to be given the opportunity to say whatever good-byes are involved. Having the chance to say actual thought-out good-byes to people, places, or a familiar family structure is among the most healing things a child can experience. Not only do such good-byes give the child a chance to review and acknowledge the good things that will be lost, they also allow the child an opportunity to express those feelings face to face with the others who are involved. Wishes and blessings can be exchanged, and the child can be given loving permission to have a successful, satisfying life. A thoughtful good-bye visit leaves less unfinished business to complicate the grief that follows the loss. Youngsters who do not have the chance to exchange good-byes or to receive permission to move on sometimes are more likely to sustain additional damage to their basic sense of trust and security, to their self-esteem, and to their ability to initiate and sustain strong relationships as they grow up. (See chapter 2 for more details on how these visits can be structured to do the most good for all concerned.)

Understanding Teenagers' Need to Turn to Friends for Support

When there is a serious illness or a death in the family, well-meaning adults sometimes suggest that children be sent to a friend's or relative's in order to protect them. But keeping children from their caregivers, for several hours, let alone days, during an emotionally charged time is likely to raise their anxiety much more acutely than would allowing them to remain at home. Adolescents, however, not only depend on their caregivers but also rely a great deal on the emotional support and protection of their friends. Consequently, some adolescents may ask to stay with a friend during an acute family illness or after a death. It is as if they need to withdraw to a neutral corner to recuperate from dealing with the constant pain, resentment, or helplessness that may be stimulated by being at home. In such cases, teens often prefer to spend time both at home and elsewhere, with the freedom to switch back and forth as their comfort and convenience dictate. Such arrangements are not intended to be disloyal or disrespectful to other family members, and if they do not conflict with the needs of others in the family, they can be quite helpful for grieving teens.

Supporting Memories and Maintaining Ties after Permanent Loss

Strengthening positive memories (without glossing over the negative ones) and validating past ties are thoughtful, kind things that caring adults can do for a child who has suffered a loss, even those who do not know the child intimately. "I remember your father always hung up your pictures and notes by his desk at the office. He was so proud of you."

Another way to help children following a separation or a loss is to plan and facilitate ways that enable and encourage the child to remember and to talk about the important person and places that are gone. Having access to pictures, talking about memories, and marking significant anniversaries all support the child and the validity of the child's relationship to those who have been important and are no longer as available.

On Mother's Day or Valentine's Day, or on other occasions, if the child chooses to write a letter or make a card, perhaps it can be sent directly or in care of the agency (or orphanage, if the child came from another country). When the loss is the result of a move or a leave-taking, it is useful to plan and talk about how the people involved will keep in touch: the parent who is leaving; the grandparents who no longer live close by; friends and classmates.

Children who have had neglectful or abusive relationships with their parents or are separated from their parents by circumstances such as mental illness or incarceration are often able to use visits to understand more about who their parents are without either denying or overemphasizing their particular difficulties. If there is concern about the child's safety when visiting, safeguards can be set up, and visits can be supervised.

For those children who are unable to maintain contact because the separation is final, due to death, family conflict, or a closed adoption, several things can be done. One is to continue to talk about the person who is gone and to keep pictures around, in plain sight. Adoptive parents often make it a point to talk about their child's birth parent(s) on the child's birthday. Many of them will express gratitude to those who gave their child the gift of life and a birthday. Some families make it a practice to include the birth parent in the meal blessing on that special day (and others). Increasingly, adoption allows for some ongoing exchange of information, even contact, between both sets of parents and may include visits by the birth parent with the adopted child or teen.

Children who have suffered the loss of someone close to them because of death may decide to decorate an area with pictures and other mementoes to serve as a shrine.

In one community, when a senior and the classmate he was driving home from school died in an accident, other students spontaneously hung a cross and a Star of David on the telephone pole where the crash had occurred. Several months later, students and their parents were still taking the time to update notes and add ribbons and fresh flowers.

Visits to the cemetery precipitate very different reactions in children and adolescents, and it is important that each child's needs and feelings be respected. Some youngsters seem to get a good deal of comfort from going to the cemetery to visit the grave of the person who has died. Others protest, refuse to visit, or go sullenly. Some children prefer to go alone rather than with their caregivers because they feel uncomfortable with the strong feelings that the adults express. Others want to go alone in order to have their own special, private time with the deceased. Clearly, there is no right or disrespectful reaction. Whatever the child wishes and needs to do should be supported.

Avoiding Cumulative Losses

At the time of a family loss or separation, when a child faces so many drastic changes, it is wise to try to maintain as much of the familiar daily routine as possible. Following the usual rules and expectations will give the child a sense of reassuring continuity and regularity. Children may want to know who will empty the rubbish or do the laundry now. Such questions stem from a basic need for reassurance that life will go on and that things (and people) will continue to be taken care of even in the current chaos of grief and change. If Friday night has been pizza night, then the sooner Friday night becomes pizza night again the better.

Following a parental death or separation, children are apt to suffer multiple losses. The primary caregiver may need to begin to work outside the home or to work longer hours. Changes in financial arrangements may cause surviving or separating parents, custodial or noncustodial, to move. The family's standard of living may drop, making it necessary to eliminate the extras that had been part of the familiar pattern of life.

Children who lose a sibling suffer massive changes. They may become only children; they may become the oldest and feel an extra burden of responsibility as a result. They have lost a playmate, companion, and rival, and all the familiar interactions and expectations that were connected to those relationships.

When a custodial parent remarries, there is often a move to a new home, school, or neighborhood for at least one set of children in a blended family. The child may have to get used to sharing a parent not only with the new spouse but also with the spouse's children. Or the child may see a beloved brother or sister being drawn into a tight friendship with a new stepsibling. Or lose a customary role as the oldest, the only girl, the youngest, the most capable. An only child may have to adjust to being one of a crowd. If the child has been used to being treated as an equal by a parent during the years between marriages, it may be a rude, unwelcome shock to be relegated to the status of a child again.

When a child moves into a new family, everything changes: the way the light comes through the window as the child goes to sleep or wakes up, the smells and sounds of the house, the colors and furniture the child sees, the food the child eats, parental expectations, routine, and tempo of daily living. It is much like being in an unfamiliar country: Nothing is the same.

It is believed that young children between one and five years of age may fear an immediate threat to their security more than they grieve over an actual loss (in part because they still believe the loss is reversible). For this reason, if it is at all possible, try to delay subsequent major changes immediately after a significant loss. Postpone the switch to a new neighborhood, a new school, or a new church, the cutting of ties with friends or grandparents. If there must be a relocation or if it is not possible to continue in the familiar place with the familiar routines, it is important to involve children as much as possible in anticipating and discussing what is to happen. Remember that, for children, the loss of their familiar home can seem like the loss of a family member; because they tend to identify themselves with specific spaces, repeated events, and familiar people, moving can cause disorientation. Include them as much as you can in decisions about the change and conversations about new routines and roles and in choosing the new home, visiting the new neighborhood, and meeting the neighborhood children.

Involving the Child in the Changes

Lauren, who is sixteen, still actively resents what she feels to have been her parents' insensitivity toward her when they separated.

16

Her mom and dad had been honest about the stresses in their marriage. She knew that they were in counseling trying to work things out. So when they had told her five years ago that her dad was moving out, she was upset but not caught off guard. Her current resentment and pain are connected to how they handled things after that. The weekend after she was told, Lauren's mom went shopping, leaving Lauren at home. Shortly after her mother left, some of her dad's friends came by with a truck. Lauren remembers standing there, watching her father go through their house, systematically taking one of the chairs, one of the bookcases, their piano, a small table, the bed from their guest room, some of the pictures from the wall. Her mother returned just before the final load was taken away and barely spoke to anyone, including Lauren. As soon as the cars were out of sight, her mother began a cleaning frenzy, enlisting Lauren's help in rearranging furniture, washing walls, and cleaning things out. "My mom was like a crazy person, opening cabinets and drawers, pitching things into different cartons, some for Dad and some for the Salvation Army. She sort of swept through the house, yanking things off walls and shelves, talking to herself about what a bastard he was. And that was just Saturday. On Sunday, he came back, and they went through the photo albums and the Christmas stuff, arguing about who was going to get what. It was the first time I knew what a 'broken heart' meant, and I wondered if they would just cut me in half, too. I'll never forgive them for that day, ever."

This is not just a divorce issue. And it is not unusual. A child who loses a sibling suddenly as a result of miscarriage or stillbirth or SIDS, may come home to find all traces of the nursery gone. Or pictures of the family member who is no longer at home may be removed from the house, the person's room dismantled, his or her belongings given away. Certainly, it is not the intention of the adults involved to inflict additional pain on their children. But caught up in their own anguish or anger or hostility or in an attempt to erase the pain by erasing the evidence that the person existed, they may force children to accept changes too quickly, depriving them of the comfort of a more gradual transition.

Whenever possible, children should have some say as to when

and how things are to be dispersed and dismantled. They should have the opportunity to request that certain mementos be left in place or that they be allowed to keep belongings special to them.

One six-year-old, when asked which of his great-grandmother's things he might like to have, requested her cane—it was the thing that brought her most clearly to his mind.

The night her brother died, a surviving sister carefully brought his hermit crab into her room because she "knew it would be lonely and Ben would want her to take care of it."

Children whose beloved grandparents had died within a few months of each other were given the chance to spend as much time as they wanted just walking though their grandparents' home, which had been sold but not yet dismantled and cleared out. Photographs were taken of the various rooms, and the children were encouraged to help the parents make a list of the things they wished to take home to use or to have kept safe.

Helping a Child Return to School Following a Death or Separation

When a classmate or a teacher dies, the child's whole community experiences the loss together. They can cry and hug and mourn with one another. But when a child who has lost a parent or a sibling returns to school, the community that the child reenters is not grieving, and the child faces what can be a difficult transition alone. Many children find returning to school after a family tragedy to be as difficult as the tragedy itself, especially at the beginning. In very painful situations, such as the sudden death of a sibling, or complicated situations, involving perhaps suicide, AIDS, or violent death, especially if caused by another family member, children are most likely to be at risk. Almost everyone knows about the loss, but no one, including adults, knows what to say. Bereaved children may become convinced that they have done something awful or disgusting or disgraceful, and this deals them an additional blow at a time when they most need and deserve reassurance that they are worthwhile, acceptable people. Their schoolmates, fearing that they, too, could suffer a similar catastrophe, may avoid them, and the resulting social isolation is likely to cause them to

18

behave in ways that annoy or irritate others, which in turn isolates them all the more. They may become more and more withdrawn, develop ever more serious behavior problems, or fall even farther outside the community's pale, where they may become scapegoats or the subjects of classmates' rejection and ridicule.

Concerned adults in the school community can make a child's return to school following a loss or change significantly easier for all the children involved. Though bereaved children may protest (out of their own need to deny or because they are following the lead of a parent who has similar feelings and is not yet ready to let others know), it is important for caregivers or other concerned individuals to let the principal, guidance personnel, and classroom teacher know when there has been a family loss or change so that the school understands and can respond in a supportive manner. Talking to the other children about what has happened before the bereaved child returns to school, explaining how to comfort and welcome the child back, and responding to their fears, curiosity, and concerns can do much to ease the grieving child back into school routine.

Because schools have such an important socializing influence on how children feel about themselves and their life situations, school personnel need to be particularly mindful about how they go about providing supports. Brenner points out that many American school systems have yet to acknowledge that multiparent families exist. Report cards in elementary schools throughout the country still are likely to list only the names and addresses of one set of parents per child. There is no space for information about noncustodial parents or for indications that a second family is to be contacted in case of emergency or informed about academic progress. When children get sick at school and need to go home, school nurses may not think of calling the other parent or a stepparent if the custodial parent cannot be reached. Sometimes only custodial parents are invited to school conferences (Brenner 1984, 36–37). Youngsters may be allowed only enough time to make one card or present on Mother's or Father's Day and then left to decide where it should go. All this makes children feel uncomfortably different. How much better it would be simply to say, for example, "Today, when we make Mother's Day cards, you may make as many as you would like so you can send one to anyone who has helped to mother you." This kind of support can be an important part of helping children resolve losses, alleviating their feelings of difference and encouraging healthy adjustments to an altered family world.

In general, schools would be wise to provide formal or informal ways to support all children who have experienced loss. Organized discussion groups can be very helpful. Teachers can make a point of referring not only to two-parent, intact families but also to separated parents, single parents, and foster and adoptive parents. They can devise class activities or initiate discussions about the diversity of family makeups. They can include books about adoption, divorce, and stepparenting in the class library.

Pains should also be taken on behalf of a child who suffers a serious illness or accident—for example, a child who is in some way responsible for the death of another, or who has almost died, or who returns to school visibly different (missing a limb, in a brace or wheelchair, brain impaired, bald because of chemotherapy or radiation). Children can be brutally cruel to one another, but they can also demonstrate a strong capacity and desire to help if someone suggests ways for them to be supportive. It is when they are not helped to understand how to respond that children are most likely to turn their feelings of inadequacy and anxiety on the hurt child, thereby compounding whatever tragedy may have occurred.

School personnel may find it particularly difficult to know how to handle talking openly with children about the death of a classmate or a faculty member as a result of AIDS or suicide. Concern and confusion about confidentiality and about reactions from the other students' parents raise difficult ethical questions. It is wise, however, to recognize the speed with which such news is likely to travel through a school community to strive to avoid the dramatic convolutions that are likely to result when such charged information travels through the rumor mill instead of being shared in an open, informed, appropriate manner. A forthright approach lets the students know that the school believes they can be trusted with information about issues that affect them or a classmate. Any such effort to share sensitive information, however, must be balanced

20

with the wishes of the family involved and a careful consideration of how to avoid making a youngster returning to school feel singled out, gossiped about, and exposed.

Children are in particular need of clear and accurate information about how AIDS is transmitted so that they won't avoid the individual who is ill or overreact in other ways. In simple terms, they can be told that the germs that cause this serious illness are transferred through getting blood or feces or, just possibly, saliva through their skin and into their bodies. (Terms such as *feces* and *saliva* should be put into the child's vernacular.) Most importantly, children need to know that they can't get these germs by just being with someone who is sick or playing with them or touching them or their things or hugging them or breathing the germs in. Tell them that it is very hard for children to get AIDS; most children who are sick were born with it because their mothers had it (stress that their own mothers don't have it). Explain how sometimes people who have needed blood transfusions have gotten AIDS because the blood they were given was from an infected person, which is how some children got it before doctors knew as much about testing blood and keeping it safe. And, finally, be sure to state clearly that people who have AIDS are sick and should get the same kindness and sympathy that we would give any person who was very ill.

It is increasingly apparent that death education should be part of the school curriculum. Just as children can be helped to understand death if their parents present the facts to them in developmentally appropriate ways, in the same way they can explore and understand more about death and normal grief reactions before they or their classmates are stricken. Given the dismaying statistics on the number of adolescents who think about or attempt suicide, it makes good sense for the school community to talk about the problem in a general context with high school and perhaps junior high school people. Discussing suicide as a social problem in the school setting can offer important protection and information to students and those who work with them. Not only do such discussions demonstrate that it is all right to talk about very difficult and upsetting things, they also support the notion that help will be available, no matter how serious the problem, as long as one is willing to reach out for it. A culture of understanding will make it less likely that youngsters will isolate themselves during difficult times.

Helping a Child Change Schools

A nine-year-old who lost both of his parents in a commercial airplane crash moved several months later to a new state to live with relatives. He was adamant that he did not want *anyone* to know what had happened to him and his younger sister. Two years later, still assuming that he had managed to keep his tragedy a secret, he became furious when another child said something about it at school. He felt totally betrayed and was convinced that he would be ostracized and victimized as a result of the news having come out. Though he was reassured that those who lived in his small rural town undoubtedly already knew, the reassurance did little to alleviate his concerns that he would become a pariah.

When children must move or begin a new school, it is important that they have the opportunity to say both hello to the new situation and a thought-out good-bye to the old. Adolescents in particular will be worried about how they will be accepted by a new peer group—indeed, they are at risk of being as damaged by negative peer relationships in the new setting as they are by the loss that may have precipitated the move. Stuart and Abt suggest:

> If a child with recently separated parents newly enters the school district, teachers need to be sensitive to the child's loss of peer support in addition to the parental loss. The child needs to feel a sense of belonging to the class and to acquire a new support system as quickly as possible. To foster this, the teacher could assign the child a valued responsibility, include the child on committees, have the class members plan a welcoming party or form a "Newcomer's Club," and a unit on the child's previous hometown could be done. (1981, 162)

This kind of responsive support can be helpful to any child entering a new school.

It is useful for hellos and good-byes to overlap, if at all possible,

so that the youngster has the chance to explore the new neighborhood before the move. Adults should consider making arrangements for the child to visit the new school (preferably while it is in
session) before they leave the old one and to meet the new principal and teacher. They might ask to have their youngster or teen
paired with a classmate and allowed to attend the school for a sam-
ple day. If school is not in session, children may still benefit from
a visit to the new school before classes start in order to meet and
talk with their new teacher, to feel welcomed, to see where their
desk or locker is likely to be, and to make sure they know how to
get to the gym, the lunch room, the nurse's office.

It is a good idea to help children identify the skills and talents
they have that they might use to join clubs or take part in other
school activities as a way to make friends. For children who move
regularly, membership or experience in a national club, organiza-
tion, sport, or hobby program provides continuity and easy access
to finding a place to belong. Participating in church youth groups
and other community activities can also help children begin to feel
at home. If the move takes place during the summer, careful
thought should be given as to how the child or teen might begin
to connect with future classmates. Often school personnel are willing to share names of students with similar interests and friendly
natures so that activities can be set up to allow the youngsters to
meet. Parents should also check out whether there is a summer
sports program or enrichment class at the new school where their
child might have a chance to meet some potential classmates in
advance.

Children also need a chance to say good-bye to current friends
and important adults, to tell them when they are leaving, and to
talk about how they might keep in touch. Sometimes caregivers
and teachers think of creative ways to help classmates provide extra
comfort and support, such as having them assemble a scrapbook
of letters and drawings as a good-bye gift or suggesting that they
sign a card or a tee shirt with their names.

Mimi Robbins, a social worker in Massachusetts, devised a good-
bye ritual for children who were leaving their school and moving
into a new adoptive family. Wanting the child to feel the good

wishes that accompanied them as they experienced this important change, she would make arrangements with school personnel to have a good-bye party in the departing child's classroom that was attended by anyone who had been important to the child during his or her stay at the school—the principal, the gym teacher, the school counselor, the nurse, and the custodian, for example. The child's foster parents and siblings might also be included. The new adoptive parents were asked to bring cupcakes or treats as their part of the celebration. When one second grader arrived at school on his good-bye day, he found his name listed under the special-events heading on the blackboard. Toward the end of the day, the adults gathered for the party. After the goodies had been shared, the child's classmates and adult friends were asked to form a circle around the child who was leaving. Mimi took out a plastic "magic wand" and asked the children to close their eyes and think of one good wish for themselves and another for the child who was to be adopted. Then she passed the wand around, telling the children that they could think of their wish for themselves as a secret to share or to keep but that they should speak aloud whatever magic wishes they wanted to give to the child and the new family. The intently furrowed brows and quiet respect that accompanied the passage of the wand around the circle, the way the participants grasped the wand and spoke their wishes, and the combination of solemnity and giggles with which wishes and blessing were shared left no doubt as to how seriously the children took their charge. Several of the adults involved found themselves fighting back tears. The ceremony ended with the new parents spontaneously hugging the child they were bringing into their family.

Helping Children through the Transition from School Year to School Year

The end and beginning of the school year create major challenges for many children who have lost or changed caregivers as they anticipate and experience the changing of teachers who have been their primary contacts at school. Starting about six weeks before the end of school and escalating rapidly thereafter, some children may begin to show behavior difficulties, grow anxious, and become increasingly defensive, both emotionally and physically. They worry aloud that their new teachers won't like them or will be mean. In some instances, problems may subside during summer only to reappear two to three weeks before school starts again. Other children appear unconcerned about school but begin to have problems as the first day approaches (or when confronted with a substitute teacher). This can happen to some children year after year after year, although it may become less intense in middle school or junior high if children have grown accustomed to having more than one teacher. School personnel and caregivers are wise to work together with children who are stressed by endings, the loss of the known, and the fear of the unknown that looms ahead, by using the kinds of bridging procedures discussed in the preceding section. It often helps if children are told who their new teachers will be midway through the last quarter or at least before school adjourns for the summer, to help them begin to settle into what lies ahead in the fall. They may still fret and begin to quiz other children about how strict the new teachers are, how much work will be demanded, and whether the teachers yell, but they still seem to derive some reassurance from knowing ahead of time a little of what's in store for them, especially if they have the chance to meet and talk with new teachers. When school is about to start, visiting the new classroom and checking in with the new teachers for a personal welcome can also make a significant difference for such children and help them worry less about going back to school and managing the new classroom situation.

There is no question that a major loss will have a tremendous impact on a child's life in numbers of ways and that the impact may last for a long while. While it may be impossible to protect children from experiencing difficult losses or separation or to prevent the grief that they will feel, we can help a great deal by being open with them about impending losses, by giving them a chance to integrate the information and say a thoughtful good-bye, and by including them in decisions about the changes that occur, respecting their individuality and the uniqueness of the way they will incorporate and manage the effects of loss and grief in their lives.

HELPING CHILDREN
FACE CHANGE

❧

2 Though he has fought hard, Tom continues to lose ground, growing more and more feeble. To him the hardest thing about dying is leaving Mary to raise their children alone and to know that he is not going to be there to help and support her or to see his children grow up. He wishes there were some way he could be sure that they know how much he loves them.

Jeff has been offered a promising new job but it means uprooting his family and moving them across the country. His children will have to be taken out of their school and away from the neighborhood where they fit in so well. He and his wife agree that the move is a good idea for their family, but they are apprehensive about how their children will react to the change.

Janet, a single parent for a number of years, met Stan at a church gathering. They began dating each other and eventually fell in love. Now they plan to marry. Although Janet's son appears to like Stan, he seems upset about the engagement and refuses to talk with his mother about the wedding plans.

There are a great many ways for loss to enter a child's life. Yet the adult faced with the task of helping a particular child through a loss and the grief and changes it may entail can find it reassuring to know that what children need is likely to be much the same regardless of the individual cause and circumstances. Nonetheless, some differences and specific concerns demand special attention.

26

HELPING A CHILD FACE A LOSS
FROM DEATH

Adults often wonder how much children can really understand about death. Overall, it appears that environmental support, family background, self-conceptions, and previous experiences with death are among the various factors that contribute to a child's ability to understand what has happened (Moody and Moody 1991, 590–92). Although there is still some disagreement among experts, the current thinking is that children under the age of two are not able to understand much about death. During the period between two and six, when the primary mode of processing is magical thinking, children appear to believe that death can be avoided or reversed. Lonetto (1980) reports that children this age think that dead people live on "under changed circumstances," which often leads to pre-occupations with how the deceased will breathe or eat or stay warm underground in a coffin. Often they believe that the deceased is simply missing and can be expected to return. Over time, as this doesn't happen, they become hurt and angry and often feel deliberately abandoned. They may want to go to heaven and bring the dead person home or convince them to return.

By first or second grade until about the end of third grade, children think of death as a person, a specter that can be evaded and fought if one's magic is strong enough (Lonetto 1980). They are likely to believe that death can take away only the old and sick who are too weak to outwit or conquer it. The skeletons, ghosts, ghouls at Halloween not only reinforce these ideas but also heighten confusions and terror.

As children move through concrete thinking, many begin to understand the reality of death but still may not realize that death is universal and that those around them can die, instead viewing death as something distant from their lives. Gradually, at around age nine or ten, children acquire a more mature understanding of death, eventually realizing that death is the irreversible end of life as they know it and that they themselves will eventually die.

When helping a child face a loss from death, remember that

the first thing to emphasize is that someone will take care of the youngster, preferably specifying who the caregiver will be. Then be sure to let the child know: (1) that the dead person did not choose to leave the child; (2) that the dead person can never return; and (3) that the person's body is to be buried in the ground or burned to ashes. Even during years of magical thinking, children can be told honestly about death. Children are lucky if their caregivers use their early interest in a dead insect or animal to lay the foundation for a beginning understanding of death. The child can be shown that the animal does not move or eat or act scared. When a pet dies, the child who is reassured that it is natural to feel sad and to wish that there were some way to bring the animal back to life receives important permission to mourn not only this loss but future losses. Moody and Moody (1991, 588) point out that children can be taught about grief as a necessary and natural emotion that not only is constructive but also makes healing possible.

When it is a person who has died, using sensory explanations help make the death real. A young child will not understand the abstractions like "soul" or "life" but can often understand descriptions such as, "The soft and warm part has stopped and can't ever be fixed. There's no more eating, no feeling, no hugging, no hurting." When you talk to a child about death, the rule about being completely honest in discussing a loss with children also applies to questions about the afterlife: If you are firm in your convictions, share them, but don't pretend to be confident about your religious beliefs if you aren't. And remember that older children may have strong ideas of their own about life after death, which you should treat with respect.

Helping a Child through the Death of a Sibling

The death of a child is devastating for a family. Parents, of course, suffer deeply, but so do the surviving siblings, who are likely to be deeply affected regardless of their developmental understanding. Loss of the sense of invulnerability that comes from youth; guilt and accusations, self-imposed or by others; confusion and guilt about the relief they may feel when the death after a long illness or serious accident that has preoccupied parents to the detriment of the child who is not dying; guilt about having survived when another has died—these are just some of the additional challenges surviving siblings may face. Research on the effects of sibling death points to four sources of particular concern: (1) the way in which the sibling dies; (2) parental reactions to the death; (3) parental feelings and expectations about the surviving youngsters that are an outgrowth of the loss; and (4) children's relationships with their siblings prior to and after the loss (Brenner 1984, 46–48).

In about half of families that suffer the loss of a child, one or more remaining siblings will develop symptoms such as depression, severe separation anxiety, and problems with going to school that seem to be connected more to the parents' changed behavior toward the remaining children than to the death itself. If a marriage founders because of the stress caused by the death, if the parents are depressed, or if the child's death is attributed to God's having "taken" the child, children may become increasingly fearful of being away from their parents for fear that something bad may happen to the parents during the separation or because they are worried that the parents may decide not to return. In many more cases than one would think, parents blame their surviving children for a sibling's death, particularly if it was sudden, and though parents often forget the accusation later, the children remember and suffer a good deal of damage from it. It is good to check with surviving siblings to determine whether any of them believe their parents blame them and attempt to see if there can be a correcting, absolving conversation between parent and child to correct that impression if it exists.

One kind of family loss where children often are or feel excluded is the loss of an infant from miscarriage, stillbirth, or SIDS. Parents are often unaware that their other children may be as distressed over the infant's death and the loss of their hopes for a relationship with the new brother or sister (even if they never knew the child) as are their parents. In the case of SIDS, children may be particularly confused if a medical examiner needs to be called in, because this may heighten their sense of guilt and concern that something they did or thought might have contributed to the death. Again, the main rule holds: Parents need to be as truthful and as thorough as possible when explaining what has happened and to recognize that each of their surviving children needs to go through a process of grief, absolution, and recovery, just as they themselves must.

Helping Children through a Death from Suicide

Talking with a child about a death from suicide can be particularly difficult because of ingrained social stigmas or taboos about taking one's own life and because survivors may feel that such a death is the result of a deliberate selfish choice by a family member who ignored the pain those left behind would have to bear. Children often feel that if the individual had truly loved and cared about them, he or she would have been more careful or would have made a different choice. Because suicide does involve a choice, children feel an even greater need to try to sort out what part they may have played and if and how they could have prevented the death.

Among others, Bowlby (1980, 384–85) has shown that those working with children who are related to or have known someone who has committed suicide may need to address special concerns. Because it is not unusual for distraught or mentally ill people to have threatened or attempted suicide before, children may have been warned by other family members not to argue with or upset the emotionally fragile person. Because most children are not able to follow that direction, such warnings and scoldings are likely to lead children to believe that they were responsible for creating or compounding the situation that resulted in the eventual suicide. Bowlby points out that in such cases children are likely to assume complete responsibility for the death, continuing to blame themselves regardless of what they are told; this is especially true when children already blame themselves for whatever had been going wrong before the death. Some children believe that it was their job to prevent the disturbed person from committing suicide and suffer enormous guilt at having failed at this responsibility. Still others become so angry, frightened, and frustrated by the constant threats of suicide that they start wishing that the person would just keep the promise—and then feel like they wrote the death sentence when the suicide occurs. Many children experience deep feelings of anger toward either the deceased or the survivors (who did not prevent the death) but think that they should not feel or seem to feel angry about the suicide because their role is to be protective and consoling toward the survivors. They may also feel that they cannot express anger toward other family members because they fear those targeted by their anger might kill themselves as well. As a result, a common choice is to turn this deep anger in on themselves. According to Bowlby, more psychological damage is likely to occur if the surviving caregivers ban discussion of the suicide or insist—even in the face of clear evidence—that the person died because of accident or illness. Such evasions appear to create tendencies for children to develop chronic distrust of other people, to inhibit their normal curiosity, and to distrust their own senses and ability to sort out what is real.

When a child's parent or some other loved one has died because of suicide, it is important to explore with the child the reasons behind suicide: most commonly, a feeling of desperation, the wish to seem important or to take revenge, or the wish to rejoin someone lost to death. Then, it is crucial that someone help the child know what other things can be done with feelings like these. According to Bowlby (1980, 389), children who survive the suicide of a caregiver may live for many years convinced that they too will kill themselves someday because the normal taboo has been broken and a parent has shown that taking one's life is a possible response to difficulty. This may be equally true if the suicide was another close family member. It is wise to discuss these thoughts and feelings with the child and to talk about the many other, less final actions that can be taken to deal with unhappiness and despair.

Helping Children Say Good-bye to the Dying

Children and teens who have a family member or close friend who is critically ill or dying should have the chance, if at all possible, to visit the individual who may die in order to say good-bye. It is extremely helpful for caregivers or other helpers to talk to the child before the death about what is happening or is likely to happen and to talk to the person at risk as well. Everyone concerned should be encouraged to take the time to think about what they might want to say to one another. Such preparation helps children and adults alike to visit ready to share their love, their appreciation, their wishes and blessings and to say a loving farewell.

Without some kind of preparation, final visits are less likely to accomplish these goals. Children's wishes that things could be different tend to override their ability to recognize the seriousness of the circumstances even when the person is obviously extremely ill or critically injured. Adolescents are especially likely to deny an imminent death, particularly if it follows a chronic or lengthy illness with periodic remission or improvement. Children and teens who are helped to plan and participate in face-to-face good-byes are less likely to berate themselves or others after the death for not having been clear about what was going to happen and thus eliminating all chance to say good-bye. If caregivers are unable to provide support or are emotionally unavailable because of their own fear and sorrow, it is important that someone else help these children face the death and say their good-byes.

The time after the prognosis is accepted and can be talked about openly is often a particularly precious time for the person—adult or child—who is dying, as well as for other family members. Often, dying parents want to leave a record of their continuing love and life wishes for their children. They make tapes, write or dictate letters, put together an album or a journal that records their special feelings and favorite stories of times shared. (Note, though, that parents should avoid encouraging youngsters to remember only the good times or to be happy for them or to be strong, because such messages may suppress the ability to have a fruitful and normal grief reaction.) Children benefit enormously from such efforts; young adults, in particular, seem to love stories about when they were little that capture the uniqueness of their younger self, delighting in talk about the kinds of things they did that were cute but slightly naughty. If the parent dies leaving these stories untold, who else will be able pass on this legacy? It is a special gift to caregiver and child alike if some way can be found to help the dying parent preserve memories and feelings for the child. For the child, that the parent made the effort is proof of his or her abiding love. If the dying parent has also thought to relate some anecdotes about

32

his or her own childhood, adolescence, and young adulthood, this allows the surviving children to continue to feel connected to the caregiver as they grow through those stages themselves.

Facilitating good-bye visits can be especially difficult for the caregivers of a child who is gravely ill, injured, or dying and for any helpers who are involved. Caregivers may want to protect themselves, their child, and the child's siblings by refusing to accept the seriousness of the situation. They may plead with medical personnel not to let their child know the potential outcome. They may resist telling others because it validates the seriousness of the situation and makes their child's death seem more inevitable. Seriously ill or injured children and others close to them often need to know what is happening but may be reluctant to ask how serious the situation actually is for fear of causing additional pain, which makes it all the easier for parents to avoid such conversations.

Even when children have an intuitive sense of their own impending death, they may be reluctant or afraid to bring it up because they don't want to upset their parents. And so the child faces the unknown, anxious and alone. Both caregivers and child wait for the other to indicate a readiness to talk about what is happening. When the topic does come up, it is not unusual for the dying child to be visibly relieved to have permission finally to ask questions and to receive the parents' reassurance and support.

Including Children in Funerals

In addition to the good-byes that precede a death, it is very important for children to be offered the chance to attend and perhaps take part in the more formal good-bye rituals, whether a funeral or a memorial service, that follow the death. Formal mourning rites allow children to see that many other people feel sorrow and love for the lost person. Being surrounded by extended support also lets them feel a sense of belonging and acceptance at a time when their security and self-esteem have been badly shaken. And the obvious concern for their well-being, which is often overtly expressed, may help relieve any fear of being somehow to blame for the death.

It is helpful if someone explains the "see-and-hear" details of what will happen at the funeral as frankly and matter-of-factly as

---

possible in order to prepare the child for what is to come and to help him or her make a decision about attending. Most children, when offered the choice, want to be included in funerals; in fact, many take comfort in being allowed to choose a memento (or to make a note or a drawing) to be tucked into the casket. Children who are excluded from participation in these final ceremonies may harbor long-lasting resentment, even anger. They report feeling that they were treated as if they were unimportant and their grief insignificant.

Bereaved children should not have to worry about what others will think about how they react at a funeral or memorial service. It is their loss, and their feelings belong to them, as do their tears. Yet older children often express concern about how people will react if they cry. They agonize over whether it is worse to cry and have people think they are weak or acting like babies or to hold back their tears and have people think that they don't love the deceased. This problem can be compounded if a child lives in a family where adults are uncomfortable with overt expressions of grief. If the child has rarely if ever seen the caregivers cry, he or she is likely to think that it is wrong to cry, that strong people don't cry, or that the caregivers will disapprove of any tears. Adults should make an effort to sort out what messages they might be sending to their child about how to handle grief. If caregivers feel uncomfortable about public or private crying, are they willing to reassure their children that it is fine to cry at funerals, even though they are in public? If they cannot, children should be asked if there is someone with whom they would like to sit—be it another family member or members or someone else—near whom they would feel comfortable and free of scrutiny.

Viewing the dead person does not appear to create unusual problems for children, although the choice should be left to the child. In many cases, children are actually relieved to see that their ghoulish fantasies of what bodies look like are not true. Be aware, though, that small children may have their fantasies that the person is just sleeping soundly reinforced unless they are allowed to touch the body. It is wrong, however, to force a child to view a body or to touch it. If part of the service takes place at the cemetery, children should be told what to expect and allowed to decide if they wish to go there. Children who seem comfortable with the open casket can become frightened and upset to see the casket closed or suspended over a cemetery plot, lowered, and covered with earth. Young children, in particular, may believe that their loved one is being buried alive. It is wise to remind them that, once dead, people do not ever breathe or see or feel again.

Play is the way children integrate and master their life experiences, and after attending a funeral, children may "play funeral" from time to time. Such behavior is completely normal. Far from being disrespectful, it marks the importance of the loss in their lives.

HELPING A CHILD COPE WITH
SEPARATION AND DIVORCE

If parents are separating or have separated, questions from their children are as inevitable and as important as they are when there is a loss through death. Indeed, separation and divorce involve both death and loss: the death of the family unit and the loss of all the normal expectations for what life would be. But because there is neither a body nor mourning rites, the grief following a separation often becomes convoluted, and fantasies are likely to abound. Things can be even more complicated when the parents themselves are unclear about what is happening, especially when one parent has plainly decided that the relationship is over but the other is still intent on working things out and reuniting. Whether one or both parents believe that they have tried to work out their problems without success, children should be told plainly that there is nothing they can do (or could have done) to have kept their parents together or to bring them back together now.

In divorce or separation, parents may put children in the middle or require them to take sides. Stressed and angry themselves, divorcing parents don't want to be the target of their children's anger, and they often try to direct it toward their former partners, making them the "bad" parents.

As with death, parents may feel uneasy talking to their children about separating or divorcing. This is particularly true if they feel responsible:

Rick, who is leaving his family because of his involvement with another woman, would rather not talk to his children about the impending separation. He feels guilty and upset about the deep distress his children will suffer. But unless he opens the subject with them, how will he be able to reassure his children that they are still important to him, that he will be honest with them, and that he is not abandoning them or abdicating his responsibilities as their father?

In cases such as this, parents must be willing to overcome their own feelings of awkwardness and speak honestly to their children, for the alternative may leave children wondering whether the absent parent ever loved them at all.

Often, embattled parents or social workers involved in custody disputes find it nearly impossible not to bring their own anxieties and biases into their conversations with children about what is happening legally. Children are usually acutely aware when both a situation and the people in it are out of control, which causes them to worry unnecessarily about their personal safety. They should be told who is moving and when and where. They should be told what will be happening in the immediate future and assured that parents will share more information as soon as things are settled. Parents should do everything possible to avoid putting children in the middle of conflicts, asking them to take sides, or pressuring them to turn against the other parent. Especially in custody disputes, it is important not to burden children with constant discussion. It is enough for them to know that their situation is secure and that they will be told if there is to be a hearing that will decide something different. They do not need to know about every meeting between parents and lawyers or for temporary review.

Though the family unit is being dissolved, continuity between parent and child is crucial. Even in the bitter conflicts that can accompany separation and divorce, it is important that each spouse accept that the other is still the child's parent. The child deserves to be reassured that, although some things, such as how often the child sees that parent, will change, children don't get divorced from their parents. Children need to be told how the non-custodial parent will keep in touch. How often will there be visits? Is the parent available by telephone (and what is the telephone number and who will help them call, if they need help dialing)? Will the parent call them?

HELPING CHILDREN DEAL WITH TEMPORARY SEPARATION

When a caregiver is to be away or unavailable for some period of time, perhaps because of business, illness, or military assignment, it is a good idea to tell the child as far in advance as possible so that the subject to be discussed and readdressed several times before the actual separation takes place. This gives the child time to understand that the caregiver will be leaving, to picture where the caregiver will be, and to anticipate what will be different while the caregiver is gone: How will people keep in contact? Will they write? Call? Send tapes and video recordings? The caregiver who will be away should make it clear that he or she trusts the person who will be taking care of the child and that that person is in charge. Children often benefit from a family discussion about what will change and what will go on as usual. It is often useful to discuss with school-age children whether they will have additional responsibilities when the parent is away and to figure out together how family chores will be reassigned and shared. Family discussions also can be used as a time to plan what each child might especially like to do with the caregiver before they must part. Pictures can be taken and audiotapes can be made, not only of these special activities but also of the child and caregiver in familiar settings doing routine things together, like playing, or sharing bath time, or reading stories.

After the departure, the remaining caregiver should try to keep the routine as normal as possible. Temporary change may be as puzzling and upsetting to children as a more permanent separation would be. Depending on their ages, children may have the normal concerns about the part they played in the separation. They may worry that the absent caregiver will not return, especially if there is reason to be concerned about physical safety. If the children are old enough to have some map skills, it can help to indicate on a map or globe where the caregiver will be, perhaps drawing two lines in different colors, one showing the trip to where the caregiver is going and another showing the trip back.

Children can be helped to keep track of time and the caregiver's travels by using a diary or a cruise calendar and having a family information center where postcards, letters, and pictures from the caregiver can be posted as a concrete reminder that, whether the caregiver is close to home or far away, he or she is still an important member of the family who loves them. Helping children make or buy (and then send) birthday presents, valentines, tapes and video recordings, photos, drawings, and schoolwork also emphasizes that the caregiver who is away is still an important person who is interested in what is going on in the children's lives.

Children benefit if the caregiver who is away sends similar packages and makes a point of commenting on things received from the children. Caregivers who will be going away can visit their children's schools or day-care centers and leave self-addressed stamped envelopes with the teachers for samples of their children's work. They can also volunteer to send postcards, maps, stamps, and letters to the class.

During Operation Desert Storm, several schools who had a child or children with parents who were to be deployed to the Persian Gulf invited departing parents to visit the school and talk about the area where they were going and to answer questions. Classes posted maps and sent drawings and mail. Not only was this supportive to the parents, it showed clear community support and concern for the children.

When a temporary separation involves children moving into the foster-care system, it is useful to share as much concrete information with them as possible. If there is some condition that a parent must fulfill in order for a child to be returned home, the child deserves to know what it is: "When your mom gets an apartment," "When your dad stops drinking," "When your parents can show us that they know how to take care of you without hurting you," or the like. This takes away some of the mystery surrounding the move and lets the child know what changes to watch for. Such information also tends to relieve children of responsibility for the separation or the outcome because they understand that they cannot personally bring the needed changes about.

HELPING CHILDREN UNDERSTAND
FAMILY CHANGE FROM
OTHER CAUSES

Many adults feel awkward when they must talk to a child about losses or separation stemming from physical or sexual abuse, parental immaturity, abandonment or rejection, neglect, mental illness, imprisonment, or substance abuse, especially if the particular cause makes them personally uncomfortable or strikes them as distasteful or inexcusable. Often, it does not even occur to them that children will continue to have feelings for these lost caregivers and may want to stay in touch with them. (Suggestions on how they can do so may be found in the preceding section.) Helpers may worry that children are too fragile, too young, or too upset to discuss what caused the separation, or, conversely, they may believe that children seem to be adjusting well and that talking about the hows and whys of the loss will simply rock the boat. Sometimes, a helper may fear that a child will feel compelled to repeat the caregiver's behavior if it is spelled out or that the child will suffer additional emotional damage from being told what really happened. Or the helper may simply lack accurate information about what led up to the separation and be confused or reluctant to interpret or intrude. A helper who is not the child's caregiver may also be concerned about how caregivers will respond to what the child is told.

In general, it is useful to remember that children are less likely to be scarred by what they are told than by the fantasies—often frightening, self-blaming, or damaging—they concoct to figure out what has happened when they are not given accurate information.

Travis, released for adoption at four by a single mother with three other children, responded this way a few years later when he was told where babies come from:

TRAVIS: Not me. I didn't grow in a mom.

HELPER: You didn't? That's amazing. You're the first kid I ever met who didn't get born that way. How was it instead?

TRAVIS: See, what happened was one day my social worker was having a snack. She opened up a box of Cracker Jack and found me inside. She pulled me out and said, "You're no prize!" and she threw me in the trash.

No child should be left to think up such damning reasons for an unexplained loss. Adult helpers can best help bereaved children by overcoming their own reluctance to be open and honest about difficult subjects and developing all the skills necessary to make that possible.

"But how can you talk to a youngster about things like that?" a helper may ask. One way to figure out what to say is to ask yourself the following questions:

- Why would an adult do something like that?
- What similar need or life situation might this child have experienced?
- If the child remembers what happened or could see a movie about the times when the caregiver was having difficulty, what would the child be likely to see and hear that would point out the adult's problem?
- How can this information be conveyed in a way that does not suggest that the caregiver was a bad person?
- Is there anything that the child might misunderstand or feel responsible for or any action by the caregiver that the child might feel compelled to repeat?

Using these questions as guides, here are some suggestions for how to explain and talk about several of the more common reasons for family change that adults sometimes have a hard time discussing with children. Depending on the particular situation, you may find that many different issues need addressing, in which case, you might want to skim through the headings below or the table of

contents to see which of the following sections relate most specifically to your concerns.

Abuse or Abandonment

One of the common conditions that lead to abuse or abandonment
is adult frustration: The child's caregiver simply finds parts of life
unfair or intolerable. A helper can connect this to a child's experience by asking: "Does anyone ever ask you to do something that is
just too hard or not fair? When that happens, what do you do (or
want to do)?" Most children will have experienced times like this,
and many also say that, when they feel this way, they want to get
away from the situation (abandonment) or fight someone or break
something as a way of releasing their feelings even if the person or
object is not the cause of the problem (abuse). Remembering their
own reactions may help them understand the caregiver's. (If parental immaturity is behind the abuse or abandonment, suggestions
for including it in the explanation can be found below in the section on neglect. Abandonment resulting from outright rejection is
particularly difficult for children to deal with; for this reason, it is
discussed in detail in a section of its own.)

It is important to remember that children may misunderstand
or feel responsible for abuse or abandonment in a number of harmful ways. "It was my fault; I was too much trouble," they might
think. The helper could talk with them about the demands all children make and the needs they all have, perhaps asking them to list
everything they can think of that they would need or need to know
about if they were to be given a baby or toddler right then and told
to take care of it. Usually, such a list will include things such as
food, bottles, dry diapers, beds, hugs, baths, and so on, which gives
the helper the opportunity to ask, "Do you suppose that you
needed those things when you were little, too? Do you think it was
OK for you to be like all babies and little children and need those
things?" Children also sometimes think that when they are older
and more able to take care of themselves, they will be allowed to
return to their previous caregivers. If it is certain that this is impossible—at least until they are grown up—children should be told
why.

Sometimes children will ask, "When things are too hard for me, I try to get away. Why did my mother hit me instead?" The helper might say, "Lots of kids feel like running or disappearing when things get too hard or are just too much to deal with. But other kids tell me they feel like hitting when this happens. Will you watch the kids you know and be ready to tell me the next time we talk which ones you think might try to get away and which ones hit?"

Some children say, "So, big deal—my parents hit me. There's nothing wrong with that. All parents hit their kids when they deserve it." An appropriate response is, "No child ever deserves to be hit as hard as your parent hit you. No matter what, kids are not for hurting. There's even a law that says that. When your father hit you because things were not going well in his life, it was because part of him had not finished growing up enough to figure out what to do instead. Let's see if you can figure out three things that he could have done with his feelings instead of hitting you. [Make list.] See, you are already doing some work on the growing-up part of you, the part that knows what to do besides hurt kids." If children cannot think of any alternatives to hitting, suggest some, and review the options with them later to demonstrate that they seem to have the ability to be the kind of grown-up that can successfully learn alternatives to abuse.

Sexual Abuse

Almost all children have had experiences of being overpowered by adults or bigger children that they did not like but could not stop, such as being tickled until it was uncomfortable or having an arm twisted painfully behind the back. They understand that some kinds of being touched hurt and feel bad and that other kinds are enjoyable. There are a number of good books available to help children understand that they have a right to say no and to tell someone who is hurting them or doing something that they don't like to stop or to get someone else to make that person stop. Such books are often helpful during discussions with children to explain why they are no longer with an abusive caregiver.

The helper must make it clear that most people want to be touched in ways that feel good to them and when they choose, but that some kind of touching is reserved for two grown-ups and is not allowed between a child and a grown-up because children are supposed to be learning how to get close in ways that are good for children. "Do you ever want someone to touch you in a certain place or in a certain way?" you might ask the child. "Like with a back rub, or a big hug, or a snuggle? Grown-ups do what [name] did because they want to be close in a special way that is fine for grown-ups but not good for children."

A child who has been sexually abused may think, "It was my fault because he got in trouble because I let him do it" or "because I told." Here, you might say, "He was the grown-up, and he should have known better and stopped. I think he knew that it was wrong, because he never did it when other grown-ups were around and he told you not to tell. But what happened was not good for you and he should not have done it at all. When you told, you helped him to do what he knew he should do, which was to stop."

If children are confused because their bodies responded to the sexual stimulation, they need to know that bodies are made to react in certain ways to certain things and that this just means they are working (McNamara 1992, 3). An example could be the way a knee jerks when a doctor taps it with a hammer.

Neglect

Often, caregivers neglect their children because of their own immaturity and because they have not learned how to take care of children. Frequently, they were neglected by their own parents and so never had an adequate model on which to base their parenting style. Helpers can explain that the caregivers had not finished learning how to take care of themselves yet, which made it very difficult for them to take good care of anyone else. When children are confused because their parents looked just as grown up as any other adult to them, they are sometimes able to understand that looking grown up on the outside doesn't necessarily mean being grown up on the inside. Sharing what is known about a neglectful caregiver's history can help a child understand: "Your dad's family was not able to take care of him so he lived in a number of different homes. I think he just missed out on learning how to take care of little children." Or, "Your mother and her mother fought a lot. Your mom kept running away, and she finally left home long before she was ready to have learned how to do the things that mothers do. My guess is that her mom had trouble figuring out how to be a mom and couldn't teach her how very well."

These kinds of conversations should be followed up with convincing reassurances that there is no reason that a child who has been neglected will not be able to be a good parent. "Do you think you will have children when you grow up?" the helper might say. (If the child says no, the helper can say, "Well, if you change your mind. . . .") "If you do have children, what kinds of things will you need to know how to do? What kinds of things do babies need from their moms and dads? [Make a list with the child.] Do you know how to fix a bottle, or change a diaper, or bathe a tiny baby?" Children often will say that they know how to do one or more of the things on the list. The helper can then ask how they learned to do these tasks. Often children report that they figured it out by watching someone else do it or from seeing it on television. If a child says that there is nothing on the list he or she knows how to do, you might want to teach one skill and then discuss how the child might learn the others before he or she has a baby to care for, pointing out the increasingly complicated things the child has already mastered as proof of ability.

Some children will feel guilty for having basic needs that were too difficult for their caregivers to manage; in such cases, discussions like those described in the section dealing with abuse and abandonment are helpful. It also helps to talk to children about how much their parents might have wished they could have been able to take care of them. A helper might ask, "Have you ever really wanted to do something, and tried and tried, but found that it was still too hard?" (Common examples are riding a bike without training wheels; hitting a home run; reading; writing in cursive; trying to stop biting nails or wetting the bed.) "I think that your mom really wanted to be able to bring you up. Here are some of the things she tried so that might happen [list them]. [Or, "Here are some of the things that people—visiting nurse, social worker, parenting class leader—tried to teach her."] But she just wasn't able to learn to do them, even though she tried and she wanted to." Responses like this are also good for allaying the common fear among neglected children that their parents just didn't want to take care of them.

There are, unfortunately, situations where a caregiver has shown little or no interest in learning how to take care of a child. If this is the case, the child needs extra support and clear information about what might have contributed to the parent's apparent lack of interest or affection.

Parental Rejection

Helpers need to take special care when a child is placed with another family because of parental rejection, because the likelihood for self-blame is so strong. Very likely there may have been something in the parent's own life or background that contributed to the rejection (for example, immaturity, poor parenting skills, addiction, a difficult childhood, or general frustration), or there may actually be something about the child that causes the parent's response. The helper also must determine whether the rejection was precipitated by something about which the child had no responsibility or choice. Perhaps the child's parent was unmarried, perhaps the child was not the preferred sex, or was born at an inopportune time in the parent's life, or was a different race, or was physically or mentally handicapped, or was conceived as the result of rape. One approach that has been successful when talking about such cases is to ask the child, "There you were, a tiny baby growing inside your first mom. You must have known that she really wanted to have a little girl. Why did you decide to be born a boy?" The ridiculous and obvious impossibility of this line of thinking seems to help eradicate self-blame in children.

Of course, children should also be helped to understand that not everyone shares the first parent's feeling. "Your first mom knew she found it very hard to feel comfortable with little boys. She made a good plan for you. She knew that other moms and dads think that boys are special. Now you have this mom and dad. How do you think they feel about having a son?" It can be very useful to ask the new caregivers in front of the child how they feel about him or her to help the child validate his or her self-esteem in the particular situation.

Occasionally, a helper will be talking to a child about a rejection that is, in part, an outgrowth of the child's behavior. The helper's task is to assist the child in understanding which causes of the rejection are in the parent and which belong to the child (many children go through a stage of temper tantrums, for example, but very few parents relinquish them for this reason). An overburdened caregiver may have found the child's destructiveness, defiance, or delinquency impossible to deal with and made arrangements for the child to live with someone else. In this case, the helper should point out to the child that there can be solutions to the problem. For example, perhaps you and the child can figure out together why the child needs to behave this way and what he or she might do instead to meet needs or express feelings. Perhaps the caregivers can be helped to understand how to handle the difficult behaviors. Perhaps another family can be located that does not see the child's behavior as so intolerable a problem.

Mental Illness

When adults are mentally ill, they are often confused about what is real and what is not, and they may have serious difficulty sorting out what is truly dangerous, leaving them frightened and desperate a good deal of the time. To explain this, helpers can begin by asking children, "Have you ever had a very scary dream, and when you woke up, you weren't sure whether it was real or not?" Or, "Do you sometimes feel scared to go downstairs [or upstairs or outside] by yourself when it's dark? Do you think that maybe something will 'get' you? When those scary things happen, how do you take care of yourself?" Most children will report that they want company when they are feeling scared or that they call on an adult for reassurance. Helpers can then explain that mentally ill adults also may need protection from their fears.

Perhaps a child's caregiver needs the help of other adults to feel or be safe or to make sure a medicine is taken, so he or she has to be in a hospital. "I'll take care of Dad," a child might think or say. A helper can explain, "Your dad needs another grown-up to keep him safe. Your job is to be learning the things kids your age are supposed to be learning, instead."

After a helper explains how fears or confusion or the need to be taken care of make it difficult for a mentally ill caregiver to think about or to know how to take care of a child, the child might insist, "Well, I'll wait until he isn't having those problems anymore." To this, the helper might respond, "I hear how hard this is for you and how much you wish it could be different. But you deserve to have the things you need right now, like food, clothes, hugs, someone to have fun with, someone to help you with school. That can't wait. This is your only turn to be eight years old [or whatever age the child is]. And you deserve to have your turn, like everyone else."

Incarceration

Explaining incarceration involves explaining that adults must go to jail when it seems that they have broken an important adult rule for which prison is the usual punishment. "What are some of the rules at your house?" the helper might ask the child. "Do you ever break any of them? And if you get punished, what happens? And then it is over, right? Well, your mom made a mistake [or "the judge is trying to decide if your mom made a mistake"] for which staying in jail is the grown-up punishment. While your mom is in jail, you need someone to take care of you, because kids don't go to jail with their parents to stay." If the news of imprisonment causes a child to wonder if the parent was a terrible person, a helper can say, "You know what lots of kids, especially little kids, tell me about breaking rules? They say that sometimes they just want to do something badly enough that they go ahead and do it and hope they won't get caught or talk themselves into thinking it isn't really so bad. I guess your parent may have been thinking kind of like a little kid in that way."

Alcohol or Drug Abuse

When separation is due to alcohol or drug abuse by the caregiver, a helper might ask a child, "Do you ever wish you could just make your upset feelings or your problems magically go away?" Odds are, the answer will be yes. "So do I. Your mom thought that using alcohol [or drugs] was the magic to make upset feelings and worries go away or that it would help her forget her problems. The problem was that the alcohol [or drugs] made it hard for her to remember to take care of you or to figure out how to make things work out. The trouble with using alcohol [or taking drugs] is that it isn't magic. It makes new problems, and the old ones don't go away. If you've ever done something bad and then lied about it, you know how it is: If you get caught, you have two problems instead of only one. You can solve that problem by deciding to stop lying. But by the time your mom might have been able to see that the alcohol [or drug] was causing new problems and keeping her from taking good care of you, she was addicted, and her body didn't want to stop." Or, "By the time she figured out the alcohol [drug] was causing more trouble than it helped, she thought her problems were so big that it wouldn't make any difference if she stopped drinking [using the drug] anyway." There are many good books for children of all ages that can help explain substance abuse. They can be found in many bookstores, libraries, or through Al-Anon or a hospital that specializes in working with substance abusers.

If a helper is concerned that a child will conclude, "If I feel bad, I can just take drugs [alcohol] and I will feel better," it is wise to check this with the child and to try to point out that the child has troubled feelings or problems and already knows other ways of responding: "When you have problems or bad feelings now, what do you try [or do] to make things work out or to help yourself feel better? I already know one thing you do now: You know that sometimes talking to someone can help things get better."

Loss from Unknown Causes

Sometimes children suffer a loss or separation, and little is known about the causes. This is frequently the case for children who have been adopted from overseas, where they may have been abandoned or separated from caregivers in wartime or as a result of great poverty. In such situations, it may be helpful to have a conversation like this: "Most adopted kids sometimes think about their birth parents. You might wonder what they were like and why they didn't take care of you until you were grown up. No one really knows about your parents because the people at the agency didn't get to talk to them and neither did we, so all we can do is guess. This is what we know for sure: A lot of kids in the country where you were born don't stay with their parents because there isn't enough money or food. Or their families don't think they can give their kids a good life. Or there is a war, and people get killed. Or the child is of a different race and no one will help the mother. I think that your parents' reason was probably one of these. What I really, really think is that they didn't leave you because you were bad somehow or because they didn't love you."

HELPING CHILDREN JOIN NEW FAMILIES

It appears that children who continue to receive the loving, involved care of at least one of their parents will have the best chance to avoid serious scarring from a loss, as long as the parent allows complete freedom to mourn. If both parents have died or if neither parent is able to care for the child, the next best caregiver is probably someone whom the child already knows and trusts. The child can expect that such a caregiver will have his or her best interests at heart. But for many children such options do not exist. Their best chance to have consistent, loving parenting will involve being placed with a new family.

The addition of a new parent or a move into foster care or from one family to another poses its own set of challenges, which can make the resolution of the original loss more complicated. Each new loss triggers memories of previous losses and stirs up the strong feelings yet to be released. For children who are separated from living parents, a new family setting may cause strong reactions not only because of grief and continued loyalty to the previous family but because children tend to hold on to deep hopes and wishes that problems may yet be resolved and that a return to the family of origin may still be possible. Replacement underscores the reality that the wish will be delayed, making the outcome less likely.

Remarriage or finalizing an adoption makes it clear that it will not be fulfilled at all.

If you are preparing a child for a relocation, a remarriage, or an adoption, you should give the child firsthand information about what is happening. When the loss involves a change of who the child will be living with, where the child will be living, or who will be the primary caregiver, the change should be discussed several times with the child, either by the caregiver or by another adult known and trusted by the child. Just because the adults involved think the new situation offers a great many benefits and is a cause for celebration doesn't mean that the child will agree or adjust quickly to the new family constellation without mourning for the old family, wishing or hoping for reunification, or regretting what might have been. An assumption particularly common to remarriage is that the child will be delighted finally to have two full-time parents, whereas the child actually may feel angry about having to share the attention of a parent with a new love and may be edgy and defensive about having to deal with another adult who can make demands, set limits, and impose discipline.

Children can benefit a great deal from having an adult open a conversation about what to call the new parents or siblings. Do they have to call the new caregiver by a parental name? How will their previous parent(s) feel about that? Isn't it weird for a kid to call a caregiver by the first name? What will other kids think? Do they say, "This is my sister or my stepsister"? How do they explain that they have a different last name? Some youngsters deal with these multiple dilemmas by experimenting with different names during the first year or more. Some avoid the issue by not using names at all.

Brenner observes that another area of difficulty is the question of who has authority in the new family. She suggests that initial stresses can be alleviated if all the important and involved adults work as a unit to sort out mutually acceptable lines of authority, communication, and rules and regulations, pointing out that such agreements help eliminate the confusion and loyalty pulls the child might experience otherwise (1984, 34).

Preparing Children for a Change of Caregiver

If a child is involved in a legal-risk adoptive placement or another kind of custody dispute, it is often helpful for the child's attorney or a therapist to relay the timing of events. But helpers working with children being placed or replaced into new families often find that there just aren't many specifics to tell: Both the planning and the outcome may be beyond their control. In such circumstances, it is wise to be straightforward about what facts are known and honest about what is unknown. Because younger children often have little sense of calendar time, they can be reassured that nothing will change about where they are living until after some major celebration that they are sure to recall. Then, if their conversation or behavior indicate concern and stress when that date approaches, they can be actively supported. If the expected date is moved forward or postponed, the child should be informed and another specific memorable date cited as the time when things will be happening: "When I told you nothing would change until Halloween, I did not know that it might be sooner. Now it seems . . ." or "The judge will not be making any changes about where you are living until after [the next major holiday]."

As with marital disputes, caregivers or others working with the child are wise not to try to force him or her to choose favorites or to take sides. One of the important and precious gifts that can be conferred on a child who is to join a new family is for the current parent to wish the child well and to give that child permission to become a part of the new family. Relinquishing parents effectively give this permission when they allow time for the child to make a gradual transition to the new family setting by visiting often before the final move. If the parent cannot give this permission in person, another helping adult can foster the feeling that it is all right to share affection with a new caregiver. Telling the child that the parents know this is a good choice, even though they might like something else to be happening, or that they would probably like this new family (if that is true) also may make it easier for the child to accept the new situation.

When a move is in part due to the child's own unmanageable

or delinquent behavior, other approaches may be more appropriate. You might try making a contract with the child, spelling out the conditions of a reunion (if this is a possibility). As discussed in the section on parental rejection, you could help the child explore the reasons for the unacceptable behavior and figure out other ways to meet his or her emotional needs.

Introducing a New Family

When a new family or caregiver must be introduced, several techniques can be used to make the change easier. Adoption workers have developed the approach of introducing a family by means of a book of photographs that a child can look through to experience vicariously what the new home looks like, sounds like, and feels like. (With modifications, such books can be equally helpful when a child is making the first visit to a distant parent, when a stay with relatives is planned while caregivers must be away, or when a family is moving to a new city or town that the child has never seen.) Later, through a gradually increasing series of visits, the child can observe and experience what the new house and new parents are like.

Robert and his caseworker sit together looking at the book made for him by a waiting family. It reads something like this: "This is the Watson family [picture of whole family]. They live in a grey house [picture of the house] at the end of a busy street. This is Daddy Watson. He likes to fish, garden, and fix the house [pictures of him at some of these activities]. He would like another child to go fishing with. This is Mommy Watson. She likes to read, cook, and sing [pictures of her]. She would like another child to bake cookies with." The book goes on to introduce each member of the family, including the pets, and to describe typical family activities, including suggestions for how Robert might share in these activities. The Watsons have wisely included a picture of the table where they eat (to show Robert he can be nurtured at their house), the room with the bed where he will be sleeping (as if to say, "There is a place for you here"), and the school he will be going to. Robert and his worker can use this book and these pictures as the basis of a number of conversations to help Robert feel less strange when he meets the Watson family.

When there is no opportunity to help a child move gradually into a new family, these books are especially useful:

At eleven one night, caseworker Peter Haney must make an emergency placement of six-year-old Becky into the Strongs' home. The Department of Welfare where he works has made it a priority to keep books introducing all its foster families, which can be used to ease the transition into new living situations. Peter makes a stop at the office and picks up the Strongs' family book. At the hospital where he meets Becky, he sits with her and says, "Your mom is hurt and has to stay here for a while. She has asked me to take you to visit with some friends of mine. Let me show you some pictures of where you'll be going and who will take care of you." They read the booklet together, looking at the pictures. Becky is quiet, but Peter can tell from her face that she is looking at the pictures carefully, and she seems to be listening. He reads the short captions under the pictures, ready to answer any questions she may ask. The book eases the shock of the sudden placement not only for Becky, who feels less as if she is being dumped off somewhere, but for the worker and the receiving family as well.

In the case of a prospective adoption, it is unfair and deceitful to arrange blind showings, where a family has the chance to observe a child without the child knowing what is going on. All but the youngest children are likely to see through this ploy and to have doubts about sharing their concerns with such apparently untrustworthy people. The use of a videotape that shows the child in a variety of situations and moods is a much more straightforward way to help a family decide whether they are interested in actually meeting the child and pursuing an adoption. Questions are sometimes raised about how to arrange such a filming or a TV appearance or a newspaper feature in such a way that children do not feel rejected if no family expresses interest in them. Children seem able to handle this risk well, so long as the adult explains (1) that the pictures are going to be used to try to help find the right family for them and that it may take a while for that to happen and (2) that not only may the pictures help find a family for this child but they also might help other children find families of their own. In addition, workers also can set the stage by telling children that it is the workers' job to try to find them a family to grow up with and that the pictures will help workers do that. If no family, or no appropriate family, comes forward, children can be reassured that efforts on their behalf will continue. If children comment or question what is happening with potential families, workers can continue to focus on the workers' responsibility—"I seem to be poky finding the right folks for you. I'm working on it"—rather than saying, "We just haven't had much response yet," which implies that there are not many interested families.

Facilitating Good-byes and Hellos

There is no question that the way a child moves from one caregiver to another can be vitally important in the attempt to reestablish continuity, sense of meaning, and self-esteem. The success of the new relationship does not depend on the fading of the memory of the earlier one; rather, the more distinct the two relationships are kept, the more the new one is likely to prosper. Yet caregivers are sometimes invested in having their children see them as the all-good parents and past caregivers or birth parents as the bad, inadequate parents. Children may feel conflicting loyalties if they think they must turn their backs on old caregivers before they can share affection and intimacy with new ones. Helping adults must respect children's needs to maintain actual or internal ties to noncustodial parents while devising ways to help them understand that it is possible and fine to have a parent-child relationship with more than one parent or set of parents.

Lucky are the children who are not only given the chance to know something about their new families before a move but are also leaving caregivers who give them permission to be close to these alternate caregivers. Who tell them directly that they are loved, lovable, and capable of loving others. Who say that it is all right for the children to love these new people and be loved in return. Who make it clear that they believe the children can do well in the new setting and that they wish the youngsters success and a good life. But such conversations can be quite painful for the adults involved, and they may dread and resist dealing with the feelings aroused during these transitions. This is especially true when the court is involved, whether with a custody dispute or with a protective-service complaint. Yet, even if the decision to sever a parental connection comes about after prolonged conflict and no matter how difficult the situation that caused the termination of parental contact or the decision by caregivers to relinquish a child, provisions should be made and an opportunity provided for the child and adults to meet to share as supportive a good-bye as is possible. If the parties directly involved in the dispute are unable or lack the skills to arrange a good-bye, then it is wise to seek a trained neutral party to facilitate one when everyone is willing—whenever that is—so that the youngster is not left with unfinished business.

My own experience convinces me that we underestimate caregivers, selling them short by assuming that they are "too limited" or "too angry" to provide what the child needs. When given a fair chance to meet with their youngsters to say good-bye, to wish them well, to confirm the reality of what is happening, caregivers frequently are able to rise to the occasion and do an impressive job of trying to help their children with the difficult transition taking place. Children benefit because they suffer less confusion, preoccupation with getting back to their previous situation, or concern that they were somehow responsible for the loss. And caregivers benefit from the chance to work out their feelings about what they have decided or what has been decided for them and to be supported and involved during the transition.

Typically what seems to work well is to have at least two preparatory meetings with the caregiver(s), at least one with the child, and finally a combined meeting. Such meetings give both the child and the caregiver a chance to think out and to practice what they may want to say to one another. It also helps them prepare emotionally for the meeting, so that saying good-bye is somewhat easier and they are less likely to make small talk instead of sharing what needs to be said. It is useful, if the adult agrees, to tape these preliminary conversations. Such tapes can be used (with some editing, if necessary) to reinforce what happens in the actual good-bye meeting and communicate any messages the adult is unable to say to the child when they meet. Copies should be given to both caregiver and child. If taping is not possible, the helper who is facilitating should take notes, reading them back to the caregiver to be sure his or her words have been recorded accurately.

With this kind of supported preparation, both child and adult are often quite able to share their thoughts lovingly and fully when the meeting actually takes place. Sometimes they may need some help beginning and sometimes they may have difficulty actually saying much at all. The supportive helper can guide the exchange as long as what the helper says comes from and captures the essence of what was said in the preparation sessions.

Donna has been involved in a prolonged struggle to get her life together enough so that she can provide safe and adequate housing and supervision for her daughter Danielle, age seven, who has been in foster care for several years. Those who have worked with her describe Donna as immature, insecure, and aggressively defensive. Although Donna contested it, the court terminated her parental rights, believing it unlikely that Danielle ever could safely be returned to her mother's care.

The guardian ad litem meets with Donna to help prepare for a termination session between mother and daughter. "Donna, I know that you wanted to take Danielle home with you and that you believe that a child belongs with her mother. You have told all of us—me, the social workers, and the judge—that you really love Danielle and that you want her to have a good life. Is that still true? I believe that Danielle loves you too and that she needs you to help her with what is happening. I want to ask you to do one more thing for her. I want you to meet with her and tell her the things that you have told the rest of us: that you love her and that you want her to have a good life. Then I want you to tell her that she will not be coming home to live with you. I know this may be very hard, but I am asking you because you are her mother in a very special way. No one else can help her believe these things as well as you can."

This approach respects and honors the special relationship that exists between Donna and Danielle, affirming that Donna has been and will continue to be an important person in Danielle's life whether they live together or not. The guardian ad litem is asking the mother who gave this child the gift of life to give her an equally important gift: permission to move on and to have as good a life as possible.

Another visit is held separately with Danielle to help prepare her for the good-bye meeting with her mother. "Danielle, you know that the grown-ups have been having trouble agreeing on whether you should go back to live with your mother or whether you needed to grow up in a different family. Even though your mother seems to really wish she could bring you home, she just doesn't seem to be able to figure out right now how to manage her life in a way that will let her take care of children. The law says that all children are important and that they must have at least one parent who can take care of all the things that every child needs to have. So the judge has said that you will not go back to live with your mother anymore. I have been talking to your mother about how she might say a last good-bye to you. Next week, we are all going to have a meeting together so that you two can talk and say good-bye to each other. I'm wondering what you might want to tell your Mom?"

At the time of the meeting, the helper begins, turning to the child and saying, "Danielle, do you remember why we are meeting with your mother today?" Danielle nods her head and looks at the floor. "We are meeting today so that you and your mom will have a chance to say good-bye to living and being together." Then, turning to the mother, the helper goes on to say, "Donna, you have told me some pretty important things about how you feel about Danielle. I'm wondering what you would like to say to her?" Donna blurts, "I love you, and I wish you were coming home," and begins to weep.

"Danielle, I heard your mom say that she loves you and that she wishes things were different and that you could come home. Is that what you heard?" The child nods in agreement. "You know what else she told me? She told me that she thinks you are a pretty special kid. And that you deserve to have good things happen in your life." Checking with mother, the helper asks, "Have I got that right?" Donna nods. The helper moves closer to the child: "Danielle, would you look at your mom for a minute? Do you think she is mad at you?" Danielle shakes her head no. "That's what she told me. She told me that you didn't do anything wrong or bad. Do you believe that?" Danielle shrugs her shoulders. "Looks like maybe you're not so sure about that right now. I think we should ask her. Donna, are you saying good-bye to Danielle because she was bad?" Donna says no. "Do you know what else your mom told me? She told me that she hopes that you have a good life and that you find a family to love you and help you grow up. Do you think she meant that? Do you think it would be all right with her if you loved them, too? Donna, I want to check that out with you: Is it really and truly okay with you if Danielle is happy and loves people in her new family the way she loves you?"

During these good-bye meetings, the helper can serve as either a silent or an active witness to the exchange of the positive things both adult and child said at the preparation meetings, until all the hard but loving things have been shared. If caregiver and child have the emotional energy, the candle ritual described later in this chapter might serve to conclude the ceremony. If they are shutting down or getting fidgety because of the intensity of the meeting, the ritual could be done separately with each of them at another time.

It is useful to tape the final session, making copies for the caregiver and for the child's caseworker, or foster parent, or therapist, so that the child can play it over and over as a way of integrating the finality of the good-bye and its blessings. It is also useful to take pictures at the meeting and to give prints both to the child's caregiver(s) and to whoever can take care of them for the child; these pictures can help all concerned hold on to the validity of their memories and feelings. If the child is adopted, his or her new parents may find it easier to support the grief process if they can hear the tape as well, so that they can directly witness the struggle of the good-bye and the courage and emotion that caregiver and child shared. It may make it easier for the new parents to leave the child's feelings for the birth parent(s) or other caregiver(s) alone and concentrate instead on cultivating their own relationship with the child.

These good-bye meetings can be hard for everyone. Helpers may find themselves moved to tears by the courage and pain involved. They need to know that it is all right for them to be visibly moved. In many ways, they are like the mourners at a funeral who share in the grieving. Two decades of working with children facing final good-byes have convinced me that meetings such as these are one of the best ways to prevent misunderstandings that we have to offer. As mentioned in chapter 1, similar meetings can be arranged when a parent or family member is dying or when there will be no more contact for some other reason. Whatever the situation, the chance for everyone to express their love and best wishes can make a significant difference to all. These meetings free adults and children to mourn their loss clearly and help to minimize the confusion, conflict, and ongoing difficulty that can complicate the grieving process seriously and contribute to long-lasting trauma.

Conducting the Candle Ritual: One good technique for letting children know that they can love a new family without giving up the love of other significant people is a candle ritual. First make enough holes in a board or a strip of Styrofoam to accommodate candles representing the caregivers in a child's life. (The Sabbath candles found in the kosher section of the grocery store work very well; birthday candles are not as good because they burn out too quickly.) Then set up the candles, one for the child's birth parents and one for each of the child's subsequent caregivers or each place the child has lived. Here is one child's story to show you how the ritual might go:

Holding a new candle, the helper begins, "When you were just born, you were born with a special gift—that was the gift of being able to love and to be loved. This gift of loving is like a light; it makes you feel warm and happy." [The helper lights the candle.] "This candle reminds us of your very own light—the special light of love inside you. When you were brand new, you went home with your mom and dad. You and your parents spent time together. They fed you, even in the middle of the night. They changed your diapers when they were wet or messy. They probably smiled at you and cuddled you. And you got close to them, and they got close to you. Of course, when people get used to one another and they get close to one another, they begin to have special feelings. They share the loving gift inside them. And you lit a love light with each other." [The helper puts the child's lighted candle next to the unlit candle that represents the birth parents until it, too, lights.] "After a while your parents began to fight a lot and hurt each other. Other people heard them fighting and hitting and finally someone called the police. When the police came, they could see that someone had been hitting you, too. They knew the rule that children are not for hurting, so they took you to see the judge, and the judge decided that you would need to find another family to belong with. Your social worker took you to live at the Robersons' foster home until the grown-ups could figure out how best to make things safe for you. At first it was strange and scary for you at the Robersons. You told people you wanted to go home. But after a while you got used to them, and they got used to you. You all got close to one another [the helper now puts the child's candle next to the second candle until it lights], and you lit a love light with them, too. The important thing is that getting close to them and loving them did not make your love light for your birth parents change. A wonderful part of the gift of loving is that you can love as many people as you get close to and never run out of loving.

"You know what happened next. After a while, the judge decided that it did not seem as if you could go back to live with your birth family and that you needed a family where you could live until you were all grown up. Since the Robersons were the kind of family that takes care of children until the judge decides whether children will be going back to grow up with their birth family or whether they will need a different family, your social worker began looking for the kind of family that could love you and take care of you the whole time you were growing up. Your social worker found the Gilberts, who have been wanting another child to bring up. You have been visiting them for a while and getting ready to move in with them. Just like when you first went to the Robersons, it may seem strange and scary and maybe sad; maybe you'll be angry

60

sometimes and wish you could go back to your foster home. After a while, I think you will get close to them and they will get close to you, and you will light a love light there as well, but you can still love all of the people who have taken care of you and been close to you for as long as you want."

The ceremony shows, in ways that even the youngest children understand, that new family constellations do not demand the death of old relationships and that differences between family members can be tolerated. The ritual is easily adapted to almost all circumstances. Variations can be used with children who have lost a parent, foster children, children who are being adopted, and step-children who are worried that if they have to share a parent with a stepbrother or stepsister they will somehow lose that parent's love. Obviously, it will be necessary to add different details if the child was not well nurtured in early life. The specifics of the ritual are as diverse as the circumstances are endless. Depending on the situation, a helper might say, "Your dad and mom stopped loving each other. Your dad went to live in a different house. But his love light for you still kept going, and your love light for him kept going too." Or, "Your mom had an accident and died. The warm, loving part of her was gone [here extinguishing the candle or moving it out of sight, depending on religious beliefs]. You kept loving her even after she was dead, and your light stayed burning." Or, "Now your mom is going to marry Ted. He will be living in your house and doing some of the things for you that your dad used to do when he and your mom were still married. In time, you may get used to having Ted help you with things. You may get close to him and he may get close to you. [The helper lights a new candle representing the stepparent.] When that happens, there will be one more person for you to love and who loves you. The important thing for you to remember is that the light of love you feel for your dad will not go out. Loving is not like soup that you dish up until it is all gone. You can love as many people as you get close to. But no one will make you blow out any of your candles. You do not have to take the love you feel for your dad away to love Ted."

Whatever the variation, the child must recognize the permission to grow close to a new caregiver. And, since children do not always get close to their caregivers and they may not have loved or felt loved every place they lived, the child should be the one to decide whether to light candles or skip over them. The beauty of the ceremony is that it makes clear to the child and to the adults involved that it is unnecessary for a child to be forced into feeling that love for one important adult must be extinguished in order to love or to please another. It also lays healthy groundwork for the notion that the child has the capacity to belong and love in a number of new family constellations, while making it plain that if the love doesn't happen, it was because something got in the way of the child and the caregiver getting close.

Frequently, children show visible relief following this concrete ritual. Even very young children have been known to object, loudly and rightfully, "Don't try to make me blow out my candle," when they are caught in a tug-of-war between different caregivers. It also helps the new caregivers understand at both intellectual and symbolic levels that they should focus on how to enhance their closeness with the child, concentrate on their own candle, and let the others alone.

Because the candle was chosen for its symbolic connection with how children perceive love—as light and warmth—it is important to close the ritual carefully:

"I can see, Andres, that you understand about loving. I don't think you need these candles any more today to help you. This candle is not really your mother. She will not stop loving you if we put it out. Are you ready to help me blow it out?"

For very concrete- or magical-thinking children, you may need to ask permission before extinguishing each candle. For others, you can say, "I think we are through with these candles for today. Are you sure it's safe to blow them out and that the loving goes on even after they stop burning?"

"Handing Over" the Child: For infants or young children who cannot understand the symbolism involved in the candle ritual, the ritual of physically "handing over" the child to the new caregiver seems to work best (Fahlberg 1991, 210–12).

The Parkers are delighted with Joy, the fifteen-month-old daughter they will be adopting. In order to help her make the transition from her foster parents, the Wilsons, the Parkers have spent part of two days visiting the Wilsons' home, and Jan Parker has closely watched Joy's routine. Sitting with Barbara Wilson at mealtime, she sits smiling at Joy while the child is being fed. Midway through the meal, Barbara passes the spoon to Jan and lets her take over the feeding. Watching her foster mother's face and body, Joy has a chance to see in her familiar parent's eyes that it is safe to take nurturing from this new person, making her feel that the familiar adult trusts the new one with her safety and well-being.

This technique can be extended to include putting the child down for a nap, packing for the move, and other routines. An important action seems to be the actual handing of the child from one adult's arms to the other's at the time of the final move.

UNDERSTANDING AND
SUPPORTING GRIEF

❧

3 | How a child responds to a separation or loss will be colored by how well the child knew the individual and by how important and supportive the child felt the relationship to be. Current research concludes that children who have healthy, happy relationships with their primary caregiver before a separation or death apparently enter the stressful situation with a sort of immunization. The years of warmth and caring have taught them effective ways of facing and handling problems, and they seem to cope more easily than do other youngsters (Brenner 1984, 43). And when children feel only tenuous connections, even with a closely related family member, their grief is likely to be short-lived and simple, which may come as a surprise to adults, who generally anticipate stronger reactions.

Each child's experience with grief will be unique. Yet every child's grief process will include three basic phases: early grief, acute grief, and subsiding grief. Though the phases may follow one after the other, overlap, or shift backward and forward, each will include several components that occur in a somewhat predictable order. Like children, adults, too, proceed through these phases even when dealing with minor losses. For example, imagine yourself running to a ringing phone and answering it just as the caller hangs up. Your first thought might be, "Oh, no. I couldn't have missed it," an expression of shock/denial, emotions common to early grief. The next reactions are likely to include some of the responses typical of acute grief: "Why didn't they hold on a little longer?" or

---

64

"Why didn't I get here sooner?"(anger and blame); "Gee, I really wanted to talk with somebody, and now I've missed my chance" (sadness and despair). Finally you might experience subsiding grief: "Oh, well, if it was important they'll call back" (understanding and acceptance). Then you might return to whatever you were doing, or call another friend, or buy an answering machine, depending on how you deal with the aftermath of the loss (integration). The whole process might take place in a few minutes, but the three stages of the recovery process have been experienced, and you are ready to continue with your life (Colgrove, Bloomfield, and McWilliams 1977, 16).

Sharing a child's journey through the stages of grief can be acutely painful for involved adults. Recognizing that their visible hurt causes discomfort to adults, children may deny or hide their feelings. Adults also are frequently misled as to the depth of a child's misery because most youngsters can only tolerate short outbursts of grief and are easily distracted, which can make it seem that they are finished mourning long before this is actually the case (Brenner 1984, 43).

Because children's expressions of grief, pain, and misery can be quite different from adults', concerned helpers need to know how to recognize common behavioral reactions in grieving children and to have a sense of how best to respond supportively. Youngsters who are supported in their grief processes are most likely to integrate losses in a healthy fashion and to move through the stages of grief productively.

EARLY GRIEF

Early grief involves a number of defense styles that occur in no particular order. The most common reactions include denial, which can involve dissociation, hyperactivity, irritability, and protest, and alarm and panic. All can entail intense distress and irritability.

Denial

Luis, age 8, has recently attended funeral services for his grand-mother, who has lived with his family since he was an infant. He still cries and talks about how much he misses her. Tonight, as he is watching TV, the doorbell rings. Luis runs excitedly to the door, exclaiming, "I'm coming, Abuelita, I'll let you in."

Carla seems to be weathering the first few weeks of her parents' separation quite well. But today she rushes inside hurrying past her mother and calling, "Dad? Dad?" Her startled mother interjects, "Carla, your dad doesn't live here anymore. You know he's in Michigan." "You're wrong, Mom. I just saw him driving down the street. He's got to be here," Carla insists. Her mother realizes that Carla has probably seen a car similar to her father's and has let her wishes take over.

Denial is the earliest psychological defense to develop. Conscious or unconscious, it is a mechanism that helps us prevent, avoid, or reduce anxiety when we feel threatened. Much the same way we may feel little pain after a severe physical injury, in times of great stress, this built-in mechanism may allow us to shut down our emotional awareness and screen out potentially overwhelming or devastating information.

Denial allows grieving children to suppress intense emotions that make them feel too vulnerable and to conserve the energy they will need to master the adjustments ahead. Denial also offers them a time-out or reprieve from the pain and work of mourning. A child's first response to the news or experience of a loss may be numbness or acute panic followed by numbness. Underneath, there is usually a good deal of apprehension, which may show in outbursts of panic, extreme distress, anger or some combination of the three. As the reality of the loss begins to register, the child may become increasingly irritable and wail and sob aloud for the lost person.

In early grief, it is not uncommon for the loss to be temporarily forgotten. Bereaved individuals may dial a familiar phone number before remembering that the person at the other end is no longer there to answer. Or they may rush toward someone thinking he or she is the absent family member. During daydreams or at night, children often imagine the lost person so vividly that it seems impossible to them that the person is really gone. Such experiences may leave the child feeling comforted and reassured and eager to dream again or may cause the child to dread sleep because of the painful awareness of loss that comes with waking. Sometimes children have bad dreams about what has happened that startle them awake, shaken and anxious. It can be helpful if others allow time to listen and encourage children to talk about their dream experiences, for they can process their losses better if their dreaming doesn't add to the difficulties of grieving.

Bereaved individuals frequently feel that they can sense the presence of a lost loved one sitting in a favorite chair or speaking in the next room. But where an adult would use the nuances of language to explain and report the experience, "For a moment, I was sure that Steve was just upstairs," a child, being more concrete, might call out, "Stevie, is that you?" and start up the stairs. Sometimes children carry on an actual conversation, insisting, like the small child with an imaginary friend, that they can see and hear the absent person, which may cause onlookers to fear that the child is hallucinating.

Children may actively suppress their feelings as a way of supporting denial, saying to themselves, "This can't be true because if it were I would feel bad. I feel fine, so it's not really happening." Or they may do so in order to please their caregivers, parroting what they have been told: "It's really all for the best. I'll be fine." Part of the denial reaction can be directly connected to how others respond to them and their loss. When there is a family loss or separation, adults tend to rally around the adults involved, often causing the children to feel that their grief is not important or valid. When this happens, children may suppress their grief rather than risk being ignored or discounted or because they believe they are responding as expected. To complicate matters, children often lack models or experience to show them how to deal with their grief. And in the case of divorce or a move from one family to another, there may be no traditional mourning rituals for the loss they have suffered.

Disassociation, Shock, and Numbing: Keisha is normally a busy, out-going toddler, constantly exploring her environment, eager to enter into shared activity and play. At the beginning of the week, however, her mother had emergency surgery. Her father has been dropping her at day care earlier and picking her up later each night so that he can stop by the hospital on his way to and from work. The day-care provider is now expressing concern about Keisha, re-porting that she is unusually quiet and withdrawn and often sits with a sad, glazed expression on her face. When she can be drawn into play, she seems disoriented and almost mechanical. What has happened to this busy, happy little runabout?

Once realization of a loss or separation hits, many children ap-pear to go through daily life like robots, smiling or responding as if on cue. Children may report that they feel disconnected from themselves, as if they were watching themselves on TV. This experi-ence of disassociation may last only a few hours, or it may continue off and on for several months. During this time, it is common for children to experience diminished body awareness. They are likely to trip, fall, spill, and drip things with greater frequency, making them seem inattentive or clumsy.

It is not unusual for children in this stage to seem spacy or list-less; to withdraw silently and show little interest in normal activi-ties; to sit for long periods gazing into space, avoiding people and conversation. Some children physically withdraw, burrowing under furniture or retreating to their rooms or to confined spaces such as closets. This kind of behavior can be especially striking in a child who is usually on the go, causing caregivers to worry that the child is experiencing some sort of breakdown.

Regression: Emily, who is six, has reverted to baby talk since her favorite playmate became gravely ill. No matter how her parents respond, it seems to make no difference. They are beginning to lose patience with her constant whining and lisping.

Telling nine-year-old Joseph to get himself ready for church wasn't a problem before his father died. But now he complains that it is too hard to tie his tie, his shirt is rarely tucked in, and he often has to be reminded to zip his zipper. Surely, he ought to be able to dress himself at his age!

Regression is a common companion to grief. Many children when faced with a loss or a life change may react by temporarily losing a skill or by reverting to old, comforting behaviors. Some show diminished physical coordination and language mastery. Like the toddler who resumes wetting or requests a bottle following the birth of a sibling, the busy, independent school-age youngster may seek the comfort of a lap, a thumb, or the return of an old security object when things are hard. Children may demand to be babied and want help with dressing or bathing. They may whine and complain that tasks are too hard or crumple on the floor, weeping or throwing tantrums. Regression may also include hitting, biting, soiling, and increased oral activity, sucking on fingers, thumbs, or hair or chewing on clothing, cuticles, pencils, or wads of paper. Some children show signs that they need additional security by becoming uncharacteristically possessive or by stealing.

Regression often causes adults to worry, fearing that the slide backward may be permanent. But not only is it normal, it also can be a positive, healthy way to respond to feeling overwhelmed. As irritating as it may be, it is not usually a conscious choice or done for effect. Major, permanent stresses, such as the loss of a parent or divorce, can set off regressive behaviors that may resurface off and on for several months and perhaps recur, even years later, when something retriggers the loss experience. Once children are allowed to express their upset and to make some of the necessary readjustments, they usually regain their previous levels of equilibrium.

Although regression can be part of the healing process for many children, caregivers are wise not to relax limits to an extreme. While they should not be overly punitive, they do need to be firm. I picked up a good rule of thumb during a conversation with Nancy Samalin, founder of Parent Guidance Workshops in New York City: Be permissive with the feelings but strict with the limits ("I can see that it is making you angry that your sister keeps getting into your things, but I cannot allow you to bite her. Let's find a way to keep these toys out of her reach"). Adults who are concerned that a child's regressive behavior will draw ridicule from other children can request that the child restrict the behavior to the privacy of home. After a reasonable time, they should convey that they are confident that the child can resume more age-appropriate behavior, perhaps focusing on one task at a time to help the child slowly resume previously mastered activities and responsibilities. The goal is to sort out fair expectations and fair timing. Four good questions to ask are: Why might my child be doing this? Am I helping my child to express feelings directly without judgment? How can I help my child grow through this period and move beyond it? Am I avoiding confronting something that might be keeping this behavior alive?

The caregiver who remains concerned about how severely the child has regressed or how long the regression is lasting should consult a professional. Short-term play therapy where the child is allowed to use regressive behavior may help caregiver and child work out ways to address grief issues without the adult becoming involved in a power struggle or capitulating to avoid tears or an angry struggle.

Protest: Tasha, whose mother left her with a neighbor and subsequently disappeared, is convinced that her mother meant to keep in touch but couldn't because Tasha was sent to a foster home. She also blames herself, "If I could just remember how to get back to Jan's, my mom would come and get me." When she was finally told that her mother not only knew where she was but had decided to relinquish her for adoption her response was, "That's a lie! No way would she do something like that! I don't believe you!" Unless Tasha is helped to give up her denial about why she no longer lives with her birth parents, she is likely to turn her anger on her social worker and then on her new parents. After all, she may reason, if nobody adopts her, then her mother has to take her back.

Children with an absent parent may deny the realities of the circumstances that caused the loss and adamantly refuse to believe that the parent is no longer available. They may cherish and review memories, mementos, letters, and pictures, sometimes obsessively. They may beg to see the parent or to call them. They may angrily blame the current caregiver and others for the absence.

When the current caregiver feels competitive toward the previous one(s), these reactions can be quite difficult. But although this behavior may cause resentment or jealousy in the adults involved, it is a healthy sign that these children are able to form strong, close attachments, accept nurturing, and return love. Whether there is a subsequent positive connection to a new stepparent or family depends on whether the children are supported in their grief and not forced to give up their memories and loyalties, so that they can make the necessary adjustments that will allow them to attach again.

Distraction, Diversion, and Hyperactivity: Eleven-year-old Leandra is a very active child. It seems to the Johnsons that she has chattered, fidgeted, or made nonsense noises with her mouth ever since she came to live with them. They find it hard to think, to carry on a conversation, or to relax. Mealtimes are especially chaotic as Leandra squirms and giggles, taps and bangs things.

After a loss, many people, of all ages, may become preoccupied with keeping very, very busy in order to avoid thinking about what has happened. Children may dislike playing alone and demand company or constant TV to help them keep their minds off what has happened. Or they may pour their energies into school, sports, clubs, and hobbies, where they can both keep busy and feel competent. Some become preoccupied with the problems of others. Adolescents often use headphones or the telephone to fill up quiet times and block internal reactions. Or they may begin to use alcohol or drugs to help them forget or stop caring about the loss. As outside conditions make it harder to keep reality at bay, youngsters can become more and more frenzied and desperate. When expected to be quiet or to concentrate, children may rock, masturbate, or sing and talk to themselves instead. Mostly this happens at night, but it may also happen at school. Wherever it occurs, such behavior can be extremely embarrassing and annoying, to the point of preventing others from sleeping or studying. Unfortunately, too often, teachers, caregivers, and pediatricians decide that children going through this phase should be medicated, not realizing that they may be experiencing a normal grief reaction. It is a

71

good idea to have such children diagnosed by pediatric neurologists, who are more able to differentiate between agitated grief, which needs time and support, and attention-deficiency or hyperactive disorders that should be treated with medication.

Children who constantly chatter or otherwise make noise may also simply be seeking attention. If so, they need help finding better ways to get one-on-one time from those around them. Caregivers and teachers may need to think about how they, too, can reach out to such children so that they don't have to resort to this kind of behavior. These kinds of children benefit when they are encouraged or learn on their own how to divert their abundant energy in positive, less frenzied ways. Activities such as swimming, roller-skating or roller-blading, and shooting hoops let youngsters release tension, distract themselves, and interact socially. Such activities also give children a chance to increase and demonstrate skills successfully, promoting their self-esteem and self-control. Other parts of life may seem to be careening out of control but here is a haven where things are not in transition or falling apart and where the child can feel intact and competent.

Alarm and Panic

It is normal for people to fear the prospect of losing their loved ones and ending up abandoned, helplessly alone. Adults may wonder if life would be worth living if that happened, but most have learned that they can go on living after the loss of someone they depend on. Children, on the other hand, have little or no such experience. Dependent on others for care, they are particularly vulnerable for, without that care, they can actually die.

Because losing a loved one heightens children's survival terrors, their bodies react as if there was a sudden danger. Children may experience increased heart rates, muscular tension, sweating, dryness of mouth, and bowel and bladder relaxation. They may feel short of breath and sigh and pant during conversations about the loss. These normal physiological reactions may make them feel even more anxious, causing waves of panic that sometimes last for hours and frequently leave them feeling weak, exhausted, and unable to go on. Some psychologists believe that the insomnia so common after major losses is connected to this internal sense of danger. No longer trusting that the world is a benign place, children may find it increasingly difficult to let down their guard enough to fall asleep. They jump to conclusions that would not occur to an adult ("He kissed me the last time he was here, so I'm going to get cancer and die, too"; "I can't sleep because I have to make sure my heart is beating"), so they need extra reassurance. Remembering that some youngsters still believe that you get pregnant by getting married or by kissing can help adults understand why children, because of their limited understanding of physiology, are likely to become unduly concerned. Watch for any signs of such confusion, explain what you can, and reassure the child that death is a long way away for him or her and for you. If the child is very anxious, you can schedule physical examinations for both you and the child, so that the doctor can make it clear that nobody is in danger of dying.

The traditional approaches used to ease puppies into new homes suggest responses that can be extremely helpful for children in early grief. First, people expect that a young pup, recently separated from familiar caregivers and surroundings, will be frightened and lonely and may whine and have trouble sleeping. Rather than feeling rejected, new pet owners try to make the transition as easy as possible. One way to do this is to feed the puppy what it is used to eating, so that at least the diet will be familiar, even if the surroundings are not. Like puppies, anxious children relax and feel more like eating when they are offered their usual diet, including their special "comfort" foods, such as those they are used to eating when ill. This is easy enough for parents or familiar caregivers to manage. If possible, new caregivers should be told or find out what children's particular comfort or familiar foods might be. Common examples are soft, basic foods such as applesauce, mashed or french fried potatoes, pasta, bread, rice, beans, grits, or grilled cheese sandwiches; sweet, milky foods such as cocoa, cereal, pudding or custard, or ice cream; and spicy or fast foods.

New puppies are often provided with a hot water bottle wrapped up in an old towel or blanket to snuggle with at night. Likewise children and adolescents who have suffered recent changes or losses are often better able to face the dark, lonely, scary bedtime if they wear soft, warm, textured garments such as blanket sleepers or sweat suits next to their skins, or if they are tucked in between flannel sheets, or if caregivers remove the top sheet allowing youngsters to sleep with a blanket directly against their skin. Like newborns, bereaved children may feel more comfortable when tucked in tightly or even when wrapped up in a cuddly blanket and then tucked in. During the day, some children may want to wear extra layers of clothing, to reduce the sensitivity to cold that grief often precipitates and to help them feel cushioned from possible harm.

Having a security blanket or toy or animal to sleep with also makes children feel less vulnerable. When a child will be sleeping in a new place because of a planned or sudden loss, it is important to make sure that a security object goes along. If no one available knows, someone should ask the child what he or she wants to take along to hug or to sleep with. Older children and adults often find that sleeping with a piece of clothing that smells like the person they long for helps ease their pain and loneliness at bedtime, making them feel safe enough to fall asleep. Care should be taken therefore not to wash everything the child brings along until the child becomes used to the smells of the new detergent or fabric softener.

One foster mother of teens began a tradition of crocheting throw afghans for each of her foster children. During their stays, they could sleep with their own afghans or wrap themselves up in them while studying or watching TV. When they moved on, they took their afghans with them.

Such thoughtful gestures help make a child feel welcomed and cared for and demonstrate concretely a true desire to take on the responsibility for the child and to respect that child's individual needs and feelings.

Like a new puppy, who is often provided with a ticking alarm clock for company, children who have suffered a recent loss often have less difficulty settling down for bed if they are allowed to drift off to sleep where they can overhear the reassuring sounds of grown-ups talking or the television going. (Obviously this is wise only if the adult conversation or television program is comforting rather than scary in tone.) Investing in an inexpensive radio to lull children to sleep softly or setting up an aquarium in the child's room can be a boon to adults caring for children with bedtime fears. Both provide quiet, soothing background sounds to fill the stillness of the night or to cover up strange noises; an aquarium also serves as a night light, comforting even older children or teens without embarrassment. Moreover, studies show that watching fish in an aquarium promotes relaxation and lowers tension, even reducing blood pressure.

Children who are not given distractions seem to find them. A child who suffers a loss during the summer may insist on going to sleep with a fan running even after cold weather has arrived. A child who arrives during flu season may continue to request a vaporizer long after all congestion has cleared, for the sake of its comforting hiss.

Unfortunately, a child's anxieties are usually much slower to disappear than those of a new puppy. Fear of the dark is common and may last for years. Children may also become afraid of sirens or have recurrent nightmares or night terrors, crying out with open unfocused eyes, even getting out of bed and attempting to escape unseen terrors, but unable to remember the event the next morning.

If a child is experiencing a heightened feeling of vulnerability, make it clear that you will look out for the youngster, respecting his or her fears (even if they seem unreasonable to you). Dishing out extra hugs and pats not only reassures and comforts most children, it may also reduce physical complaints. If the child's needs threaten to overwhelm you, try to be clear about what you can give, attempt to bargain cooperatively for something that will work for both of you, and see if you can find someone else who can share in helping you meet the child's needs. It is also a good idea to encourage the child to ask directly for what is needed: "I need to talk to you," "I need a hug," or the like. Even if you can't meet a request at the moment it is made, you can reassure the child by saying when you will be able to respond: for example, "I can't listen now, John. How about if we talk after supper?" When such a postponement is offered, it is imperative that you follow through as promised. Otherwise, the child will wonder whether you can be trusted to do what you say, and this doubt will add to his or her vulnerability. And obviously, you shouldn't agree to respond to requests that cannot or should not be met: to bring back the absent family member, to stay home from work, to allow the child to stay home from school for an extended period of time. But you can suggest other alternatives that may help the child feel more peaceful: "I can't be Mommy, but I can cuddle with you." "I have to go to work now but we can plan to have extra time together when I come home."

Physical Responses to Loss: Many bereaved children and adults require more sleep than usual. They may fall asleep early and wake feeling unrested. It is wise to plan for a quiet time or nap in the afternoon, or perhaps an earlier bedtime. Children also find it restful if they are helped to alternate active pursuits with more passive occupations like playing in a warm tub, or listening to music, or reading.

Children who have suffered a recent loss seem to be more susceptible to infection, having one cold, ear infection, or gastrointestinal upset after another. Their noses run, they begin to cough or clear their throats constantly. They may suffer from skin rashes, heightened allergic responses, bleeding of the gums, and frequent bronchial infection. Such physical symptoms of stress may appear within forty-eight hours after a child is told about a separation or loss, or they may not occur until the child begins to believe that the change is real and is likely to be long-lasting or permanent— perhaps at the time of a remarriage or the finalization of an adoption. Physical symptoms of stress may reappear at anniversaries of the loss and at holidays (reactivation of grief is discussed more fully in chapter 6).

It is not unusual for children to become oversensitive or to react with unusual intensity to real or imagined injuries in the period following a loss or major change. Minor bumps and scratches may acquire unusual importance and need solicitous care. These feelings of physical vulnerability may be reinforced by their caregivers: In *One Hundred Fifty Facts about Grieving Children* (1990), Erin Linn points out that parents who lose a child often become overprotective of remaining children. Or bereaved parents may become underprotective, feeling that since they couldn't save one child, it is futile to try to protect the others. Thus the surviving children may be deprived of normal care or a concern for a period of time.

Separation Anxiety: The classic kinds of separation anxiety often seen when a caregiver is away for a short time and then returns or when parents have recently separated, such as children needing to be sat with at night until they fall asleep or wanting to sleep with a caregiver, are often heightened if a child is confronted with several sequential changes or losses or suffers a permanent loss. About one-fifth of the grieving children Bowlby has studied showed intense separation anxieties and experienced acute night terrors; about one-fourth clung excessively during the day or insisted on sleeping with a parent or sibling at night (1980, 316).

Children as young as six months may show separation reactions such as regression or deep depression when they are separated from their caregivers, and these reactions may persist long after caregiver and child are reunited, because the child fears that the caregiver might leave or be lost again. And regardless of the type of loss or separation, some children become overly concerned about who else might leave them and disappear. If a grieving child's caregiver becomes ill, the child may fear that this person too will be taken away or will decide not to return (Linn 1990, 25).

Michael's caregivers became completely frustrated when their new son screamed and struggled as soon as either of them began to put on a coat or tried to get him into his snowsuit. When they began to understand that he was terrified that he would be moved to another family or left behind, they began a routine of saying, "Two coats. Two people going in the car. Two people coming home." They would then give Michael his snowsuit to hold while they put on their own coats and then say to him, "Now it's your turn to get ready to go to the store, and then we'll both come home with the groceries."

It is not unusual for children who have suffered a recent loss or change or separation to call or peer through the screen door or the window repeatedly after they have been sent outdoors to play, in order to reassure themselves that their caregivers have not disappeared. A parent may be unable to leave the room without hearing a frantic child calling, "Where are you, Mommy?" When the parent goes to the bathroom, the child may hover outside, talking or knocking on the door.

Chad, who has a new caregiver, refuses to leave her side. He hangs around, constantly underfoot. When told to go outside and play with the other children, he cries, "No! I'll be good. I'll be good."

Bereaved children often stay close to their caregivers or listen in on their conversations, worried at the prospect of some new loss or separation. In families where one child has died, it is not uncommon for previously well-adjusted brothers and sisters to show anxiety and reluctance about going to school. Sometimes strongly attached children will reject the absent parent, whom they feel has rejected them. One very young, nonverbal child responded to his mother's return from the hospital by ignoring her the first day she was home and then giving her a smile, followed by a kick, when she joined him in the kitchen the following morning to fix his breakfast as usual.

Separation anxiety may also cause children to have difficulty falling asleep when caregivers are away or when sleeping away from their caregivers.

Kim, age ten, truly wanted to stay overnight at friends' houses or to make it through the night at sleep-over birthday parties, but the separation anxiety arising from leftover feelings about her adoption as a young child and her anxious attachment patterns made her unable to do either of these things successfully and she would end up having to call her parents and go home. She couldn't even stay overnight at her grandparents' house while her parents took a weekend vacation, despite the fact that she had been given the telephone number where they could be reached and permission to call them day or night.

Separation anxiety is also seen when children need to make a transition from one caregiver to another, for example, at the beginning or the end of day care or school or at the beginning or end of the week when it is time to relinquish one normal routine for another.

Jorge is still having trouble going to his day-care center following his father's deployment overseas. In the past he has looked forward to seeing the familiar staff and playing with his friends. Now he whines and begs his mother to stay home. Most recently he has begun to cling to her as soon as he sees the center. His mother, who must go to work, feels guilty about tearing herself away from him when he is so obviously distressed. What can she do?

One way to reassure a child who is experiencing separation anxiety is to be absolutely reliable about returning when expected. If you are delayed, call and ask to speak to the child personally in order to explain what has happened. Not only will this reassure the child that you are on your way, but the sound of your voice will assure the child that nothing bad or dangerous has happened to you.

It helps young children to be talked through the day's routine so that they can anticipate when their caregivers will return. Jorge's mother might say, "After lunch you have nap time. Then there is the sharing circle, and then time in the play yard. Next I come and get you."

Rachel, who has experienced a number of changes, wakes up each Monday morning looking for a fight. The smallest thing can set off a major temper tantrum. At first her family thought her behavior had to do with how she felt about going back to school. But recently one of her parents was away on business in the middle of the week, and her reaction was the same. Now her parents are making a serious attempt to forewarn her and to talk about upcoming family separations. Sunday evening after supper, her mother begins a conversation: "Rachel, today is Sunday. And you know what happens tomorrow. Dad goes back to work, you and Shelley go back to school. Do you think Dad is going to work because he is mad at you? Is Shelley riding a different bus because she doesn't want to be with you? And what happens tomorrow night? Dad comes home from work. Shelley will be here after field hockey."

Rachel may still be sensitive and sulky about family partings; she may also continue to throw temper tantrums. But if she is like many children who are given this kind of specific reassurance, Monday mornings may no longer pose as strong a threat, and she may start the week more easily.

There are various ways to help children monitor the passage of time concretely. Children who are old enough to tell time appreciate having a watch to help them keep track of time. A caregiver who must be away for several days could set up a calendar or make a chart so that the child can cross off the passing days and keep track of when the adult will return. A similar technique that works with younger children is to make a paper chain with a link for each day the caregiver will be away. Each evening, as the child cuts off that day's link, it is easy to see that the days of separation are dwindling and to count or see how many remain. Some parents write a short note inside each of the links: "Jason, I hope you had a fun day today. I was thinking about you. Love, Mom." Be aware, however, that it is not unusual for young children to display magical thinking in these circumstances, wanting to cut off several links at once to make the time go by faster.

Another reassuring gesture is to leave something important with the child for safekeeping (a duplicate house key, for example), because the child is sure that the caregiver will not disappear for good without this talisman.

ACUTE GRIEF

This second phase of mourning has several components: yearning and pining; searching; dealing with sadness, anger, anxiety, guilt, and shame; experiencing disorganization and despair; and finally beginning the job of reorganization. Each helps the child recover from the loss, accept what has happened, and move toward healing. Although children may have a mixture of these feelings, shifting among them over time, it is not unusual for one reaction to predominate at first, and then for the child to begin work on another as the first subsides. Some children feel overwhelming anxiety or sadness first, while others begin with anger or guilt. Whether the feelings are mixed or successive, each component of grief must be worked through, and none suppressed. This can be a lengthy though intermittent process, taking as much as two to three years in adults and longer in children. Older children may need more time than preschool children, and adolescents can be especially vulnerable to separations and losses, because so much in their lives is already in flux. In addition, research indicates that serious ambivalence or internal conflicts about the relationship with the lost person severely complicate the grief process, extending the time it may take to move through it. When there is no physical body to take leave of, this, too, tends to prolong the grief process.

Children need to know that their feelings and reactions are common and normal to grief, that the return to creative, healthy living involves pain, and that there is no short cut—the greater the loss, the longer it takes to get over it. Unfortunately, in these days of fast food and instant gratification, many adults as well as children have had little experience with tolerating discomfort patiently. Children should be reassured that they will feel better eventually, although they may not believe it. It is honest to tell them that crying and hurting are part of the cure, though they may not understand how that can be so. Often it helps them to know that what they are experiencing and feeling is normal so that instead of trying to fight their feelings they can become more comfortable expressing them.

The outcome of children's grief experiences hinges to a large extent on whether adults are able to tolerate their expressions of strong feelings about what has happened. Complications seem most likely to arise in children who have not felt permitted to let themselves know and express their genuine feelings or have not had their awareness and expression of these feelings encouraged and supported. Remember that when the loss has stricken the caregiving adult or adults deeply, children may be reluctant, resistant, or unwilling to share and process their feelings at home. In such cases, it is important that children have supportive adults to talk to and that their need to keep their feelings separate and private from their caregivers should be respected.

Whatever their age or their circumstances, grieving young people need authentic empathy, respect, and support from caring adults. Give children as much time as they need with all their feelings; don't try to rush them into "more productive" emotional states or urge them to speed their reactions up or tone them down. Feelings are, after all, just signals of an emotional state—our response to something that has touched us, like the itch that results from a mosquito bite. To say to a child, "Don't be sad [or angry or upset]" is as useless as saying, "Don't itch." Be firm, however, about not allowing children to discharge their feelings in hurtful or destructive ways.

Here are some suggestions for the adult who wants to provide encouragement and support to a child who is experiencing or dealing with acute grief:

- The child's feelings and concerns should take precedence over almost everything else. As soon as the child tries to share feelings, stop what you are doing immediately (or as soon as you can) and focus on the child. It is important to send the message: "Your feelings are important to me, and I will find time to listen to them. You are not bothering me."
- When the child shares sadness, anger, guilt, or shame, whether verbally or physically, don't ask that those feelings be postponed, denied, or concealed. Stifling grief requires precious energy better used to deal with all the changes accompanying loss; moreover, grief driven underground can return months or even years later to haunt the child.
- When the child's feelings or the duration or timing of those feelings differ from your own, respect the differences, and don't criticize or appear upset by the child's statements and feelings and actions. It is the recognition, acceptance, and validation of each emotion as it occurs that lets the child move from one emotional state to another so that grief can be completed.
- Remember that children often just want someone to bear witness to their pain and grief. If you have a close relationship with a child, what you say may not be as important as what you do. The touch of a hand on a knee, an arm around a shoulder, a lap to sit on, or a shoulder to cry against can offer profound comfort.
- If a child seems to be playing up grief for attention, this is a signal that some other need is likely not being met. Giving extra

support and showing ample authentic positive interest will usually make the problem disappear.

If caregivers are inclined to encourage the suppression of feelings, sending the message, overtly or covertly, that some feelings are good or right and others are bad or wrong or responding to expressions of feeling with recrimination, withdrawal, or retaliation, then the child will need to have another trusted, supportive person to talk with.

Yearning and Pining

Sara's mother died two years ago. Since then, Sara has found life very difficult; her father is remote and demanding, and she spends a lot of time dreaming that things could be the way they used to be. One Saturday afternoon she goes with a friend to see Walt Disney's *Snow White*. "I'm wishing, I'm wishing," sings the heroine, and tears roll down Sara's cheeks. Snow White is just like her, she thinks; people are always asking her to work hard, and no one notices her or cares about her feelings and her needs. She is left in a dark forest, scared and alone. When will a prince come to wake her from her glass coffin and take her away to live happily ever after?

There is a core deep within children who suffer a loss that half-believes (or wants to believe) that a different ending is possible. They feel that what happened was not what was supposed to have happened, that things have not worked out as they were supposed to. Hope keeps flickering that somehow things will return to the way they were, that the lost one will return. The child's feelings keep shifting between anxiety and despair, moved by this recurring hope.

Like Sara, a great many children identify with characters from books, television shows, and movies who suffer a loss but are somehow reunited or find a happy outcome through the love and appreciation of others. Stories such as *Snow White*, *Annie*, *Oliver*, and *An American Tail* frequently become favorites. Such stories say, "It may be bad now, but it will be fixed by and by."

The particular story or theme that the child identifies with often relates to the kind of loss the child has suffered and the child's developmental age at the time. Sara's life, for example, shares many features with Snow White's story: the death of a mother, the lack of an understanding protective father, the need to reach outside her family to be noticed and appreciated. In addition, Sara's mother died when Sara was at the peak of the magical thinking stage when children often believe that death is some sort of transient suspended state—which is certainly the case with Snow White. Like the dwarfs whom Snow White has mothered, Sara is unable to bring her parent back but waits and mourns.

Other children identify with stories whose themes mirror their own experience. Many foster children see their own stories in *An American Tail,* in which a lost mouse child and his family search desperately for one another and are ultimately reunited. Children who feel a keen sense of being different because of their particular loss often identify strongly with E.T., the young extraterrestrial who openly longs to get home and be among his own kind. Some children will ask to see this videotape over and over; others adamantly protest, "I hate E.T.," because the character reminds them of feelings about themselves and the ways they seem abandoned and different that they would just as soon forget.

Searching

Sam was removed from his parents' care when he was nine, because of severe neglect and abuse. Now that he is fifteen, he has taken several bus trips back to his old neighborhood. He knows that his parents moved away years ago, but he likes to visit the corner where their old apartment was and to wander the nearby streets. Sam would laugh scornfully if he were accused of looking for his parents, but still he finds himself drawn back time and again to the place where his loss occurred. Perhaps he is looking for the memories that vanished along with his family. Perhaps he feels that now that he is older, he could work things out if he could just find them. Perhaps he needs to go back and face down insecurities from the past that haunt him.

Such needs are normal, regardless of the cause of the loss. Throughout his work, Bowlby points out that biological precursors may influence this behavior. He reports that situations that seem to endanger the continuation of our bonds to loved ones are likely to elicit instinctive actions to prevent the loss, resulting in immediate, automatic, and intense efforts, first to recover the family member and then to discourage that member from leaving again. These reactions seem particularly strong in situations where a child was quite young at the time of the loss or where there was little preparation for the loss or a lack of ongoing contact after it.

Searching behavior may occur soon after a separation or loss and can continue for years as part of normal grieving. It may be unfocused and involve an aimless restlessness, an inability to sit still, a constant searching for something to do. Or it may be marked by an increased preoccupation with the lost person and a heightened interest in the places the person frequented or where the person might be found. Searching behavior may appear compulsive and irrational until we think about our own searching impulses when we lose something. Our frenzied activity when we misplace a needed item, such as car keys: We can't believe that they aren't on the desk where they belong. We check our coat pockets. Still no keys. If a second check of the desk proves unsuccessful, we rush to look somewhere else, only to return to the desk for yet another look. We persist in this kind of behavior long after it is quite evident that the keys are not on the desk. Unable to stop ourselves, we behave in much the same way that children do when they are in the searching stage in the grief process.

Bereaved children commonly experience a compelling urge to recover the lost loved one, even when they are aware that the attempt is hopeless, that such behavior is futile. The drive is often particularly strong in children separated from a loved one through abandonment, separation, divorce, foster care, adoption or those whose loved ones are MIAs, hostages, or kidnap victims or otherwise unaccountably missing. In such cases, searching may allow children not only to try to retrieve but also to test or attempt to confirm the reality of the permanency of the loss. As long as they continue to believe that a loss may yet be reversed, they are impelled to action. Divorcing parents, for example, often recount how while they were having a tense meeting to discuss division of property and financial settlements, their youngsters were busily putting on soft music and turning down the lights to help them get back together again.

When youngsters are convinced that retrieval is impossible, they may respond by trying to replace the missing person. They may begin to dress like, act like, or take over the roles and responsibilities of the person who is gone. They may become pseudomature caretakers or project personal concerns about safety on to other people or animals ("Poor puppy. Don't worry, I will take care of you"). Jealous of other families that are intact or feeling deprived (as they may very well be), they may set about trying to complete their family by urging their parent to remarry or to have another child. It can feel to the parent as if any individual of the right age or sex will fill the child's bill. Young children in particular are likely to feel that a person can be replaced as easily as a lost pet. The phenomenon is so strong that children who have spent their lives in orphanages and hence lack much, if any, experience of regular family life may settle securely into an adoptive family, thrive there, and then begin to ask a single parent, "When are you going to get us a daddy [or mommy]?" Or only children may ask for a sister or brother. The experience with adoption has been positive; the children feel themselves part of a real family. Now they want it to be even more complete, and they expect that their parents will just go out and find the extra piece.

The searching phase draws to a close only when children accept that they have mustered every effort available at this point in time but nothing has changed. And even when overt behaviors have diminished, children may make an internal contract, conscious or unconscious, the terms of which involve some action on their part that will cause the lost loved one to return. Bowlby gives an example of how such an internal contract was enacted by a fifteen-year-old girl whose mother had died suddenly of a cerebral hemorrhage. Before the death, there had been tension and disagreement between the two about the girl's weight, the mother feeling that the girl should make an effort to slim down. As the young woman's seventeenth birthday approached, she began to diet diligently and became quite slender. On the eve of her birthday, she appeared noticeably dreamy. She took a long walk. The day following her birthday, however, she began a serious enough eating binge that her family became concerned for her. This binging lasted for many weeks. "Having conformed with her mother's wishes over the dieting, it appeared she had been expecting her mother to return on her birthday; it was a bargain which had not been kept" (Bowlby 1980, 372).

Impatience with children who are preoccupied with searching can delay or impede rather than facilitate grief work. Curt remarks urging a child not to dwell on the past only drive the feelings and behaviors underground and leave the bereaved child feeling misunderstood and unsupported. Helping adults need to understand that searching helps children accept the change. Through repeated attempts at recovery and repeated disappointments, children gradually relinquish the fantasy of reunion (although it can be a slow and painful process) and come to accept the inevitability and permanence of their loss. If denied the chance to do this, they are likely to continue to expend precious emotional energy in futile attempts to regain their lost loved ones long after the time when this energy would be better spent elsewhere.

Anger, Deprivation, and Blame

Brian has been very upset about his parents' separation. His mother, trying to talk to him about it, tells him that both his parents are concerned about him. "Oh sure!" Brian yells, jumping up from his chair and knocking it over. "You and Daddy just care about your own selves. I hate you, I hate you both!" He runs to his room, sobbing as he slams the door.

Merdyth, who was just beginning her senior year when her parents divorced, is so upset with both of her parents that she has moved in with a friend and is refusing to talk to or live with either one of them.

Desiree, whose older brother died in a car accident following a party, alternates between sorrow and cold terror as she listens to the mounting quarrels that punctuate her parents' grief. What will become of her? How could her brother take such a risk and do this to them all? She sits in her room talking to his picture, "Damn you, Dennis. You've ruined everything. I'll never forgive you, not ever!"

87

Then, filled with an overwhelming rush of pain for her brother, she hugs his photo closer.

Bowlby found that about one-fourth to one-third of the children he studied following a significant loss were overactive and aggressive, engaged in unprovoked violence toward peers or adults, and destroyed property (1980, 316). Anger is an almost universal response to loss. Parents who have spent frantic hours trying to find a child who is very late arriving home only to greet the returning child with anger and threats understand from personal experience that the standard response to the loss of a loved one is first to find them and then to scold them. Day-care providers and working parents frequently observe children's scolding response. The child who has been fine during the day becomes surly, demanding, rude, even hostile when the parent arrives to pick the child up. Similar anger can be seen during a visit with a noncustodial parent where the child ignores or in some way makes it clear that the visiting parent is in disgrace. When a loss is irreversible, grieving children, unable to express their anger to the one who left, will lash out at those who remain.

The grieving child is often overly sensitive to perceived slights, counting up grievances. Children whose anger at being deprived as a result of loss may act as if the world owes them, yet nothing is good enough to please them. No matter what they are given, nor how generously they are treated, they may explode when told no: "You never give me anything." "You never let me do what I want." Unable to focus on what they have, all they can see is what is missing. Children may become preoccupied with ensuring that they are not shortchanged or overburdened. They may make it a point to be sure that they have exactly the same number of candies, the same length of turn sitting by the car window, or that they have no more dishes to wash or socks to fold than others.

Anger may flare up unexpectedly, triggered by observing others' joy. Youngsters who have suffered a loss may dislike and want to avoid community gatherings where other children are having fun and enjoying their families. Holidays that focus on families coming together may cause strong reactions in children and caregivers alike when part of their family is missing or when the previous family structure has been lost.

Anger at God is common, often accompanied by guilt over the disrespect it entails or anxiety that God will retaliate. While some bereaved children take great comfort in their religious beliefs, others may find their faith deeply shaken. They may want to stop attending religious services or simply refuse to go, posing questions about what their religion teaches and expressing doubt about the usefulness of a religious affiliation.

One child, raised in a hymn-singing family, talked about the conflicting messages he found in two of his favorite hymns, "What A Friend We Have In Jesus," which he believed promised him that all his grief and pain would be taken away, and "Jesus Walked This Lonesome Valley," which told him that, like Jesus, he "had to walk it by himself." He poignantly described his struggle to figure it out and then demanded to know which was true.

Avoidance

Kory, age eight, and her father had lived alone since her mother's death two years before. Recently her father remarried. Now Kory avoids going inside the apartment as much as possible, preferring to play outside. Her father is horrified when his new wife reports that a neighbor has seen Kory defecating underneath the bushes between their buildings. What on earth has gotten into his child?

One way children defend themselves from things that stir up too much discomfort or conflict is physically to avoid them, much the way children in early grief may avoid going to bed. Kory may not actually have been pressured to accept or to love this new mother, but she is old enough to know that it would please her father if she did. Not ready to do that, she minimizes the time she spends alone with the new wife. She avoids going inside to use the bathroom because it means facing the reminders of the new situation, which compromises her ability to suppress her feelings about the change. Unaware that her behavior has been noticed, she takes care of her toileting needs in a way that seems reasonable to her, if not to those around her. Unlike the self-soiling that can be symptomatic of deeper disturbances, Kory's toileting behavior is situational; a way to take care of her feelings as well as those of her father and new mother.

Avoidance behaviors can also help children who feel they must deny their reactions release some of their rebellious feelings. If Kory were given an invitation to talk about her mixed feelings about losing one mother and getting another and the grief that the marriage may have reactivated, it is likely that her toileting behavior would change. She might very well benefit from being in a group with children dealing with similar family issues who will not take her mixed reaction as a personal affront.

Avoidance reactions occur even in children who are quite young.

Tiffany, who joined her adoptive family when she was three, would cry, struggle, and pull away when her family tried to induce her to ride in a blue car. Too young to explain her fear, she was reacting to having moved from her foster family in a blue state car. Part of her remained convinced for some time that such a car would wrench her from the familiar and plunge her into the unknown.

Children may have unpleasant memories or creepy feelings about the place where a death occurred or where they first heard the news of an impending loss, not wanting to go near that room or building or space. They need to have their feelings respected and to be reassured that the reaction is neither stupid nor silly.

Reading provides children with a means of withdrawal, escape, and avoidance. Books allow children to give themselves a mental break from all the difficult adjustments and realities in their lives. Children may avidly read at the breakfast table and effectively tune out the rest of the family. Or they may read in the car, oblivious to the person who is driving them to wherever they need to go. They read during chore time or when it is time to be getting ready for school or bed. Sometimes, getting such a child's attention can be difficult. It can help to make physical contact, such as touching a shoulder, then speaking the child's name. And it may be necessary to remove the book (or turn off the video or television, if that is the distraction and means of escape). The adult who accedes to a child's request just to "finish this page" or "see the end of this program" may need to remind the child to close the book or turn off the TV at the end of the page or the program, before another chapter or program beckons seductively.

Sadness

Sadness is the response that adults commonly expect to see in grieving children, and often the one they often feel most competent to handle. Even so, a bereaved child's sadness may pain the adult, stir up similar feelings, and activate a strong urge to protect the child. Adults should be careful not only to allow children to express sadness but also to monitor their own reactions and to avoid anxiously trying to provide constant amusement or to cheer the child up. Children who are feeling sad may turn to adults for comfort or they may want to be by themselves. When a child withdraws into a quiet space or wants a quiet time, adults are wise to recognize that sometimes this is part of the healing process, much as resting is part of recovering from a virus.

Disorganization

Kristen seems to be over her early upset following her family's relocation to a new city. She complains less and less about missing those left behind, and her irritability and angry outbursts are tapering off. "She's weathered it," her mother says to herself, with a sigh of relief. Then Kristen's teacher requests a conference. Formerly a good student, Kristen is falling behind in school. She seems to be finding it hard to settle down and get to work. She doesn't complete her assignments and seems to daydream instead, jumping when she is called on as though her mind has strayed somewhere else. What can be the matter?

During the disorganization stage, it is quite normal for previously competent children to become vague and unfocused. Apparently the preoccupation with the loss, the effort needed to accommodate to it and the physiological changes connected to grieving (or not being allowed to grieve), reduces the ability to concentrate, to organize thinking and work habits, and to memorize or remember. Grieving is extremely demanding work. It takes so much energy that little is left to attend to other aspects of living.

Many teens, preteens, and adults who have suffered major losses as children have little or no memory of what happened in their lives during the period following the loss, perhaps as much as one or two years. School-age children will remember who their teacher was before the loss and after the major grief adjustments are over but be unable to remember the names of the teachers they had during the major adjustment stages. Because of the shutdown that occurs during the denial state of early grief and then the demands of active grieving, many children begin to fall behind, not only academically but also in the development of physical skills.

Adults in this stage often stop reading the newspaper or listening to the news because they find it too difficult to follow what is going on. They sometimes report that there is so much happening in their own lives that they have temporarily ceased to care about much else. Simple decisions such as what to wear or what to buy at the store can seem exhaustingly difficult. Tackling something new, finishing a project (or finishing it without error), organizing one's day seem like monumental challenges.

Adults who are experiencing the disorganization phase may be impatient with themselves or alarmed by the cognitive changes and worry that the disabilities will be long-lasting or permanent. But difficult as this may be, adults have some latitude. They often can simplify their lives by postponing complicated decisions or delegating detailed or overwhelming tasks to someone else. At work and at home, concerned friends and colleagues may cover for them, sharing or taking over tedious, precise, or analytical tasks until this stage subsides. Children rarely have these options. For them, little or no covering is possible. Their worksheets and assignments must be done. If their classmates try to help, all concerned may be accused of cheating.

Social studies, where facts must both be teased out separately and organized into a cohesive whole; English, where themes must be explored in depth; classes that require abstract reasoning as well as attentive concentration, such as math or chemistry, can become particularly difficult. Some children seem to have an interesting symbolic reaction to arithmetic: Math problems involving subtraction or division that mirror the loss or splitting up that is occurring in the child's life will sometimes set off internal defenses, wherein the grieving child, who may have no trouble adding and multiplying, is unable to perform the opposite operations.

Grief-related learning difficulties may be so severe that afflicted children often enter the next grade lacking important information and study skills, which intensifies their struggle and may contribute to a continued decline in their performance. As children watch their grades slip or find their teachers increasingly irritated with them, they are likely to feel that they are no longer the competent people they used to be, and their diminished self-esteem and their frustration with themselves exacerbate the original loss.

Teachers will generally give the child who is undergoing a major separation or loss some leeway. Too frequently, though, the duration of this stage of disorganization is greatly underestimated. Because it often lasts so long and because the symptoms come and go, teachers and caregivers tend to expect the child to settle down in an unrealistic amount of time. In addition, learning gaps or difficulties may not show up clearly for over a year. By then, the child is likely to have a different teacher who is unaware that the loss is still having a major impact on the child. The new teacher may feel that the child's difficulties are a result of procrastination, poor self-discipline, a lack of application, or just plain laziness. Yet a study conducted in Arlington, Massachusetts, found that almost every one of the forty-nine bereaved elementary school children in public schools there showed a decline in grades, aside from being passive and withdrawn from relationships in general. With good support from the home, one-third of the group recovered from their trauma at the end of the first year, but two-thirds were still set back and working on resolving their grief issues (Grollman 1975, 164).

It is not helpful to assign labels to these children. It is more productive to simplify directions and to show children what is expected and how to do it. Try to figure out what techniques you use to keep yourself on track when you are fatigued or when your attention wanders; this exercise may uncover methods that can help children through this difficult period.

Ten-year-old Buddy continued to have trouble concentrating

and following directions three years after the loss-related changes in his family. As a result he was doing poorly in school. Yet his ability to pay attention, listen well, and follow directions when he was playing basketball in gym class and to remember and repeat accurate information when he talked about what was happening with various pro football teams seemed fine. Rather than accusing him of deliberately fooling around when he should be paying attention, Buddy's counselor talked with him about how sometimes athletes have to get themselves up mentally and focus themselves by thinking through the plays before a game. It was decided that Buddy should pick which adult he could best ask to serve as a "coach" who would give him a pep talk each morning: "OK, Buddy, you can do it. You can beat that old math. Go to it!" Buddy imagined that his math assignment was the team he had to beat. He pictured cheering himself on (clapping his hands together and shouting "Go!") as he sat down to work. If he found his mind wandering, he snapped his fingers quietly to bring himself back to his task. These methods did not interfere with or shorten his grief process, but they did help him keep his mind on his schoolwork enough that he no longer forfeited his recesses.

Adults are unwise to expect children to exert this kind of focused effort throughout an entire school day; such exercises are extremely tiring, and children may not have enough energy or success over an extended period to be motivated to continue with them.

Similar concrete suggestions, drawn from a child's interests and experiences, can be as creative as the adult can make them. Some children benefit from wearing a thick rubber band around the wrist to snap when they begin to lose their trains of thought or notice themselves falling behind or having trouble paying attention. Other children make a contract with themselves and an adult at home or at school to work hard for about fifteen minutes and then take a break such as stretching or watering the class plants or running an errand. They use a kitchen timer to mark the time. Gradually they can be encouraged to try to extend the concentration period, a few minutes at a time.

Listening skills tend to suffer during the disorganization stage, compounding its difficulties. It is often extremely helpful for children in this stage to have directions written down, on the blackboard or on a worksheet or in both spots to prevent information overload and confusion. It may help to talk youngsters through assignments one step at a time and then to ask them to repeat the directions to see if they missed or don't understand something. Methods and directions that allow the child to break tasks into small sections and then focus on following and completing one instruction or task at a time often help the child perform more successfully. Children can be shown how to set up their notebooks, keep track of homework assignments, and use outlining and other memory skills. The school's study specialist can be of enormous help here, if one is available.

Grieving children may have trouble making smooth transitions from one activity to another. Caregivers and teachers are wise to recognize this and help children by following predictable schedules and warning children ten to fifteen minutes before a transition, particularly one from something that they enjoy to one that they dislike: "Juan, recess is almost up today. It will be time to line up soon."

Children who are experiencing disorganization often benefit from having a set time to talk about their problems and loss with a caregiver, a school counselor, or a therapist. This helps them compartmentalize grief work and school work, improving their ability to focus. Children may benefit particularly from having a place at school where it is all right for them to think about the loss, instead of always having to attend to academic responsibilities. The normal physical release and social interaction that comes with recess or other less structured school activities are also important, and makeup work should not be scheduled to interfere with the parts of school that the child may find energizing and releasing. In this way, children come to see school as a supportive, caring place rather than a demanding, punitive environment. Many children blossom if they have a supportive concerned person to check in with at the beginning of the day to help them connect to the daily routine and expectations and to have a similar check-in before they head home to see if they have all the necessary books and assignments. Some children benefit from a five-minute check-in after lunch to help them refocus as they make the transition back to the classroom. Such support offers children the chance to feel successful rather than dumb, competent rather than hopelessly confused. Sometimes school personnel argue that, with all the other demands on their time, these added responsibilities are too much. Experience shows that it is as time- and cost-effective to provide such services when needed as it is to hold countless conferences or to spend staff energy chasing after or disciplining children who are underperforming. It is also much more humane and satisfying to the teacher and others involved.

Grieving children often suffer from disorganization at home, too. Daily responsibilities like washing or brushing teeth, no matter how routine, may be neglected or performed haphazardly or sporadically. Sent to get three items in the living room, a child may return with only one or yell, "What was I supposed to get?" Youngsters may not hear a request until it has been repeated a number of times and then complain that they're always being yelled at. Caregivers are bound to get exasperated. What often works is to come up with ways to help the child remember responsibilities.

"John, look at me. I want you to go into the living room and [holding up one finger] pick up your jacket, [holding up a second finger] pick up your shoes, and [holding up a third finger] pick up your backpack. Now, tell me, what are you supposed to do?" John successfully recites his list and then singsongs to himself, "jacket, shoes, backpack," as he goes to fetch the items.

Evoking a mental image of the three fingers might also help John remember: "Now, let's see, there was one more thing. Oh, now I know."

Written lists are another useful concrete way to help children remember daily routine. Younger children can draw pictures to remind them of the tasks to be completed before bedtime or before the school bus arrives. These pictures or lists can be posted in logical, easily visible spots—on the refrigerator, on the bathroom mirror, or alongside the front door—for quick review. Not only do they spare caregivers a good deal of nagging, they put responsibility back on the child in a way that allows the child to feel a sense of mastery and competence.

Despair

Despair is perhaps the most difficult stage of grief to experience or to witness. The bereaved person sinks into a bleak, hopeless state of mind that resembles clinical depression. A child in despair may speak and move more slowly, seem pessimistically resigned to the bleakness they experience, and lack energy or motivation. Normal interest in eating, grooming, and socializing diminishes sharply. The child feels helpless and hopeless: It seems as if the worst possible thing that could happen has happened. Life seems both meaningless and overwhelming. Why get up? Why go to bed? Why eat? Why care?

Mornings become difficult for children and caregivers alike. James Whittaker reports that children may be reluctant to leave the warm security of bed and enter the cold, less manageable world. He suggests that caregivers help children face the demands of the day gradually by waking them gently, moving slowing, talking softly. The key, he says, to helping children who wake surly or with difficulty is to avoid rushing or pushing them. The morning should be a time of quiet activity with a known dependable routine. Cheerfulness and exuberance is better saved for later in the day (Trieschman, Whittaker, and Brendtro 1969, 121–23). Try to establish a routine that suits a child's personal style: Some children benefit from not having to make decisions as to what to wear or what to eat. Some draw strength from being allowed to dress where there is company, while others are best left alone until they are ready to be around other people.

It is not uncommon for mourning children and adolescents to think about dying as part of this stage of their grief, usually in fantasies of dying by accident or illness as a way of rejoining a lost loved one, and this does not necessarily indicate that the child is suicidal. If such youngsters become increasingly reckless or physically careless or seem serious about killing themselves as a way to end the pain, rejoin the lost person, or demonstrate how desperately they need the lost loved one to return, it is very important to refer them to a professional who has experience determining whether apparently suicidal people are at risk of acting on the thought.

Renee buried herself with leaves and lay in the road not once, but several times, following the death of her sister in a car accident.

Eddy rode his bicycle into a bridge abutment so hard that the frame broke into two pieces after he was told that his best and only friend was moving away.

A trained therapist should be able to suggest better ways for such children to handle their despair.

Food can become a focal issue to some children during this stage. Some children lose their interest in eating. Others eat and eat as if to fill up the emptiness they feel inside themselves. In either case, comfort foods may help with the problem. When children hoard food in their rooms or wander at night and forage while the rest of the family sleeps, it is a good idea to stock up on tasty, healthy foods, such as fruit, raw vegetables, unbuttered popcorn, peanut butter sandwiches, and juice, all which may be consumed without restriction.

In a conversation with me in 1975, Vera Fahlberg suggested that, when dealing with children who overeat, caregivers should watch to see whether they keep helping themselves to food or whether they only take what is offered. Either way, food intake can be controlled by handing each diner a dished-out plate, rather than passing food at the table. If children ask for more after having been given an ample amount, try helping them to differentiate between feelings of hunger and feelings of emptiness, without making an issue of weight. "I wonder if you're really hungry," an adult might ask. "Let's see if a snuggle [a hug, a back rub] might feel even better." Caregivers should be careful, however, about deciding how much children should be eating. If a child is new to the household, for example, a caregiver may underestimate how much food the child actually needs to maintain normal weight and growth. Adolescents can consume a full meal and get hungry again before the table is cleared or the dishes done.

A technique that seems to work well for both heavy and light eaters is learning how to cook. Heavy eaters begin to recognize how to nurture themselves in a grown-up way, which may lift some of their feelings of helplessness and hopelessness. Light eaters sometimes regain an interest in food if they have prepared it themselves. Like early grief, the despair stage often involves physical symptoms that indicate the level of stress and fatigue being experienced.

Todd spends every other weekend with his mother. Although he has lived with his dad for some time since his parents separated, he still finds having to split his time between them extremely painful. He leaves his dad's too subdued and quiet. He parts from his mother with his eyes brimming, swallowing shuddering sobs. Following the past two visits, he has been morose and lethargic after returning home. His mood has been accompanied by bleeding gums.

A dentist sensitive to physical symptoms of grief in children would be careful to rule out other causes but would not be surprised if such bleeding turned out to be grief related, subsiding as Todd becomes more accustomed to making the transition from one loved parent to another. Sometimes children in similar situations have temporary skin eruptions, such as rashes and hives, or suffer from stomach upsets or diarrhea.

Children in this stage of grief need caring adults to stand by them and reassure them through response and action that they are worth caring for and comforting. Fortunately, for most children, this difficult stage of grief is short-lived, often lasting only about ten days to three weeks, although, in adolescents, as in adults, it may last for two or three months. If it persists much longer or if the youngster talks about killing or hurting him- or herself, it is likely that the child is having trouble getting the internal healing mechanisms going and that it is time to seek professional help. If the helping adult becomes frightened at the child's despondency, futile hopelessness, and increased dependency, here, too, it may make sense to consult a professional.

Whether it is the caregiver or the caregiver and a helper working together, an adult's protective presence and willingness to share a child's feelings may help sustain the child. But it is important for both laypeople and professionals alike to recognize that, although helpers can validate a child's hopeless and helpless feelings, they will not be able to lessen the feelings of abandonment, isolation, or despair: that pain is part of the grief work itself.

INTEGRATION OF LOSS AND GRIEF

Jerome seems to be in a much better frame of mind now than he was several months ago. He is much less likely to explode angrily, and there is a marked decrease in his irritability. He is interested in what is going on around him, and his pep and enthusiasm have returned. He does not act as if he has blocked out the loss but rather as if he has come to grips with it. His fifth-grade teachers report a notable improvement in his self-control, attentiveness, and performance. He seems both to understand himself and to be more sensitive to others. He no longer automatically discounts either his own abilities or the helpfulness of others. After twenty months, Jerome has reorganized himself enough to go on with his life without his missing parent.

For fortunate children, the experience of separation or loss is eventually mastered, and they can reorganize themselves and get on with life. Having survived the worst, they are ready to get back to the business of living and growing. When this happens, there is a noticeable return to a more balanced perspective and better physical and psychological well-being. The reality of the loss becomes part of their makeup but no longer has such a profound impact on their outlook or self-esteem. Life and people become enjoyable once again and there is increased focus on the present and the future instead of the past. There are many steps, even leaps forward, in the ability to cope. There are also setbacks, but observers sense that, overall, things are moving forward in a positive way. There appears to be more ability to create a new life, one that takes the loss into account but is not as preoccupied with it. There is also more autonomy, as well as renewed capacity to get close and to renew attachments or make new ones. Children may change some or all of their friends, gravitating to those who have stood by, comforted, and understood them and leaving behind those who were unable to support or share the healing process. Often there will be a notable growth or maturational spurt, emotionally, socially, and physically. It is not uncommon for children who have been in limbo during a court settlement or in a temporary placement to grow, sometimes as much as three inches, after they have balanced some of their grieving and adjusted to their permanent family settings. This growth spurt is so common that therapists and social workers often watch for it as an indication of how settled children are feeling.

During integration, children often seek to find meaning in the loss, to fit it into their understanding of life, of God, or of what is good. Their need to go to the cemetery (or to avoid such visits) may change. Children who have clung to mementos may pack them carefully away or replace them with something new. They may express pride and satisfaction at having survived a challenge and grown through the experience (many will come to feel that their loss opened them to a fuller appreciation of life). Pain has been replaced with feelings of poignancy and caring.

FACILITATING THE GRIEF PROCESS: HELPING CHILDREN WITH SADNESS, ANGER, AND AGGRESSION

❦

 For the first six to eight months following a loss, children are immersed in their own style of mourning, and, through the first year, they will show the common and somewhat predictable responses discussed in chapter 3. As the first anniversary approaches, however, children who are moving forward in the grief process will show fewer episodes of anxiety, sobbing, and angry, inappropriate, or destructive outbursts (although their ability to concentrate and organize may still be impaired).

For many children, however, additional help may be needed before they can positively integrate loss. Such children may remain angry or depressed or seemingly suppress their feelings. Or they may be unable to move on, feeling that it would be disloyal to give up their pain and be happy. They may lack the ability to become involved with others, or stop developing as they should, or persist in an unhealthy preoccupation with physical aches and pains. They may continue to be unusually fearful of additional separations. Caregivers may find themselves having trouble controlling their children, or children may become helplessly discontent and appear just to give up, discounting themselves and their feelings, underachieving, or behaving destructively toward themselves or others.

Gloria Burns left her husband some time ago. At first she and her two children lived with her parents; now they are sharing an apartment with her friend Donald. Gloria feels that she has finally found a relationship that is good for her and the children. But she is concerned about nine-year-old P.J., who resists doing anything he is asked. He constantly stalls and complains. A conference with his teacher confirms that this is happening a lot at school, too. In fact, P.J.'s teacher tells Gloria that unless P.J. buckles down, he will end up repeating third grade. Feeling frantic, Gloria wonders what on earth to do.

Caregivers who seem to want children to accept loss may be resented as keenly as if they had caused the loss in the first place. To grieving children, nothing but the eradication of the loss will bring true comfort, and efforts that do not yield this result are seen as useless and provoke angry outbursts and blame. Tempting as it may be, this is not the time for adults to try to defend against accusations or to argue about them. Instead, they should try to understand why they have become a target for anger. This will be easier if they do not lose sight of how intense or lengthy the recovery process is likely to be, so that they can pace themselves and their patience accordingly. The truth is that loss is as traumatic as a major physical assault. It is no easier to recover from and restructure one's life after loss than it is to adjust to the amputation of a limb, the loss of vision, or paralysis after a spinal cord injury.

All grief takes a long time to abate, but it can take even longer to repair the damage that results from trying to shorten the process. Beleaguered caregivers may want to consider seeking counseling for children if the feelings being directed at them begin to interfere with their ability to remain supportive. It is a good idea to consult someone who specializes in issues of separation and loss, because even people used to working with children may feel overly protective or helpless in the face of a child's traumatic loss or their own reaction to it unless they have experience with grieving children or children's grief. In order to work productively with grieving children, helpers need to be willing and comfortable directly addressing what has hurt or confused them, what is happening now to impede or complicate their emotional lives, and how they feel about the loss or change. By approaching such subjects head on, helpers avoid sending the message that what has happened or the feelings it has aroused are too terrible or powerful to be discussed.

Signals that suggest outside help might be warranted include: (1) deteriorating relationships between child and caregiver or sibling or peers; (2) much more frequent illness or injury than is normal for that child; (3) constant clearing of the throat or a lingering cough when the child has no apparent infection (which may indicate that the youngster is choking back feelings and experiencing related bronchial constrictions and/or throat spasms); (4) activities generally indicating that a child is trying to relieve distress and anxiety, such as physically picking at him- or herself, licking or sucking the skin around the lips, biting the nails or cuticles, twiddling or pulling out hair, picking and biting at clothing, increased masturbation, or daytime soiling or wetting in a child who has been toilet trained for some time; (5) distress or refusal to talk about the loss or the people involved or to allow others to do so, signaled by increased agitation, flopping around or falling off furniture, bolting from the room, changing the subject, tuning out, or distressing others to distract them from the unwelcome subject; (6) facile, superficial conversation about the loss with little inflection or in a singsong voice, as if reciting something by rote; (7) serious episodes of aggression toward peers, siblings, caregivers, or animals; (8) fire setting; (9) apparent disregard for personal safety and/or references to dying or hurting themselves; (10) indications that a child's caregivers do not have the personal stamina, fortitude, and objectivity to allow their child to express a full range of strong feelings. Children learn how to grieve from watching others grieve and from experiencing the disappointments and losses that are normal parts of growing up. But many children who suffer a significant loss, with its overwhelming impact on all areas of life, have never before experienced grief of such magnitude or seen it in another. They are unaware that others experience the same kinds of reactions that they are experiencing. As Linn points out, grief has a way of isolating young and old alike into thinking that they are the only ones having these painful feelings. Thus, there is a tendency to try to endure these feelings in silence (Linn 1990, 36) or to release them in ways that caregivers may not be able to recognize. This is one of the reasons that a support group or counseling can be so helpful.

104

Children can be reassured that they are not alone and that what they feel is normal.

BEGINNING COUNSELING

Anyone who works with grieving children is wise to draw on the rich source of important information and support that can come from a child's caregivers. Yet one mistake too many helpers make is to work alone with the child. Not only does this tend to reinforce the notion that the child's feelings are to be kept secret, it also prevents the helper and caregiver from learning from one another. A better way—unless the child is caught in the conflict between angry, divorcing parents or is part of a custody dispute—is to include the caregivers from the outset. Although the beginning meetings may be done separately with the child, caregivers, and other family members, it is most effective to do actual treatment work with at least one caregiver present with the child (at least for alternate sessions) for a number of reasons.

As the helper models a nonjudgmental stance that gives reflective feedback and involves actively making connections among scattered themes, thoughts, and feelings, caregivers learn both to respond to behaviors and to ask questions in an increasingly therapeutic manner and to become more alert to patterns that may trigger future difficulty, so that when old material surfaces they are able to respond appropriately and with increasing confidence. Observation of the interactions between the child and the helper also helps caregivers understand more fully where the areas of difficulty actually are, how they began, and how to respond to them. Their children will begin to turn to them when stressed or excited by new discoveries in the therapeutic process, thereby heightening their mutual sense of attachment and belonging with each other. Such participation may help promote a sense of mutual respect, understanding, and forgiveness in both caregiver and child for past grievances or concerns that have troubled or disrupted the family. The approach also discourages the child from playing the caregiver and helper off against each other, which can undermine the therapeutic process.

Frequently, it is useful to begin the work by meeting with the caregiver(s) alone to take a relationship history, to determine how well they understand the issues that appear to be troublesome, to explore their styles of problem solving and what they have found to be effective, and to clarify their particular concerns in order to begin to formulate a treatment contract with the family. If this is done, the helper should report the results to the child, which reinforces the notion that there need be no secrets and also makes it easier to begin the questioning process ("Kira, I saw your Dad last week, and he told me that he was worried about several things. Can you guess what some of them might be?"). The helper can then fill in the information that the child is unwilling or unable to share.

Some children who have had outside helpers when they changed caregivers in the past may be apprehensive when they first come to see you, fearing that you intend to make them move again. If this is not the case, you need to make it very clear: "I guess you know what happens after you come to see me. We have our turn, then we finish, then you go home. That is what I think will happen every time I see you—you will always be going home." If you are or might be involved in helping the child make another change of caregiver, though, it is important that the child understand this and that past changes be explored before the child is asked to deal with a new one.

From the first call or visit to the helper through the completion of treatment and termination, it is important for the helper to communicate clearly that the personal needs, feelings, and thoughts of each family member will be given respectful, equitable attention and that all attempts by any family member to impose a point of view on another will be discouraged. For things to work well in family work, the helper must always be mindful that *the whole family is the client* and that each member is equally important.

Checking Out Family Rules about Feelings

Any helper working with a child who appears to be repressing or inhibiting a particular feeling has a responsibility to try to determine what part the child's caregivers or significant others might play in the repression. Families often have unspoken rules that certain feelings are unwelcome or dangerous, making it complicated for the child to own or talk about those feelings. Moody and Moody (1991) suggest that the helper observe the coping style of the caregiver(s) to decide whether intervention should begin with them or with the child. Only after caregivers are able to express their own grief is the rest of the family freed to grieve as well; those who fail to resolve their own feelings of loss may complicate and add to their children's discomfort.

When worn down by grief or depleted from struggling to master new roles and responsibilities, caregivers may find it hard to help their child sort through pain or to figure out how best to support their child's strong emotions and the accompanying behaviors. Dealing with the child's pain is likely to intensify concern or regret in those who have been unable to protect a child, especially if they, whether caregivers, social workers, or other helpers, feel partially responsible for the loss. Instead of being able to allow the child to experience and express feelings freely, involved adults sometimes send subtle (or not so subtle) clues to the child that they need the child to support and validate the actions or decisions that led up to the loss or change, encouraging children to act as if what has happened to them is unimportant or is a relief. Children are likely to assume it is wrong for them to experience or reveal emotions unless the important adults around them do the same. Some children have difficulty because prior expressions of strong feelings have met with negative responses. Others need more permission and a model before they can try, particularly if they have rules or fears about particular feelings. And even children who talk about their feelings may not be experiencing and processing them. Some children learn to parrot appropriate words about feelings in order to satisfy adults enough that they will drop the subject.

In order to work well with a child and family, helpers must identify family rules and work with them respectfully. It is useful to ask caregivers, either privately or in the child's presence, what rules govern the expression of strong feeling in the family and what styles of expression are allowed: "If I were a child in your family,

---

107

how could I let you know that I was upset [sad, angry, scared, etc.]?" As different feelings are discussed, the helper can watch for glances exchanged between child and caregiver and comment on what they might signify: "I noticed you looked at your mom just then. I'm wondering if you think it's OK with her for you to feel angry?" Or, "I noticed that David looked at you when we started talking about being scared, Mr. Sadler. Maybe he's wondering how you feel about him sometimes having that feeling. Could you tell him what you think about that?"

Another conversation that helps establish guidelines for discussion and display of strong feelings might go like this:

"Mrs. Jensen, Peter and I have been talking about the kinds of things that might make him or a boy like him have different feelings. I know that everybody has some things that bother them or make them angry. I'd like to ask you what people do when they have these feelings in your family. Can you tell me what Peter is likely to do when he feels mad? [Mrs. Jensen responds.] You're saying that he most often cries and runs to his room. Thanks, it helps me to know that. [The helper turns to Peter.] What about your mom, Peter? What does she do when she gets mad? [Turning back to the mother, the helper asks:] Is he right, Mom? OK, it sounds like you've been watching each other and you know that both of you get mad sometimes, and that each of you has certain things you most often do when you're angry. Now let me ask you, Mr. Jensen, what about you? Do you sometimes get mad, too? Well, what do you do?"

This kind of dialogue not only gives the helper a sense of family patterns and rules about dealing with anger (or any other feeling that needs to be discussed) but also establishes that members in the family can watch each other, be aware of each other's feelings, talk about their actions and reactions openly. Holding a family meeting for this kind of discussion often clarifies for the helper who in the family makes the rules about expression of feelings, who enforces those rules, what happens when they are broken, how comfortable the caregivers are with their own feelings as well as the child's, and what the child is frightened may happen if he or she lets a particular feeling out.

108

Families may need help understanding that it is extremely important to free up family customs and rules so that each family member is allowed to grieve in his or her own way, authentically, and without being limited to feeling what others feel. Even in families that usually avoid emotionally laden conversation, new permissions can be shared that can promote better health in the family in general. If there appear to be strong rules against expressing, noticing, or remarking about feelings and reactions to feelings, the helper can encourage the family to experiment with doing so in this special time together or this special place.

FACILITATING CONVERSATIONS WITH CHILDREN

When a child and family are in crisis or serious difficulty, getting down to the challenges at hand can be extremely important. Too many helpers waste valuable time waiting for the child to bring up the problem. It is helpful to establish a respectful, businesslike but playful, interested, and honest relationship with the child or adolescent as quickly as possible. One technique is to use a kitchen timer with a young or school-age child. The child is told, "Here we take turns being boss. You get a turn, and I get a turn. Would you like the first or the second turn ?" During the child's turn, the child picks the activity, and the timer is set to what seems appropriate to that particular child (usually from ten to twenty minutes). The helper's turn is the same length, also monitored by the timer. Children respond well to this: It is fair, it respects their need to be in charge or to learn to take charge, and they may find it is easier to deal with difficult material if they can predict when the helper will stop talking or asking about it—at least until the next turn. In addition, if a variety of inviting, versatile props are available for children to explore and play with (such as drawing materials, dollhouses and action figures, puppets, and noncompetitive sharing games), what they choose to do with their turn may furnish useful insights into their states of mind and suggest avenues of conversation that the helper may want to pursue.

Common, useful diagnostic projective drawing techniques (such as the Kinesthetic Family Drawing or the House-Tree-Person series) may be used during the helper's turn to gauge further where difficulties lie. Most children do not feel they are being examined or tested when asked to draw such pictures, and parents should be reassured that projective drawings often provide useful clues as to what might need additional investigation and clarification and can suggest a diagnosis or course of treatment to trained helpers using them.

It is unwise to assume that children who never talk about what has happened and how they feel about it are untouched or handling their grief in a healthy way. Even children who are likely to seek help and comfort when they are physically hurt may find it hard to ask for support when they are suffering emotionally. There are a number of reasons why this happens. Children often have great difficulty putting their feelings into words because they lack the maturity or the communication skills to know how to begin. Young or regressed children may fear that by openly acknowledging their rage or terror or intense pain, they will somehow cause another calamity to befall them. School-age children, mindful of the stresses that weigh heavily on their parents, may stifle their grief feelings to avoid creating additional pressures that they fear might overload their caretaker. One eight-year-old boy, who appeared to take his sister's death quite lightly, when finally asked if he was glad his sister had died, explained that he felt terribly sad but that he was heeding the advice of an adult at his sister's funeral who had impressed upon him that it was his responsibility to cheer his parents up during their terrible time of sorrow (LaTour 1987, 14).

Understanding Conversion Responses

Children should be encouraged and helped to give direct voice to their feelings, not only in the months immediately following a loss but again and again. Expressing, revisiting, and readdressing feelings over time is one of the most vital components of a healthy healing process. Otherwise grief may fester indefinitely. One very common response in children who have no model or cannot give themselves permission to express their feelings is to convert feelings that cause them discomfort into some other feeling.

During the first meeting, the helper asks, "Tell me a little about Tara. You say that she seems to get angry very easily. What kinds of things seem to make her angry?" Charlotte recites the list. "OK, that seems on target. Now, I'm wondering, what kinds of things make her sad?" "It's funny," Charlotte answers slowly. "I don't really know. Oh, she gets mad, especially at her little sister, but sad. . . . Even when I spank her, she never cries." "Does she ever talk about feeling sad?" the helper inquires. "No. Even when you can tell her feelings are hurt, or when she's really disappointed, she just sort of shrugs it off and says, 'I don't care.' Do you think that could be a problem?"

Given that Tara's behavior is causing concern, and given that children often show rather than say how they feel, both Tara's mother and the helper would be wise to follow up with Tara to see if she can own and share the usual range of feelings, including sadness.

Mike, who is six, had a major change in families several months ago. His new mother complains that nothing seems to please him. Mike weeps and carries on about everything: He cries when he is frustrated by a stubborn button or loose shoelaces. He cries about imagined slights. He cries about the tiniest bump or scratch. He cries because it isn't his turn to sit by the car window or because it is his turn to set the table. "You'd think he would rust," says his mother in frustration.

There is a chance that Mike has an internal rule, "Don't be angry." When he feels angry, he may convert that feeling into an allowed feeling of sadness. Some of his tears, then, might come from genuine sadness, others from anger. Other children, frightened by the vulnerability of sadness, may convert it into rage, releasing their sorrow as hostility, irritability, annoyance, or complaining. Some behave in ways that are sure to draw punishment, providing them with an excuse to release the tears and anger they are having trouble releasing.

111

Although such conversions of feeling are quite normal for many children, they pose problems for those around the child, who may find it increasing difficult to respond supportively to the unceasing blaming, raging, or weeping. Compounding the difficulty when a child releases converted feelings is that it has no effect on the original feeling. The child pays the price, continuing to act out discomfort without gaining relief and irritating those who could be available to support and help if it were clearer what was really going on. Luckily, after conversions are explained to them, children and their caregivers are often quick to recognize that anger, for example, is often a second feeling (first you feel put down and then you feel angry) and can work together to help plan ways for the child to express and release the underlying feeling appropriately.

Children who decide that they should hide or repress their feelings have often concluded that a particular feeling is bad. They may suppress their grief until they feel they are old enough to be taken seriously. Only when they feel certain that they will finally receive validation, support, and comfort will they bring forth and share their memories and pain and resentment. Whether they convert or repress their feelings, they often benefit from learning that feelings are feelings, neither good nor bad.

Helpers should be careful not to assume from a history alone that a child will have trouble discussing feelings. Instead, they should draw their conclusions from the level of reluctance with which the child responds to approaches that usually help children express themselves. They should also understand that exploring areas that have been sealed off for a long time may be frightening to the child or that they may be asking the child to break a strong internal survival rule. One child drew a sign while her helper was trying to engage her in conversation about her feelings: NO TALKING IN SCHOOL. PRIAVISI [privacy].

The Five Feelings Technique

When children are uncomfortable or unpracticed in talking about their feelings, combining discussion with an external activity, such as using visual props, often helps them open up. One simple but effective way to begin is to use the five feelings technique.

Begin by saying, "This doesn't have to be hard. There are five important feelings that grown-ups and children are likely to have [hold up one hand with your fingers spread, and move one finger and then the next as you recite the feelings): sad, mad, happy, scared, and lonely. Let's check it out. When you think about not living with your dad anymore do you [hold up one finger] have any sad feelings? [If the child shakes his or her head, continue.] OK, no sad feelings. [Hold up a second finger.] What about happy feelings? [If the child shrugs, follow it up.] OK, looks like you're not so sure about happy." Proceed through the entire list, each time putting the child's reaction into words or repeating his or her words.

It is important not to anticipate or to feed the child answers. If you are unsure about what a child is sharing, try to clarify: "I'm mixed up. Your mouth said no, but your head went up and down in a yes. Will you help me out so I'm sure I understand?" Then restate the question. This kind of respectful checking not only avoids confusion but makes it very clear that the helper is truly interested in understanding what the child feels. And if you are a caregiver trying to help your child through such conversations, especially if no outside helper is involved, remember that it is extremely important not to use the information your child shares to embarrass, control, or demean the child in any way at a later time. If caregivers share their own feelings, whether a helper is involved or not, the likelihood of this happening is reduced.

The Five Faces Technique

Another excellent way for a helper to begin talking with children about their feelings is to use an activity that combines seeing, hearing, and doing and alternates feelings work with other activities in order to pace things out. An early conversation might sound like this:

HELPER: Hi, Ling Sung. Let me tell you how it works here. We take turns being boss and deciding what we want to do during our turn. I'll set this timer to keep the turns fair. Do you want to be boss first or do you want me to? [Interestingly enough, being offered the opportunity to be in charge seems to relax children, and they often want the helper to begin so they can scope out who and what they have gotten involved with.] OK. One of the things you'll find out about me is I like to talk with kids about how they feel. So I want to see how good you are at that and where you might need some help. Let's see [taking out three-by-five index cards and markers]. I know that there are at least five feelings kids are likely to have. Have you got any guesses about what some of them might be?

LING SUNG: I don't know. Happy, I guess.

HELPER: Sure, happy is one. Let's write that on the bottom of this card, and then we'll see what a happy face might look like. Do you want to draw it, or shall I?

LING SUNG: You do it.

HELPER: OK. What color shall I use? [The idea is to proceed with the activity and invite the child to make as many verbal choices and inputs as you can. Many times the child will just take the activity over.]

LING SUNG: I don't know. Blue, I guess.

HELPER: Sounds good. OK, there's a happy face. We'll write each feeling you can think of on one of these cards, and then we'll draw the faces to match. . . . Let's see, you also thought of angry and scared. Do you have a guess about what some of the other feelings might be? [Ling Sung can't or won't answer.] Can you write the words for other feelings on these cards if I tell you what they are?

LING SUNG: OK. [As the helper recites the feelings, Ling Sung writes *sad, mad, glad* (or *happy*), *scared,* and *lonely* (or *left-out*), one word across each card.]

HELPER: Good. Now we need to make faces to go with the words. You know, when people have something to say, a lot of times they show you with their faces instead of telling you in words. What about you, do you ever do that?

LING SUNG: I don't know.

HELPER: Well, think a minute. Show me how your face would look if I told you that we were going to take the day off and just do something that was fun? I see. [The helper mirrors Ling Sung's expression.] Your mouth would go up, and your eyes would look like they were smiling, like on this *happy* card. Let's try another one. What if I said that everybody but you got to take the day off and have fun, but you had to stay in and clean up your room? Oh. That would look a lot different. Which one shall we do first? [If the child selects the order, interesting diagnostic information may be suggested, such as which feelings are easily accessible and which are being avoided.] You picked *angry*. Will you draw it or shall I?

LING SUNG: I will. [He draws a face.]

HELPER: Great. Now which one?

Helper and child can proceed through the drawings, which will usually look something like this:

SAD   MAD   HAPPY   SCARED   LONELY

If you're stumped as to how to draw a face or if the child is confused, it is a good idea to ask the child to show you the facial expression he or she uses for that feeling and then to draw it. Or you can show the child how your face looks with that feeling, and have him or her draw it.

Children who have trouble sharing a particular feeling will give clues through their drawings in this game: "Your sad face is hard for me. It looks almost like your happy face [or angry face, the other common variation]. Is that how you look when you're feeling sad [an good opener to conversation]?" Conversions in a child's drawings may point to which feelings act as a mask for others. It is not unusual for a child to describe one feeling with the word for another. A very common example is the substitution of the word *boring* for *lonely* or *painful*.

Even if the child only watches and the helper does most of the talking and drawing, the child may benefit from learning that feelings and their expression can be safely discussed with this person in this place. Helpers might also want to add neutral comments with questions: "I'll show you what a lot of people do when they have sad feelings [adding tears to a *sad* drawing]. Do you ever look like that?"

Sometimes you may need to add other emotions to the basic list of five. Some common ones are confused feelings, silly or giddy feelings, embarrassed feelings, and helpless feelings. Often these additions will be suggested by comments from caregivers or teachers on how the child has reacted to the separation or loss; sometimes they will arise in conversations you have with the child. As conversations progress, either child or helper may decide to add other cards and faces.

After they are completed, it can be helpful to use the "feeling faces" cards as a check-in at the beginning of each session. They will remind the child that talking about and working with feelings is a primary task. Both child and helper are reminded that feelings are part of life in general, not just important when connected to grief. By talking with the child about what is happening between sessions, both child and helper have the chance to focus on other joys and woes, triumphs and disasters, as they come to know one another better.

Doing feelings check-ins with the caregivers present can help keep youngsters focused, aware, and accountable. When asked, "How did your week go?" the child may answer, "Fine." If you then ask, "Any time you felt angry?" and the child answers no, caregivers may jump in quickly to remind or challenge or express their own observations: "What about when you punched Jimmy and told him to mind his own business?" Including caregivers also gives them a regular time and place to share their own feelings with both child and helper. They may even want to add new cards. One mother began a session by drawing a picture of a light bulb with a face on it, which she labeled "Aha!" and other parents and children have used her card to talk about an insight they've had about themselves or another.

Both the "five feelings" and "five faces" techniques can be used at home to help continue the work that is being done in counseling. Typical assignments might include asking a family to set up a time each day to check in with each other about their feelings, perhaps at a meal or while driving together, where the caregiver asks each person in the family, "Did you feel [angry, sad, lonely, etc.] today?" After each person, including the caregiver, has answered about that feeling, a second family member initiates a question about another feeling. Or the family might be asked to watch a TV program or cartoon with the sound off and see what each of them thinks the characters are feeling and whether the guesses agree.

It is not unusual for children who initially seem timid, reluctant, or guarded when it comes to talking about their feelings to relax visibly when they have the opportunity to figure out how to share their experience, confident that the listener will let them take their time and speak their own truth without judgment. Sometimes children will end preliminary conversations with deep sighs of relief; sometimes they will share copiously as if they had only been waiting for someone to open the door; sometimes they will grab a hug or spontaneously turn and wave happily as they leave; sometimes they will open up in a session but later express reluctance about returning for more conversation because they feel anxious about having shared more than they intended.

I frequently joke with children about how adults are likely to do things the same way over and over. When they go to their doctor with a pain in their knee, their doctor is still likely to look in their ears and check their chest. I tell them I am more interested in feelings than ears and noses and I will be wanting to check their feelings almost every time I see them. I end early sessions by telling children that their homework is to notice which feelings they have during the coming week. Then we start off the next session by looking at the "feeling faces" cards and checking them out in random order: "OK. Any glad feelings? Sounds like that sleep-over will be really fun. What about scared feelings." And so forth. I sometimes keep a separate set of cards for each young child. But there is also a stack that sits on the table where we are likely to spend part of our session, and these cards are used to introduce "feeling faces" and do feelings check-ins with older children. Blank index cards and markers are also available. As new children draw their first faces, some of their cards can be exchanged for old ones in the stack. Or children may decide to add cards for feelings not yet represented, so the cards in the check-in stack change and multiply. In this way, the check-in demonstrates concretely that other children have a full range of feelings as well and that this is normal and healthy.

"Feeling faces" cards are a good way to begin talking about some of the things that might be troubling the child. Spreading the cards on the table, a helper might ask, for example, "When you heard that your mom had decided not to live with your dad anymore, which of these feelings did you have?" Or, indirectly, "What would you tell someone about how kids might feel when they don't live with one of their parents any more?" The child can then use the cards to explore and explain feelings, even if only by pointing. The helper could also use the cards to reassure the child that it is normal to have several different feelings about the same event. Many children under age ten still think in either/or terms yet experience mixed feelings. The cards can help them recognize and share all their varied and perhaps conflicting feelings.

Experienced helpers might not only give children permission to express feelings but also try to clarify that what they feel is fairly normal and nothing to be ashamed about: "Lots of kids have told me that they had some really strong feelings when they stopped living with their dads. Was that how it was for you, or was it different?"

It is important to remember that children can often show how they feel more clearly than they can verbalize it. As you ask the child, "Did you have any sad feelings?" watch carefully for body signals such as nodding or shaking the head or shrugging the shoulders (which often means "I'm not sure" but may also mean "I don't want to tell you"). The helper can then mirror back the physical signal and give words to what the child seems to be communicating physically: "Some sad. OK." If the response was a shrug, you can say to the youngster: "When I asked you if you felt any sad feelings, your shoulders went like this. I'm wondering if that means that you don't know?" A second shrug usually means "I don't want to talk to you about this."

Another useful technique in gauging the depth of children's

feelings is to prompt them to use their hands to show how much of the feeling is experienced. Hands spread wide apart would mean "a lot"; hands held close together "a little." You can then put words to the physical communication: "Did you have any sad feelings?" Then spread your hands, and say, "A lot?" If the answer is no, bring them together, and ask "A little? Or something in between?" Then, "How about lonely feelings, were there some of those? A lot, a little? I understand. You have had a lot of sad feelings and a little bit of lonely feelings." And so on through the list. With adolescents, it can be useful to ask, "How would you rate that feeling on a scale of one to ten?"

With help isolating common feelings and addressing them individually and from hearing their body language put into words, children often gain confidence in talking about their feelings in general as well as sharing specific reactions. At the same time that the helper is paying close, respectful attention to what and how a child responds, however, the helper needs also to be very careful to stay aware of his or her own responses. Even a subtle lapse of attention, a flush, a shiver, a hurried attempt to comfort or too quick a looking away or changing of subject is likely to communicate discomfort and to squelch the child's sharing even when it comes from someone who sincerely wants to help.

Storytelling as a Way to Bring Out Feelings

When children have difficulty talking about or sharing their own feelings, one way to help them become more relaxed or fluent is to make up a story, tell part of it, and then have the child point to which feeling comes at that place. For example, "Once upon a time, Gertrude the green giraffe woke up on a Saturday morning. She could see the sun shining brightly through her window. She jumped out of bed and said to herself, 'I feel so . . .'" After the child chooses a card, the storyteller continues, "because . . ." and goes on with the story. Or the child may draw a card and then be asked to continue with the story. What the story is about is not particularly important. It simply provides a nonthreatening way to understand the child's experiences and feelings better, to look for major

119

themes (feeling left out, feeling anxious, and so forth), or to gauge which feelings the child avoids or returns to again and again.

Another way to use storytelling is to make up a game that involves dealing with feelings. As you tell a short made-up story, pause when a character might have strong feelings, and ask the child to point out the face or name the feeling that illustrates what those feelings are. Then ask, "What do you think Gertrude [or any major character] could do to make things better?" This can help you understand better what the child knows about defending or helping himself, in what ways she or he feels helpless, and what kinds of fantasies the child might be using to handle the feelings brought about by loss and separation.

A number of commercial board games promote the sharing of thoughts and feelings. The Ungame and Life Stories are two popular examples. Some children who do not have trouble waiting for their turns or talking about other topics will be noticeably fidgety and uncomfortable while they wait for their caregiver(s) or other family members to answer the questions in games in which there is more intimate sharing. Some children can wait for one caregiver to share but not the other. Their discomfort and their need to control the flow of sharing of personal and feeling information causes them to regress and act much younger. They may also behave intrusively, blurting out the answer to a caregiver's question or saying, "I know!" or rattling the dice impatiently. Often this is because they are anxious about knowing or hearing about their caregivers' feelings or because they are acting on an internal rule that it is not right or safe for family members to do this kind of sharing.

Using games allows the helper to establish healthy ground rules for sharing thoughts and feelings: No one is allowed to answer for anyone else. Each person will take a turn and speak his or her truth without interruption or distraction from other players. There will be no verbal or physical put-downs. As children become more familiar with intimate sharing without negative consequence, it becomes easier and easier for them to follow these rules, until finally there is no need for reminders. And since these rules are also the basis for healthy family conversation and for respecting the individuality of each family member, it is likely that family members will become more aware of how and when they break these rules in their daily interactions and begin to remind or confront one another outside the therapy setting when a rule is broken, which will lead to a basic healthy change in general family functioning and communication.

Some children have such strong internal rules about not letting themselves or others know what they think and feel or have had such traumatizing experiences that they need a good deal of support for the courage it will take them to address their feelings and to share them.

When approaching painful or defended topics, helpers should lower their voices and slow down their speech, as if they were on holy ground, and give some empathetic forewarning: "I know that this is really hard for you to talk about." Helpers also need to recognize that sometimes children really are unable to get in touch with their feelings and thoughts and just blank out. Unable to respond they may agree with everything helpers say or shrug and say, "I don't know." An appropriate response is to say, "You can figure this out. Let yourself know," and then to pause and see if something comes. If a child still is stuck, the helper can say, "In time, I think you will know. And you can take whatever time you need." When a child seems unable to own or talk about a particular feeling, the helper might observe, "Seems like you know and understand the things that make you feel [for example] angry, or sad, or lonely, but being scared never seems to get a turn in your life. I wonder where that feeling goes?"

One child who had lost her father tragically when she was quite small and then had needed to take care of the remaining adults around her by not creating difficulties was completely at a loss when it came to identifying and dealing with her feelings. She had reached a point of desperate unhappiness and had become severely aggressive, both verbally and physically, with her younger stepsisters and classmates at school. Although she was pleasant during sessions and would perform as requested, the usual activities that engage most children in claiming and discussing or demonstrating their feelings proved fruitless. Knowing that another way to engage a child's involvement is for the adult to begin to draw something related to what is happening and to let the child just observe, her helper began some symbolic work to acknowledge what appeared to be happening. The helper thought about how the child's two responses—hidden/guarded and explosive—might be represented pictorially. Then she began a story that went like this: "Elana, this is what your life reminds me of. Once there was a deep, deep cave." She drew a brown cave covered with grass and bushes. "Outside that cave something terrible happened that caused a terrible hurt." She drew a pool of red for blood, with drops leading to the mouth of the cave. "And now that hurt lives inside this cave. I can feel it there, but I don't know if it wants me to come in and see how to help it. And I keep hoping that it will come closer to the door so I can tell it how sorry I am about how it hurts and how alone it is and keep it company until it feels safe enough to come out. I think you know a lot about this hurt and this cave. If the hurt were an animal that lived in there, would you draw me a picture to show me what kind of an animal it might be?" Elana drew a picture of a fawn lying close to death, and then she said, "Wait! There are two animals," and drew a chipmunk frisking about. "That's to keep the deer company," she went on. "I think maybe it would like to come out just to the door and see you because it can always run back inside really quick." The helper responded, "I'll try to be very careful so that maybe it will have a chance to play outside in the sunshine sometime." To which Elana responded, "I think it will like that. Someday maybe it will tell its friend that it is safe to come out and eat some grass."

In the next session, the helper said, "We've talked about how sometimes I see you in this cave. The other thing that I think about when I think of you looks like this." She drew a volcano and then, coloring in the bottom of the cone, she said, "Deep down inside, there are some bubbling, building feelings, maybe angry. And, like a volcano, every so often the feelings build up and build up until the pressure inside spurts them out, and they erupt over the edges, and the hot, burning feelings move and swallow up things and seem out of control and dangerous. I think those volcano feelings inside may make you pretty uncomfortable, and I know that the eruptions scare the people who live around and near this volcano.

I'll be glad when you can talk about the feelings so that they don't need to build up and explode because then you can decide to let them out a little at a time as you want and need to."

BRINGING OUT AND MANAGING
ANGRY FEELINGS

When grief causes anger, many children run into trouble. Sometimes they are afraid that if they get angry, they will get in trouble. Sometimes they are very uncomfortable about feeling angry, so they convert their anger or deny it and stuff it away. They may blame themselves relentlessly, torturing themselves with all the things they ever did that were wrong or displeasing, immersing themselves in their guilt, and convincing themselves that they deserve to be deprived and unhappy. Or they may turn their aggression on themselves, picking at or biting themselves or their clothing. Sometimes they can't control the intensity of their anger, and the level of their anger and the way they release it frightens and intimidates those around them and causes retaliation or rejection. Helping children voice and release their angry feelings appropriately while discouraging inappropriate or dangerous expressions of feelings can be a challenging part of helping them work through their responses to separation and loss.

In order to be effective at this work, adults must be comfortable being around children who are angry. They also need to understand and accept that although some children can talk their anger out, other children need to act on it, just as adults may shout or yell, slam a door, bang a dish, or drive around to cool off or sort things out. Adults often try to be helpful by suggesting that an angry youngster punch a pillow. Although this approach reassures the child that the adult recognizes and respects that the child may need to discharge anger physically, unless it matches how the child needs to release anger, it is likely to leave the child feeling supported but misunderstood and the adult frustrated and confused.

It helps to know that when children get angry they seem to feel a surge of energy in one of three zones of their bodies: their mouth;

their arms and hands; or their feet and legs. If you watch children when they are angry or listen carefully when they talk about when they were angry, you may discover that their emotional energy travels to a preferred physical zone: they may grind their teeth, bite, spit, scream, or insult; or they may clench their hands, pinch, yank, punch, or tear; or they may swing their feet back and forth, get up and pace, run or stomp around, kick, or trip.

If you explain this theory about energy zones to children, they are often fascinated. All of a sudden, their behavioral reactions make sense to them. It is not unusual for children immediately to be able to identify their anger zone. Children who can't do this can be helped to figure out which energy zone brings them the most sense of release through questions such as, "When Susie told on you what did you do [or wish you could do] to get even?" Sometimes more than one zone may be involved. It helps to ask the child, "When you get into a fight and hit and yell at Susie, if you could only do one of those things, which one do you think would feel best?"

The best way to help children physically release their angry feelings is to respect their preferred energy zone and to devise a permitted expression for such feelings.

Dean appears to be a low-energy, passive youngster, out of touch with his feelings and only vaguely aware of himself and his surroundings. It seems that his problems might be connected to feelings of hopelessness, helplessness, and inexpressible anger. The helper working with him introduces a way for Dean to begin to share his feelings and then to release them, physically and verbally, using large reinforced-cardboard blocks (which are carried by nursery and kindergarten supply companies):

HELPER: Dean, you're getting so you can do that angry face really well. I'm wondering what kinds of things make you angry.

DEAN: I don't know.

HELPER: Lots of kids tell me they get angry when things are not fair. Does that ever happen to you?

DEAN: I guess so.

HELPER: I have a mad game I play with kids sometimes when they have those feelings. It goes like this. You stack one block for each thing you can think of that isn't fair or makes you angry. Let's see if you can tell me one. It's not fair when . . .

DEAN: I have to stay in at recess.

HELPER: [Slams block down.] I have to stay in at recess. [Holds up second block.] And it's not fair when . . .

DEAN: I get blamed for something I didn't do.

HELPER: [Stacks block loudly on first block.] And . . .

DEAN: [Louder] It's not fair when my mom likes Brad better than me. [Helper adds, "And . . ."] It's not fair that I always have to do the dishes. It's not fair that I never get to pick the program on TV.

After Dean has built a tall tower of blocks, his helper says, "Now, I'll tell you something fun to do. You look at that big stack of blocks, and then you kick them down, hard, like this!" (aiming a kick at the stacked up blocks). As the blocks tumble and fall down, Dean shouts gleefully, "Let me do it!" Together the helper and Dean rebuild the stack (children can also rebuild by themselves). Prompted by "It's not fair when . . ." or "I feel mad when . . ." Dean verbalizes his stored-up resentments, building his stack again and again and crowing with delight as he kicks it down. He is taking charge of releasing his feelings. Within a week or two, his caregiver reports that Dean is sleeping better and that he appears less tense and has more positive energy available. Dean asks in his counseling sessions, "Can we do some more mad games today?"

As children think about their grudges, they are likely to find it easier and easier to enumerate them. If not, helpers can make guesses based on their other complaints or can make a hypothetical stack: "Other kids have told me they hate having to wash their hair. And they've said, 'It's not fair that I have to go to bed so early.'" When the time seems right, whether it is the first time the game is played or a session or two later, the helper may add with the final block on the stack, "It's not fair when someone you love goes away," or whatever fits the child's situation.

Whether they have been inhibited about expressing anger or have shown outbursts of out-of-control anger, children who do this activity with caregivers present may glance at them to check whether it is OK to be doing it. If the caregivers are waiting in another room, the child may report to them at the end of the session, "I got angry in there today." If not, the helper should take responsibility for informing the caregivers of the session's activities ("Dean and I practiced getting angry safely today"), so the child does not leave guiltily assuming that he has done something wrong.

After the cardboard-block game, children might be encouraged to investigate other areas and types of release. Their helpers might try talking to them about other anger zones and then helping them check them out for themselves:

HELPER: Sounds like you're not too sure where your anger wants to come out. Let's try something. Come stand here by me, and let's stamp our feet to see if you can feel your anger going down there. OK. Now let's stack these blocks and try kicking them down. How was that?

DEAN: Can we do it again?

HELPER: Which, stamp or kick?

DEAN: Kick.

HELPER: Sure, go to it.

After Dean has tried kicking the blocks for a while, the helper says, "Let's try something different. How about stacking up the blocks one more time, only this time I'd like you to bop them down with your hand. Woooow! How did that feel?"

DEAN: Good.

HELPER: Which feels best so far, stamping, kicking, or bopping?

DEAN: Kicking.

For each child, there are likely to be certain sensations and sounds that feel expressive, satisfying, and under control. In Dean's case, his helper might ask him to kick something soft, such as a pillow, and to jump up and down on something that can be squashed, such as a grocery bag stuffed with newspapers or a small plastic trash bag stuffed with plastic bags. As Dean explores and observes, he is likely to reconnect with those parts of himself that are tucked away and to be able to figure out which kinds of sensations are most releasing for him. This kind of sharing and reclaiming of the authentic self is of itself therapeutic and vitalizing. It can be equally useful with youngsters who are discharging their anger inappropriately, as it seems to help them focus their release in a way that is not harmful or frightening to others.

It is useful to have different materials on hand to use as props for the physical release of anger and to help children identify what activities and objects feel and sound most satisfying to them. When children are hand releasers, they should be encouraged to try tearing paper and wadding it up; pinching, poking, and pounding Play-Doh or soft clay; or splatting it against a piece of cardboard or on a cookie sheet. Adults can help by watching closely to see how the child moves: Does the child swing the whole arm? Up or down? Does he or she want to throw something or feel an impact with the fingers, the inside of the hand, the side of the fist, the knuckles? Any of these areas may be where the child needs to feel the energy release.

Cheri likes hitting the blocks because she likes the arm swing. At home, one of her patterns is to slap or pull hair. Her helper got her to try spreading her arms wide and then bringing her hands together in a slap. She also had her hit a table with a foam bat so that Cheri could feel the handle smack in the palm of her hand and use her full arm swing. (Foam bats available in toy stores during baseball season are inexpensive and durable and can be used to hit chairs or blocks without causing damage. Bats can also be made from rectangular foam cuttings available at mattress suppliers and upholsters, by wrapping the handles with electrical or duct tape.) Cheri was clear that she liked being able to whap with the bat best.

Whenever a child has been working on releasing anger physically with a helper who is not the caregiver, the helper should have a conversation with both child and adult to establish clear guidelines as to whether the child will be able to continue such expression at home, and to plan where and how it will be allowed.

"Cheri and I have been figuring out how she might let out some of her angry feelings without slapping or pulling hair or hurting anyone. It seems that what might work best for her is to have something that she could pound with so that she could feel an impact in the palm of her hand. I'm wondering if there might be something we can think of that she could use at home next week if she feels angry?"

Most caregivers will try to think of something that fits in with their rules. In Cheri's case, it might be a foam bat or an empty plastic bottle with a neck. For other children who hit, bopping their beds with a stuffed sock or sack or banging a tree with a stick or a short piece of old hose work well. Children also need to know where they are allowed to do their hitting and what they are allowed to hit (or kick or bite).

For children who need something to kick, reinforced cardboard cartons, such as those used for bottled beer or wine, can be wedged into the corner of a room for kicking at home. Such cartons are inexpensive, easily replaced, and will not cause damage if they fly around. Being given permission to stomp to their rooms and slam a door is a technique that often works well, and it can be a useful substitute for children who release through temper tantrums. Punching bags and inflated clowns are sometimes useful for hitters, but good punching bags are very expensive and the others tend to leak if they are hit. You may want to experiment to see if they fit your needs. For children who release through chewing, a piece of old toweling or a rubber dog bone (a child can bite right through teething rings) may do the trick. Although sometimes caregivers feel funny about giving school-aged children something to chew, they often change their minds when children stop chewing holes in their clothing or experiencing the kind of behavior problems that accompany undirected anger release.

One interesting side effect of children having the right object to kick or hit or chew is that those who have had problems with bedwetting after a loss often stop or decrease the wetting. Sometimes they will only wet the night before they are to see their counselor.

If a system for releasing anger is agreed on, everyone involved needs to be comfortable about it and confident that the child is not likely to use the release object on other people; if this is not possible, the release should be confined to the therapy setting. If the child will be releasing anger at home, caregivers must be empowered to restrict the activity, perhaps limiting it to the child's bedroom or to some other specified area. Caregivers should be encouraged to leave the room if they discover that they feel uneasy or uncomfortable watching or listening to the child's venting of anger. If a caregiver is clearly upset by the idea of the child giving physical release to anger, the helper should arrange with the child to confine the behavior to their sessions together. "Different grown-ups have different rules," the helper can explain, "and your grown-up prefers that you do your kicking [or other releasing activity] here and not at home." Most children can take such restrictions in stride, especially if they have previously hidden or repressed their anger, but they may arrive at their counseling sessions nearly bursting with accumulated grievances. In such cases, they should be allowed to get angry and to release it right away so that they are not distracted by built-up feelings during other therapeutic activities.

If overt priming of anger appears to increase rather than decrease inappropriate physical outbursts, this type of release work should stop for the time being, and other activities pursued instead.

Releasing Anger Appropriately at School

Until the child is able to talk about or to talk out anger and frustration, it is wise for those involved to help the child plan how to release anger appropriately at school. Most children who are mouth releasers find their own way, releasing tension by sucking on their hair, chewing wads of paper, or biting their nails, cuticles, or pencils. So long as they understand why they may be doing these things and are not made to feel self-conscious about what they do, any of these outlets may work just fine. For children who need to release anger with their hands, caregivers and teachers might discuss what could be allowed in the classroom or at school. Perhaps the child could have scrap paper to scribble on or wad up. Perhaps the child could be excused to go into the hall or bathroom to slap the hands together, pound fists, or stamp feet. Release can also be found in games such as tag and dodgeball and in races, unless the child is subject to ridicule or scapegoating in such situations or becomes overly aggressive or competitive.

Schools that give bereaved children a forum where they can talk about and express their feelings seem to find this kind of support effective in reducing acting out and depression as well as sending a message that the school (or community) really cares about its students. Schools would be wise to provide release supplies and to use support groups and check-in times to give bereaved children a chance to talk about their feelings or dissipate them in a way that does not pose problems for the children, classmates, or staff. Many children could settle down and work more productively, as well as feel better about themselves, if there were approved verbal and physical outlets for their anger.

Redirecting Aggressive Behavior

When adults coax, embarrass, threaten, or punish children in order to get them to stop being aggressive without having some understanding of the source or function of the aggressive urge or offering appropriate suggestions as to better ways to respond, children are likely to stop one activity only to replace it with another that may be just as unwelcome. A better approach is to talk with children about the ultimate outcomes of the aggressive behavior so that they are motivated to find other ways to handle things. Ultimately, it is hoped that children will learn to discharge their anger by talking about it and gain the satisfaction of knowing that they can control themselves and talk through their angry impulses.

Help was sought for Karen, whose family setting changed shortly after she turned thirteen. Karen seemed to have a chip on her shoulder. She had been kicked off her school bus after several incidents during which she stuck other students with pencils. During the first interview, the helper slowly led Karen to a more accurate understanding of the consequences of her behavior:

HELPER: I heard that things were not going so well on the school bus.

KAREN: Yeah! Those rejects can take their bus and stuff it.

HELPER: How are you getting to school? [Karen enjoyed school and had always done well academically, so getting kicked off the bus did not appear to be a way to avoid school.]

KAREN: I'm getting a ride, but now my parents say they're going to make me walk, and it's three miles!

HELPER: How come you stuck those kids with your pencil?

KAREN: They're a bunch of stuck-up weirdos. They think they are so great. Well, they can't push me around. I showed them!

HELPER: You did? How?

KAREN: They gave me their funny looks, like I don't belong on their dumb bus, and I got 'em. I stuck 'em. That'll show 'em, those rejects.

HELPER: Let me see if I've got this right, OK? You have to get on this bus every day with a bunch of weirdos who don't think you are as good as they are, hmm? That must make you pretty mad, hmm?

KAREN: Yeah!

HELPER: So when you get that mad, pushed-around feeling you want to get even and show them not to mess with you?

KAREN: Yeah.

HELPER: So you stick them with your pencil?

KAREN: Uh-huh.

HELPER: Small problem occurs to me: Who's off the bus?

KAREN: What?

HELPER: Looks like you got even and they got you off the bus.

KAREN: Ohhhh.

A similar conversation took place with eleven-year-old Brandon, who was spending many of his recesses in the hall outside the principal's office where he was being sent for fighting with other children on the playground. "So maybe you're the kind of kid who really likes spending a lot of time with the principal. Maybe you want to be a principal when you grow up, so you need to stick around and watch what he does?" the helper said good-humoredly. "No way? Well, if you'd rather be outside with the other kids, it looks to me as if we should figure out why you need to hit them. Maybe there's some other way you can take care of yourself instead that doesn't end up with you losing your recesses so much. Are you interested in working on that?" In working with aggressive children, it is good to emphasize freedom of choice, since much

131

aggressive behavior, especially in bereaved children, grows out of feelings of helplessness. It supports such children to know that their behavior may be an outgrowth of legitimate feelings and needs; that what they are doing involves making a choice; that they can look at their choices and decide which of those choices work and which might need to be rethought; that they can figure out more successful ways to meet their needs if what they are currently doing doesn't work well, hurts other people, or gets them in trouble. This avoids the impression often given to these children that they are somehow out of control and cannot change, an impression that makes them feel even more threatened and helpless.

Helping adults, however, may need to forbid dangerous or harmful behavior: "People are not for hurting." "When you have that hitting feeling, you *may not* hit Tim. You may hit your pillow or bang your fists on the table." "What you are doing is not safe [or not good for you and others]. I want you to take better care of yourself." Setting limits in this way recognizes the child's feeling or need, gives permission for a sanctioned expression of that feeling, and allows for more than just one outlet, avoiding the conflict that sometimes occurs when the child is told, "Don't do that [your thing]; do this [my thing]." When children seem about to lose control of their choices, adults need to lend support: "It's getting hard for you to stop. I want you to sit down or go to your room until you cool off." Helpers can often defuse the situation and help children solve problems in a way that saves them face and does not take sides: "You think it is your turn; Timmy thinks it is his turn. You two have a difference of opinion. Both of you want the next turn. How can we solve it fairly?"

Often, in order to change behavior, several small steps toward the ultimate goal are necessary. Children deserve time and support as they replace one behavior gradually with another. Adults who decide to stop smoking often find that it helps to know when the urge to have a cigarette is most likely to occur and then to plan substitute behavior to deal with the urge when the time comes; in the same way, children find it helpful to recognize what sets off their aggression and to plan how else to react. Like the adult who bridges from cigarettes to carrot sticks, gum, or candy, children may need to adopt some similar, but less harmful, activities as a bridge when they are asked to give up aggressive behavior.

The helper working with Karen thought about what else Karen might do with her pencil instead of sticking people, since it seemed that Karen's immediate response was to whip out her pencil. Knowing that an appeal to Karen's concern and empathy for the people whom she felt were giving her a hard time was likely to be fruitless, the helper asked Karen if she was interested in getting even in a way that was not so likely to get her kicked off the bus. "When they look at you funny," the helper suggested, "I want you to take out your pencil [current behavior], open your notebook, and write *REJECT, REJECT, REJECT* in big strong letters [new behavior]. Then close your notebook, and look right at them. I think it will drive them crazy."

Children who have been hitting other children can be taught to slam a fist into the palm of the opposite hand (which often encourages the other child to back down) or to hit their own hip or thigh with a closed fist and shout, "Stop that! I am getting really angry!" Children who kick others might kick at something else instead, or stamp their feet, or shift rapidly from one foot to another.

Children who are not able to stop their aggressive behavior by themselves may need to be restrained: "Can you stop or do you need help? You're showing me that you need me to help you stop." The ultimate goal is to bridge the child into a verbal venting of feelings. Eventually, words should be added to or exchanged for the substitute behavior. In Brandon's case, a helper could ask, "Are you willing to try something and see if it works to keep you from ending up in the principal's office? OK, here's what I want you to do. When you have that feeling, try making a fist and pounding your hand, and saying, 'I'm angry, I'm angry, I'm angry!' Let's practice that now." If the helper models the new behavior and takes the child through it several times, perhaps using role play, the child is likely to feel less awkward and to find it easier to remember to try the new reaction when pressed. Children can be asked to report on how the new response works out for them, either at their next session or on a daily basis if the helper is a caregiver at home.

When a substitute behavior has been planned, agreed to, and

practiced, children may spontaneously bridge themselves from the physical behavior to a verbal reaction or even to a mental one. Such was the case with Karen. When asked to report how the pencil and notebook trick had worked, Karen, who was back on the bus without incident, said she didn't know. "Every time I get the feeling," she said, "I just burst out laughing thinking about the looks on their faces if I pulled that notebook thing, and I chill out."

Given their tendency to think concretely, children may need help understanding that anger does not have to be directed at someone but can simply just be felt. Adults can help by sharing that they, too, sometimes have impulses to get back at or even with someone or think about acting or speaking out in response to frustrating situations. Children often don't realize that almost all people get aggressive impulses but that as they grow up they get better and better at deciding not to act on them. When caregivers choose to share some of their own challenges and reactions and talk about what they do with their aggressive feelings instead of acting on them (such as fantasizing or exercising), children have a much better model on which to base their own actions. Such conversations might begin, "When I couldn't get the stuff I needed to finish that job today, I felt like. . . ." Or, "When Mr. Lee chewed me out about the dogs getting into the trash again, I wanted to tell him. . . ." Or, "Sometimes I say to myself, if she does that one more time I'd like to . . ." and then continue with, "But then I said [something appropriate and reasonable] to myself and decided to [do something appropriate and reasonable] instead."

Working with Passive-Aggressive Behavior

Instead of blowing up or becoming directly aggressive, some children hide their anger, pushing it down inside where it churns around and builds up. Over time, the accumulation of this anger makes children feel uncomfortable and guilty, and they begin to release or express it indirectly by frustrating those around them through what is called "passive-aggressive" or "passive-resistant" behavior. Not daring to be openly aggressive, these children are likely to release their anger and frustration through hostile procrastination: not getting dressed, constantly losing things, moving very slowly, demanding that adults listen to endless, meaningless stories or participate in interactions that immobilize or frustrate them or cause them to spend a great deal of time and energy reminding, correcting, and checking up on the child (Bettelheim 1950, 210). Passive-aggressive children may constantly "forget" to follow normal daily routines or do their chores or homework. They may lose track of time and schedules, daydreaming or playing when they are supposed to be dressing or undressing. They may bed-wet (sometimes when wide awake). They may become unusually clumsy, breaking things or "accidentally" hurting themselves or others. And they may take so long to do something within their ability or perform the task so ineptly that adults cave in and decide to take over.

Children indulge passive-aggressive behavior for one or a combination of at least four reasons: (1) to vent anger; (2) to get punished in order to relieve internalized feelings of guilt or badness; (3) to get even for perceived betrayal or neglect; and/or (4) to regain some sense of control. Caregivers are unwise to react to such indirect expressions of anger with punishment or threats. It is more useful to help children release resentment and anger directly, using the methods discussed earlier. Another useful technique is to employ Dreikurs' (1974) technique of mutual problem solving.

Caregivers and child meet together, with or without an outside helper, and figure out solutions to their problem following specific steps. First, they agree that there is a problem and specifically state what that problem is—say, that evenings are spent fighting about whether it is time for the child to get ready for bed instead of doing fun things together. Second, they agree to see if they can beat or outsmart the problem together (which makes the problem the enemy and allies caregivers and child as a team). If a helper is involved, the helper may want to challenge the family to take charge of getting something better for themselves and to come up with a minimum of four or five suggestions that might work to resolve the difficulty. Third, family members brainstorm together, calling out any ideas that occur to them on how their problem might be solved. (Sometimes, when children are feeling helpless, they are reluctant to participate in this process. They may mumble, talk softly, use incomplete sentences, and say "I don't know," or "I don't care." Such children should be encouraged to use their energy and power: "When you say that, you give away all your power, and then everybody bosses you. How about holding on to that power and being your own boss?") Each idea is written down, and no one is allowed to comment or react to any suggestion until all involved have run out of possible ideas. Fourth, family members discuss each item on the list. If anyone objects to a suggested solution, that suggestion is crossed off the list without discussion. This defuses the conflict of "your way" versus "my way" and engenders a sense of teamwork that allows caregivers and children to think of new solutions they may have overlooked in their struggle for power. If someone questions whether a suggested solution might work, that idea is signalled with a question mark in the margin. Usually, this culling process leaves one or two suggestions, which may or may not have been flagged with a question mark. (Occasionally, the process yields no solution agreeable to everyone. The helper can then say, "Well, it looks as if this problem is still smarter than we are. Let's give ourselves a week to see if we can't come up with something to beat it." The following week, the technique can be used again.) Fifth, the family takes a vote on the remaining suggestions to see which one the family likes best or thinks might work best. If any family member questions one of the remaining solutions, the family brainstorms some more or simply discusses ways to eliminate the concern. Sixth, when the family has agreed on one approach to try, they encourage one another to think about what might happen to sabotage the trial solution. Finally, family members check to determine if each person involved is willing to agree to experiment with the new approach for a set time (often one week). At the end of the trial period, family members meet again to evaluate how the proposed solution has worked. They may discover that it has solved the problem and agree to continue with it; if, however, they find that it has solved parts of the problem but that difficulties remain with other parts or if they decide that the solution has not worked at all, they restate the problem as they now see it and begin the process all over again.

This technique works surprisingly well. The interaction between caregivers and child that begins with a problem and/or complaint ends on a positive, cooperative note, leaving all concerned with energy to work on the proposed change.

BRINGING OUT SAD FEELINGS

Researchers are increasingly in agreement that crying is an excretory process, like sweating. And there is even chemical evidence that, among other purposes, tears reduce stress in the body. Dr. William Frey of St. Paul–Ramsey Medical Center in Minnesota found a definite chemical difference in the content of irritant tears as opposed to emotional tears (LaTour 1987, 32). Yet, because they are most likely to feel sad or cry when they are injured, in pain, frightened, or lost, children frequently connect crying with being vulnerable and may avoid crying or expressing sadness to protect themselves from their own internal feelings of weakness. Sometime they seem to think that, since tears mean pain, if they can control them, they can control the pain. Parents, other adults, and peers also are likely to have tried to distract or discount the distressed crying child by promising a treat if the crying stops or by cutting the feelings short: "Hush, hush, now" (over-soothing). "Why are you making such a big deal of this; it's not that bad" (minimization). "You know you love your new school" (contradiction). "Don't be so sensitive" (criticism). "Stop that crying, or I'll give you something you can really cry about" (threat). "Be a big boy" (embarrassment). "Crybaby, crybaby" (peer pressure). It is not at all uncommon for children (and adults) to do practically anything to keep from crying in an attempt to protect themselves from such criticism and attacks.

Helpers working with children who are having trouble expressing sadness or allowing themselves to cry may want to begin by using body work to start the flow of feelings and to help these children connect or reconnect with the repressed or guarded feeling:

"Serena, you've told me that when your mom left you felt really upset. I was thinking that 'most anyone that happened to would

137

feel sad. I bet you looked sad, too. Can you show me a really sad face?" Other lead-ins are also possible:

"Serena, we're just getting to know one another. One of the things I've been noticing about you is that lots of times your face tells me things. Like I can really tell if you like doing what we're doing because you give me a big smile. But I bet you're like most kids. I bet sometimes your face says other kinds of important things about how you're feeling. Can you show me how you look when you're really sad?"

Many children will show their sad faces readily, but some will have more trouble. In these cases, it may help to make the activity into a friendly contest:

"That's as sad as you can look? I can look much sadder than that. [Helper makes a sad face.] See if you can beat me. Hey, that's better. Bet I can look sadder. Now you try."

A mirror can be helpful here, unless it makes the helper or the child self-conscious.

The activity may begin to release inhibitions right away, but sometimes it needs to be repeated: "You're getting better, but you still need some practice." Often the child will begin to find the contest fun, and adult and child may end up both practicing sad faces and laughing with each other, a sure way to reduce the child's anxiety about expressing the feeling.

Once the child is able to make a sad face, the helper should add sound effects: "You're getting pretty good at that sad face stuff, but I bet I can *sound* sadder than you: Waaaaaah!" Many children who have hidden away their sadness will begin to tear up as soon as they make a sad face and add a sad noise to it. This gives the helper a chance to move from playing to real sharing and feeling: "Ohhh, that doesn't look like pretend sad. That looks like real sad. And you certainly have had some things happen that are really sad." If the helper speaks to the child in a warm voice, reaches out with a hand on the child's chair or knee, the child may begin to cry or even to sob. The plug has been pulled: The child is ready for comforting.

Sometimes just joining the child compassionately by recognizing unspoken pain will open the floodgates.

One nine-year-old girl came for therapy because of uncontrolla-

ble rages and serious verbal and physical threats toward her siblings. When asked at her first session if she knew why she was there
she answered tentatively, "To make me a better person?" When
encouraged to go on, she replied, "To make me behave myself?"
The helping adult said gently, "If you want to change how you are
behaving, I'd like to help you with that. But I think you are here
because things are being very hard for you. I'd like to see if we can't
figure out together what is going on that is so hard and how to
make things feel better and work better for you at home." At that
point, the youngster burst into deep sobs, put her head on the
table, and cried for almost ten minutes. When she had finished,
she sat up, squared her shoulders, and said, "How do we start?"

If a caregiver is involved, either as participant or helper, it is appropriate for him or her to be the comforter. For some children,
this will be the first time they have let a caregiver share in this part
of their loss. If the caregiver is not involved or is unable to respond
to the child's distress even when encouraged, the helper should
provide comfort as best he or she can.

A great benefit of this activity is that the child shares the tears.
It is much harder and often less satisfying and healing to overcome
grief or despair by crying alone. There is a normal, deep need to
have someone understand, support, bear compassionate witness,
and validate the right to the hurt and to the pain. The helping
person must be prepared to stand by the grieving child in this stage,
not only physically and very frequently at the start but also during
the following weeks or months. Consequently, this method of
bringing out sad feelings probably should not be used by anyone
who cannot promise to be available consistently. Caregivers can be
invaluable here, whether as primary helpers or as participants in
counseling sessions, because they can be there to comfort when
the sadness wells up between scheduled appointments.

Another way to bring out sadness is through a child's identification with another person or animal who has suffered a loss or separation. There are many good television programs, movies, and
books dealing with loss and restitution. Fiction addressing these
themes can be used to prime both feelings that are easily triggered
and those that are heavily defended. As the child or adolescent is

moved to tears, the helper can make a connection between the fictional character's pain and its similarity to what the child may be feeling.

The helping person does not have to see tears to know that the child is letting sad feelings out. Some children are very reluctant to cry in front of others. If they are primed for sadness and their tears are noted, they may be frantic to change the activity or the subject in order to keep control of themselves. This anxiety or avoidance can be acknowledged with a suggestion that the child keep letting the sadness out, even if this has to happen in private: "I think you don't want to talk about sadness anymore today. Let me tell you one thing that I've heard from lots of kids. Sometimes people want to do their crying by themselves. They're not as likely to get a hug when they do it that way, but they think it works better for them. Kids who feel like that often tell me they save their crying for after they go to bed. Some of them say the shower is a great place to let the crying out; no one hears you and no one can tell afterward." Adolescents, in particular, seem to respond to the shower suggestion, reporting matter-of-factly later, "I tried that shower thing; it worked"—which may be all they want to share.

There is no right way for grief to happen, and helpers should not demand more expression than the child is ready to reveal or demand that it take a particular form. For most children and adults, though, tears provide a healing release and signal a need for comfort, alleviating some of the sense of aloneness and vulnerability engendered by loss or separation.

DEALING WITH CHRONIC SADNESS OR ANGER

When children are actively sad or angry eighteen months to two or more years after a loss, it is likely that they have become stuck in chronic sadness or anger that needs addressing. There are several reasons why strong emotions can become chronic. For some, as the stress of the separation or loss makes them long to return to an earlier, easier time and as they go through the yearning and search-

140

ing stage of grief, they seem to come to a piece of magical thinking that is based on fairy tales. A great many fairy tales do involve losses; what is unique about them, though, is that the central character eventually gets what is needed to fill the gap left by the loss. In the Cinderella story, for example, Cinderella loses her mother, gains a wicked stepmother and two selfish stepsisters who exploit her, finds her father unavailable to her, and is forced to do everyone's work. Finally, when she has been miserable long enough, her fairy godmother appears and enables Cinderella to meet a prince, almost lose him, but eventually triumph to live happily ever after. The formula clearly established, in this fairy tale and in many others, is that in order to get what you want you must have bad things happen to you long enough that you earn a happy ending. Chronic anger or sadness, then, may be based on the theory that, if one cries or rages loud enough and long enough or collects enough deprivations and injustices, all wrongs finally will be redressed. So long as this thinking continues, a loss is unlikely to be seen as permanent, and hope lingers on.

The techniques used to diminish denial and disbelief, discussed in chapter 3, can be a way to start easing a child through this stage. Gentle confrontation is also a help: "You've been being really sad [angry] for a long, long time. I'm wondering how that sadness [anger] can be good for you. You don't know? Well, let me tell you what other kids have said and see if any of their guesses fit you. Some kids have told me that they think it might make [the absent caregiver] mad if they stop being sad [mad]. Is it like that for you? [If so, the child needs work on giving him- or herself permission to move on, as discussed in chapter 6.] Other kids have told me that it's like a deal they make, where if they just stay sad [mad] enough long enough they can make things different. Do you ever feel that way?" If this last is the case, ask the child about the terms of the deal and how they can be sure the deal is workable when one or more of the parties involved have not actually agreed to them. "What about it, do you think maybe somebody could make your mom change her mind about the divorce?" you might ask and explore the possibilities if the child says yes. Sometimes caregivers can be brought into these conversations, so that the child can check out or be helped to check out directly whether things can be changed by the behavior. With or without the caregiver's input, the child needs to know that in the end he or she is the one who is going to have to move on. "Sounds to me as if you are going to have to be a fairy godmother to yourself and fix up the things you can fix, so you can have some happier times."

Another helpful tactic is to point out to the child that she or he is using an awful lot of time in feeling bad. "That doesn't seem very fair to me. I don't think you are being a very good friend to yourself. Seems like it must be about time for you to get a turn with some better feelings, think so?" Sometimes these conversations will release a child's hold on sad or angry feelings. When they don't, you might ask, "How long do you think you are going to need to be this unhappy? For ten more years? Five?" and then follow up with, "I'll sure be glad when you give yourself a turn to have some more comfortable feelings."

When approaches such as those suggested in this chapter are used to help validate children's rights to have and to understand their own needs and feelings, whether those reactions involve sadness, anger, or aggression, and when children are treated in ways that not only respect these rights but also allow the appropriate expression and discharge of strong feelings, a major part of the grief process is facilitated and supported. Children are less likely to become stuck, unable to incorporate their loss productively. By developing techniques that help them during their bereavement, they learn more about themselves and what to do with their strong feelings in general, which will serve them well throughout their lives.

RESPONDING TO PROBLEMS
OF SELF-ESTEEM AND
CONTROL

❦

5 Since Bowlby first discussed attachment in children in 1968, there has been a clinical effort both to observe and to understand better how children forge emotional bonds with their caregivers and the other significant people in their lives and how those attachments (and subsequent losses) affect children's lives. Although some disagreement remains as to how much of a child's temperament and reaction pattern is innate and how much is an outgrowth of life experience, attachment appears to influence individual development and lifetime responses—emotionally, socially, and cognitively.

Children who form secure attachments in the first three to five years of their lives are more likely to be trusting, confident, competent, and resourceful. They also expect others to work from similar foundations of self-esteem, which makes it easier for them to enter into and maintain healthy relationships. They think logically and perceptively, which allows them to maximize their intellectual potential and to develop strong consciences. Because their lives have continuity and meaning, these children feel able to count on the predictability of people, things, and events, which makes them more likely to develop the internal and external resources needed to cope with stress and frustration and the ability to handle anxiety, jealousy, and disappointment. Predictably, they also seem to rebound from life's adversities more fully than do children without strong attachments.

Attachment is an outgrowth of repeated interaction and response, initially between child and caregiver and later between the child and other important people in the larger social setting. Perhaps the child has a need, which causes emotional or physical discomfort or distress, and signals this discomfort or distress with physical clues (crying, complaining, etc.). The caregivers respond to the child's signals and take prompt, appropriate action to relieve the problem. When the interaction or intervention is successful, the child signals this by relaxing or openly expressing relief. Or perhaps the child feels delight and excitement, and the caregivers respond with approval and pleasure. As this cycle repeats itself over and over, the child comes to trust that the caregivers will be a reliable source of support, safety, and comfort, making it more likely that the child will turn to them in the future. And because the caregivers feel increasingly competent, successful, and important to the child, they are ever more likely to respond. When both child and caregivers come to enjoy their growing sense of connection and closeness and the child develops the basic belief that the caregivers will continue to be a primary source of emotional and physical well-being so long as they all remain available to one another, the child is said to be securely attached.

In addition to how successfully and how promptly caregivers respond when the child is distressed or delighted, another component that affects the development of secure attachment and solid self-esteem is the positive interaction cycle: that is, who initiates play and enjoyable learning experiences between child and adult, who responds when the child initiates such interactions, and how often these positive exchanges occur. Children with caregivers (and concerned others) who take a positive but not intrusive interest in their discoveries and experiences and who obviously enjoy their children and the time they spend with them are likely to become securely attached between one and five years of age. Many children will have primary attachments by the time they are eighteen months old. Through the process of attachment, the child comes to see him- or herself as a worthwhile, interesting individual who is lovable and who can function in competent, responsible ways in relationships with others and with the world.

Research supports the opinion that these feelings form the original foundation of positive self-image or self-esteem. When children with these foundations feel expansive, happy, triumphant, or want to share activities, or are distressed, disheartened, in need of help, they will seek out the people to whom they are attached because they connect them with positive situations and outcomes and involved, respectful responses. Such children are also more likely to behave responsively, to be flexible individuals, cooperative leaders, curious learners, and to become socially competent individuals who are sensitive to the distress of others.

When children cannot count on continuing, dependable, positive interactions, they tend to form insecure or anxious attachments characterized by *ambivalent* or *avoidant* interactions. Children with ambivalent attachment interactions are likely to seek constant attention, to be highly sensitive to criticism, and to have anxious reactions to separations from their caregivers, while at the same time being quick to criticize how their caregivers respond or to react belligerently to overtures and offers of help. In avoidant attachment interactions, children may appear unusually self-sufficient and competent. Such children often outwardly reject parental attention or offers of help and seem to resent interference while remaining quite insecure inside. They may seem angry, distant, or estranged.

Self-esteem appears to depend primarily on the quality of the interactions in the early years of a child's life, but it is not fixed and can change as the quality of those interactions or the positive interest or responsiveness shifts because of childhood trauma or loss or if the child feels he or she has failed to measure up in academic or peer relationships. Thus even children lucky enough to have started out with secure attachments who experience a significant loss or separation may suffer damage to their developing senses of attachment and self-esteem. Instead of feeling lovable and likable, they come to feel unappreciated, or a burden, or, in the case of divorce, like the prize in a power struggle between their parents. Instead of feeling worthwhile, they may feel like helpless victims of circumstances whose needs and feelings are unimportant or discounted and misunderstood, which often leads them to conclude that they are worthless. The disorganization and regression that accompany grief often set children back, taking a toll on developing cognitive, motor, and social skills. This makes it all the more difficult for them to keep up with their own and others' demands and expectations and often causes them to feel even more inferior.

Should previously attentive, responsive caregivers become seriously ill or less available because of a major life change or stress, the strains of managing the changes in their lives and the lives of their children may leave them with too little energy to respond effectively or reliably to their children's attachment signals. Some may fail to respond at all. Those interactions that they do initiate are likely to be connected primarily to work (such as nagging about daily routines, chores, and schoolwork or demanding that children take on more personal responsibility). Often the lighthearted, positive interaction cycle is replaced by curt, annoyed, or impatient exchanges. Enjoyable mutual activities may be replaced by fighting or arguing. The interaction cycles come to be primarily negative—grim, mechanical, and controlling rather than encouraging and expansive. No longer secure in their relationships with their caregivers, unable to count on what used to be automatic, children begin to feel inadequate. They are likely to blame themselves for what has happened or to become distraught when they are unable to do anything to fix it.

A child's attachment patterns and self-esteem may also suffer if the individual who has been the primary caregiver or the primary source of positive, playful interaction (perhaps a sibling or a grandparent) is no longer available. Those who try to take over the role may not be as familiar with the child and may not notice or understand signals of need or interest or invitation to connect. In such cases, although cared for physically, the child is likely to experience a profound sense of misconnection and deprivation that intensifies the pain and potential damage of the loss. Children under three or four, with their more limited sense of life's dependability, are even more likely to experience difficulty with attachment and self-esteem following a significant loss, and this difficulty is further compounded by the increased use of temporary substitute care often needed for children at this age.

Sometimes it is the child who shuts down parts of the need or play cycles. Caught in the throes of grief, children may continue to signal their distress but become impatient, resentful, and blameful when no one is able to relieve their pain and longing for what they have lost. They may be unable to initiate or respond to positive interactions for extended periods of time because of the intensity of their grief and the accompanying disorganization or because of the demands of the new life circumstances they must master. Grieving children may show little zest for normal pleasures and exploration. They may not play well, and their play may be further inhibited if they feel guilty about having a good time when other family members are actively grieving.

Children of loss, therefore, are at risk of seeing themselves as unlovable, unwanted, and unworthy. Those who reach out to such children may find themselves frustrated because it can be so difficult to engage them in positive interactions, and eventually they may give up trying to reach out. As a result, when these children suffer subsequent adversity, they may expect others to become impatient and to blame or misunderstand them. As children struggle to incorporate what has happened to them, their limited ability to understand, the internal adjustments they must make to deal with the demands of grief, and the deprivation that they feel or actually experience often lead them to develop reactions and behaviors that cause them ongoing difficulty. Children who come to believe that they are unable to make and hold on to relationships may continue long after the initial grief experience to act in ways that make this belief come true. Some children come to defend themselves against the pain of separation and their feelings of vulnerability by depreciating or devaluing the person who is gone or by trying to deny their feelings. They may act as if they don't care about what happens to them or to their relationships. "It looks like we need to find another family for you," the child is told, to which the child sullenly responds, "So?" This denial or depreciation may be encouraged by current caregivers who send overt or covert messages that children should act as if nothing bad has happened or should deny their feelings and pretend to be pleased or grateful for changes. "I really don't like it there, I'd rather be here with you,"

147

children sometimes say to please. Some children will go so far as to deny that the absent caregiver exists or ever existed. Believing life to be harsh, punitive, or unjust, many develop extreme internal and external defenses against what they perceive to be actual or potential threats to their well-being or even survival.

All children ask themselves, "Am I lovable?" "What is lovable about me?" "When am I lovable?" "What do I need to do in order to feel/be lovable?" Caregivers and other adults are wise to evaluate what messages they are sending children in answer to these unspoken questions.

They might think about their three most recent intense conversations or interactions with their youngsters and note the focus of the conversations (positive or negative interaction, approval or disappointment, congratulations or criticism). What might their children have decided about themselves as a result of those conversations, in terms not only of how lovable they are but also of the other three elements of positive self-esteem. They might also check directly with their youngsters, asking them when they last felt lovable (worthwhile, capable, responsible). The following checklist may help clarify where children might be having trouble maintaining self-esteem.

Indicators of Self-Esteem

People with Low Self-Esteem

Discount their needs, wishes, and feelings.
Don't ask for what they want.
Don't ask in a way or at a time that allows them to get their
    needs met.
Don't accept positive input.
Reject criticism or accept it without consideration of validity.
    ("You're right—I'm a total loser.")
Don't appreciate and share what they have to offer. ("What do
    I know?" "They are all better than I am." "They'll just
    laugh.")
Put themselves down and are quick to accept put-downs.

Don't try new things or quit or blame others if they make
    mistakes while learning.
Don't praise themselves or give themselves and others credit
    where it is due. Don't love themselves.

People with High Self-Esteem

Recognize their own needs, wishes, and feelings and act on
    them positively.
Ask directly for what they want.
Ask in a way or at a time that allows them to get their needs
    met. ("It's OK to ask." "I should ask; they can't read my
    mind.")
Accept positive input. ("I need and deserve that.")
Consider criticism and sort out what is valid and helpful.
    Appreciate and share what they have to offer. ("Some
    of my ideas and actions are good. They are worth sharing."
    "It's the thought that counts.")
Evaluate themselves fairly and in a balanced manner.
Experiment with new things and learn from their successes and
    mistakes.
Praise themselves and give themselves and others credit where
    it is due. ("Good job." "I like how you did that." "That
    was a really good idea.")
Love themselves realistically. ("I am lovable. I am doing the best
    I can, and I am getting better.")

Adapted from Levin 1974.

Record keeping can help caregivers and helpers figure out the symbolic or specific triggers that begin the roller coaster of what appears to be a nonsensical reaction. Sometimes just marking the daily ups and downs on a calendar reveals rhythms and connections. Does the behavior happen on a particular day or days? If so, what is different about those days? Does the behavior happen at a particular time of day? Before or after a particular part of the daily routine? As a response to an identifiable interaction?

UNDERSTANDING AND EASING
DISPLACEMENT REACTION

One type of behavior that can often be identified by keeping track of the answers to these kinds of questions is displacement reaction. Some children, whose loss or separation has made them think that other people always want to get rid of them, may overreact or become hypersensitive to being displaced or feeling left out or rejected. When they believe that someone is pushing them away or telling them to get lost, they fight back as if their very survival depended on it, often to the confusion of those involved, who have no idea what could have caused such a violent outburst.

When Shauna was eleven, her father brought her for counseling, exasperated by her out-of-control temper tantrums. The person working with them was at a loss as to the root of the problem until one day when Shauna was overheard asking her dad, who was reading the paper in the outer office, if she could sit in his lap. When her dad said no, Shauna blew up and starting screaming, kicking the floor, and hitting herself. What she had heard was a global "I have no room for you in my life"—now or ever. And she fought for her space as though her life depended on it.

Children like Shauna who are sensitive to displacement may also have difficulty if they are asked to give up or share their room, their bed, or their place at the table. They respond poorly to discipline that involves sending them to their rooms or asking them to remove themselves until they can behave.

Nine-year-old Derrick, who had experienced several changes of caregivers, was in a special class for behaviorally disturbed children. When he began to act out and disturb his classmates, he was asked to move to a small adjoining time-out area that was regularly used as part of the behavior modification program in his class. Unlike the other children, however, the request set him off, and he would explode. When his helper talked with his teacher about symbolic displacement issues, the teacher agreed to experiment with a different kind of time-out for Derrick. His caregivers were asked to buy him a bath towel, letting him pick the color. They ran it through the wash so that it would smell like home, cuddled him in it several times over the weekend, and then sent it along to school with him. Derrick and his teacher found a safe place for him to keep his towel, and when he needed a time-out, he was told to sit with it or on it outside the time-out space at his teacher's side. He was able to respond cooperatively. It seemed that what he needed was a physical reminder that his caregivers were supporting him and the knowledge that his teacher would help him calm himself without sending him away.

Patterns, rhythms, and triggers frequently become clearer if the answers to the following questions are also recorded:

1. What keeps happening?
2. How does it start?
3. Then what?
4. How does the child seem to feel at the beginning and at the end of the exchange?
5. How does the adult feel?

Because no confusing or difficult behavior is continuous, it is also important to record the answers to two more questions:

6. How/when does the problem behavior stop? (Does it just run its course, or does the child, caregiver, or both do something to help it end?)
7. After the behavior subsides, what needs to happen so that both child and caregiver reconnect positively (or at least neutrally)?

If the patterns or interventions that lead to the beginning and ending of the problem can be identified, it becomes more possible to figure out ways to head things off or to help the child stop sooner or more easily.

Brenda's parents and her third-grade teacher were all concerned about the major temper tantrums she was having at school. Brenda's mother had remarried, and then the family had moved to a new town. Brenda seemed to adjust well to her new home life with only occasional difficulties, but she had become increasingly aggressive at school. Periodically, when something set her off, she yelled and hit other children. School staff also felt that Brenda milked minor or even imaginary injuries to gain attention. School personnel, at a loss, referred Brenda for a therapeutic assessment to find out what was happening and how the school might best respond.

After meeting with Brenda and her parents for several sessions, the helper decided to visit Brenda's school and observe her interactions there. On the day of the scheduled visit, Brenda greeted her helper at the door to her class, eager to introduce her adult friend to classmates. She seemed able to share the adult attention and did not need to claim clear possession of her guest or to try to monopolize the helper's attention or demand that others leave the helper alone.

The helper sat at a corner table and watched how Brenda interacted in a group that was doing a play from a book. Brenda appeared to have no trouble sharing the teacher's time and attention with other children or waiting her turn, which again suggested that competition was not an issue. When the activity was over, Brenda settled near the helper and worked independently on her arithmetic until her reading group was called by the class aide. As Brenda stopped at her desk to gather up her books, another child sat at the round reading table in the chair that directly faced the helper. Brenda immediately shouted at him, "That's *my* seat! Get out of it!" As seats were usually chosen randomly, the boy was caught off guard and hesitated. The aide intervened when it became clear that if he didn't move, Brenda was likely to push him off the chair. The boy took a different seat, with some confusion. When Brenda was able to take the place she obviously had planned to be hers, the rest of the day went smoothly.

Later, the helper asked if the school personnel had noticed that Brenda seemed to be particularly sensitive to not knowing where her place was (literally and figuratively) or to having her place preempted. Her teacher thought about the question briefly and then exclaimed with relieved understanding, "That's it! That's exactly right. She blows up when she feels displaced. You know what else? I think she pulls that 'poor me, I've hurt myself' routine when she needs to enter or rejoin a social situation. Maybe she doesn't know any other way to do it. I've watched her over and over on the playground standing on the sidelines watching the others play but not joining in. You can see her getting frustrated. Then she loses control, and she pushes someone or trips and 'hurts herself.' I can think of a bunch of things that might help her besides being aggressive or behaving like a hypochondriac. Let's work on helping her know how to find a place for herself and say what she wants, like 'Can I play, too?' or 'It's my turn' and see what happens."

UNDERSTANDING SCARCITY ISSUES

Many of the behaviors discussed in this chapter are connected not only to how children express their feelings of helplessness and anger about their loss but also to how they deal with the reduction in positive, helpful interactions that results when a significant person is no longer available or less available than before. One way to understand how loss affects children is to imagine that each child enters this world with a tiny arm through the handle of a tiny bucket. As children grow larger, so do their buckets. Much of how they react and how they see themselves is determined by what goes into this bucket. If children make secure attachments, positive energy pours into their buckets. As they continue to experience good nurturing and positive interactions, their buckets fill up with good feelings about themselves, which enhances their self-esteem, promotes ample physical and psychological energy, and allows them to give freely of themselves. In time, they begin to dip into their buckets and ladle good feelings into the buckets of those around, tentatively at first and then more freely as they discover that their sharing brings other good feelings. As long as things go well, the outpouring and receiving become life patterns that work successfully.

Separation and loss interrupt or end the interactions with the person who is gone, temporarily or forever, lowering the level of good feelings and energy and challenging the security of children's attachments and their positive self-regard. Moving into new family settings sloshes children's buckets. Even if those around them are concerned and supportive, it isn't the same. The connection they long for has to do with the particular interactions they shared with the person or family that is gone. Bowlby tells the story of a pre-school youngster who complained a month after her mother died that no one loved her. Her father tried to reassure her by naming a long list of people who did, to which the child responded aptly, "But when my mommy wasn't dead, I didn't need so many people—I needed just one" (Bowlby 1980, 280). This young child knew that her bucket was low and why, and she expressed her sense of scarcity.

If a child lives in a situation where everyone's bucket is low—that is, where everyone is stressed and preoccupied—the level in the child's bucket is likely to remain low, and there may be little if any ladling of good feelings from one person to another. The closer the bucket is to low, the more tightly the child clutches it for fear that someone will slosh out some of its precious, life-sustaining contents. It may become impossible for the child to share directly and reciprocally. Some children go so far as to construct covers for the tops of their buckets to prevent any more loss. Unfortunately, such covers also prevent any good feelings from getting in. Positive interactions just hit the surface, roll off, and are lost.

However the depletion occurs, it makes children needy, demanding, and reluctant or unable to give much back to anyone. This behavior often causes those around them to pull back or to respond negatively. Each withdrawal or ongoing negative connection then lowers the buckets' contents even more. In time, children may come to believe that there is not and will never be enough positive emotional connection available to them. Since to survive we all appear to need some degree of connection, be it positive or negative, children who perceive themselves as unable to forge positive connections are likely to focus on generating negative exchanges instead.

Curtis was having marked difficulties at school following his parents' separation. Although manageable at home, he frequently blew up at school, sometimes throwing chairs at people and knocking over desks. When asked what he thought made him so angry and out of control, he told his helper that he hated being told to stop doing something "fun," such as playing with Leggos, and to start doing something "hard," such as working on arithmetic. His teacher confirmed this, saying that at such times Curtis would begin to mumble loudly and avoid switching tasks as long as possible. It was clear to the helper working with Curtis that he was experiencing and replaying old feelings of scarcity. He didn't feel good about himself in the academic area, in which he was behind, and when his self-esteem plummeted he reacted in ways that his teacher could not accept. As a result, he often stayed in at recess and missed his snack. Being denied the good time of recess and more especially the symbolic treat of food, Curtis blew sky high.

Once Curtis's teacher was aware of how past scarcity patterns were being triggered for him, she began to encourage him to get to his arithmetic promptly so that he could have two snacks, one when he finished his work and another at recess, which built in an appropriate reward system and also guaranteed that he would not go without his treat, regardless of his academic performance.

Combating Scarcity

Provocative children need help to learn to interact in positive, bucket-filling ways. Caregivers, too, may need help to understand how to establish more positive patterns. The best gains occur when the helper involves the caregiver in changing the child's perceptions and in helping to enhance the child's sense of belonging, competence, and self-worth.

Mrs. Prentiss is having trouble handling her nine-year-old daughter. She complains that Marissa is fresh, refuses to comply with simple requests to pick up her room or put away her laundry, and lies and argues when called to task. Mrs. Prentiss finds herself locked into "Did so"/"Did not" conversations that make her feel like a nine-year-old herself. Marissa often threatens to run away following these sessions. Eventually, Marissa and her mother come for counseling.

HELPER: Wow, Marissa. It sounds as if you are really good at making your mom mad. True?

MARISSA: [Grinning] Yeah.

HELPER: Let's see how good. What are three things you can do that are sure to get your mom upset?

155

MARISSA: [Without having to pause to think] I can be late for school. I can leave my clothes all over the floor. And, I know, I can forget to put my dishes in the sink.

HELPER: [To mother] Is she right about those? [To Marissa] Your mom is nodding. I guess you know her pretty well. OK. Now, I want you to tell me three things you can do for sure to get a hug or a smile from your mom.

MARISSA: [Looking quite confused] Huh?

HELPER: What are three things you can do that are sure to get a smile or a hug from your mom? [Marissa shrugs her shoulders, a blank look on her face.]

HELPER: [Looking at mother] I think we've got part of the problem here. Can you help Marissa figure this out ?

MOTHER: [Genuinely surprised] Why, Marissa, there are lots of ways you can get hugs!

HELPER: Tell her three.

MOTHER: You could pick up your room in the morning. And you could set the table without complaining. And you could say you were sorry once in a while.

HELPER: What about it, Marissa, do you think those things might work? [Marissa nods.] OK. Which of those would be easiest for you to do?

MARISSA: Setting the table, probably.

Marissa is asked if she would be willing to experiment to try to find out if she can get her mother to respond differently by setting the table occasionally during the coming week. She is told that she is to use this as a way of checking up on her mom and that she will be asked to report at the next session if she got a smile, a hug, or a pleased thank-you when she practiced this behavior. Listening to this conversation, Marissa's mother is being primed indirectly to respond to table setting and to reward it, knowing that Marissa will be watching. Mrs. Prentiss is also encouraged to try to catch Marissa doing other positive things during the week and to let Marissa know that she has noticed them and that she appreciates them. Each time Marissa's mother shows pleasure when her daughter does something positive is likely to make Marissa believe just that much more that she is able to control things in a way that feels better.

This intervention is an extremely powerful, concrete way to help adults understand that their children may be truly stumped as to how they can please instead of frustrate their caregivers. Sometimes a single exchange like this will be enough to start a caregiver figuring out how to begin turning things around. Or the helper can move into helping the caregiver and child begin to rework their provocative connective pattern and reestablish more positive interactions. Caregivers often report, sometimes even by the next session, that they are feeling more hopeful because they are able to see that their youngsters do care and are trying. As caregivers become more encouraged, they have more energy with which to respond positively to their children, who in turn respond more positively to them.

In order for this approach to work well, goals and homework must spell out clearly and concretely what is to be done. General, ill-defined outcomes should be avoided. Say Mrs. Prentiss said she wanted Marissa to "be more respectful":

HELPER: How would I know that Marissa was being more respectful? What would I see or hear that was different from what is happening now?

MOTHER: Well, she'd stop telling me to shut up, when I ask her if she has done her homework.

HELPER: When do you ask her that?

MOTHER: After supper, before she goes to bed.

HELPER: And about what time is that?

MOTHER: About 7:30.

At this point, the helper makes sure that both parent and child know what specifically is being requested and then assigns the homework:

HELPER: Marissa, your mom is asking you to stop telling her to shut up when she tells you to do your homework. Seems to me you have two ways to get out of that habit. One is to tell yourself to do your homework right after supper or some time before she asks at 7:30. That way your mom will hush about it because you have taken charge. If you'd rather choose to put your mother in charge and to have her know that you need help with this problem, all you have to do is ask her to remind you. Or you can let her know you need to be reminded by not having your homework done at 7:30. If that is your choice, your mom would like you to not say "shut up" to her for doing the job you have given her. Would that be hard or easy for you? Are you willing to try one or both of those ways and see if it helps stop the fighting? [Marissa nods.] OK then. Here is your homework for this week. Marissa will take charge of doing her school assignments by 7:30 so she won't have to be nagged and there will be no fight. Or Mom will notice that Marissa needs help because she hasn't done her homework and remind her to get to work. Either way, Marissa is to remember she is in charge of whether things are peaceful or there is a fight. And she is not to say "shut up." Anybody got a question? No? Well, then, I'll be interested in finding out which way Marissa decides to be in charge this coming week.

As a rule of thumb, if the helper, child, and caregiver are unable to count the number of times the assigned behavior has taken place, the homework assignment probably isn't specific enough or there has been a lack of follow-through. When homework is assigned, helpers are responsible for remembering the assignment and checking how well it has gone at the next session.

Exchanging "Target Strokes": When child and caregiver work together, they often become quite good at discovering as a team how provocative behavior can be unlearned and feelings of scarcity reduced, and they often become quite skilled at keeping a positive flow of feelings going, even when stressed. A handy fail-safe is for each to be aware of the other's "target stroke." Every one of us longs for particular kinds of affirmation and the kind that is closest to what we want is called a "target stroke." A helper might want to check with child and caregiver to discover what kind of positive responses—verbal, visual, or physical—feel best to them.

HELPER: Marissa, your mom gave us some ideas as to what you could do that would feel great to her. Now I want to ask you something. Different kids tell me that they have different ways they really like to have their parents let them know they are pleased. I'm wondering which ways you like best. Would you rather see a big smile on your mom's face, or have her compliment you or say thanks, or give you a hug, or would you like all three? OK, you think you'd like a hug and a compliment best. That's good for her to know. Would you try something for me? Would you go over to your mom and stand beside her? Thank you. Now, Mrs. Prentiss, will you give Marissa a good hug? Thank you. OK, now I need to ask each of you, did you like that?

The helper waits to see if either Marissa or her mother is uncomfortable with this physical closeness. Neither one of them speaks up or withdraws, and in fact both seem to enjoy and lean into the hug.

HELPER: OK, you both looked like that felt pretty good to you. I liked the way you hugged your mom back, Marissa, and I bet she liked it, too. Is that right, Mrs. Prentiss? Now, Marissa, I want to tell you an important secret that not all kids know. One of the ways you've been practicing getting hugs is by setting the table without complaining. The secret is, any time you want a hug you can just ask for one. You can give a hug and get one back or say, "Mom, I want a hug." Will you try that for me now and see what happens?

In most cases, beleaguered caregivers are only too glad to be asked for a positive interaction and respond willingly to such requests. To help children see that they are not only able but downright encouraged to take care of their needs for safety and nurturing, caregivers might respond further by saying, "I like to hug you [or perform whatever target stroke the child prefers], and I like the way you ask for what you want."

Children and caregivers need to know that there may be times when it is not convenient or possible for one or the other to respond to a request for a hug (or whatever). They should be encouraged to respond if they can or to explain why it is not possible at that particular moment. If Marissa asked for a hug at an inconvenient moment, for example, her mother could respond, "Not right now, but after I drain the spaghetti [or finish this phone call or whatever], I'd love to hug you." This would prevent Marissa from interpreting the answer as "No, not ever." Of course, all such promises must be kept.

The chance to practice new behavior at a safe time and in a safe place is another strength of having children and caregivers meet with a regular helper. Indeed, the concept of practice is useful in itself, because it implies that nobody has to be immediately comfortable with or perfect at the new behavior. Children and caregivers need to be warned that new things may feel awkward or artificial at first, that they will take time and practice to master, and that sometimes people will forget and fall back into doing things the old way. These initial corrective interactions will set the stage for starting over and trying again, which is essential to mastering new ways of behaving. In time, as there are more episodes of positive interaction, children can be confronted when they act in a way that has negative results. A caregiver might say, "You are making this chore of picking up your room into a war. Which would you rather have right now, a hug or a fight?" When caregivers become aware that children are beginning to slide into old patterns, they can say, "I think you are acting like a kid who needs a hug, and I have one right here for you."

Dealing with the "Good/Bad" Split in Children: The "good/bad" split is another common manifestation of scarcity, most classically seen in siblings who have experienced life as a plate of sweets that never holds enough to go around. It is not unusual for two children in the same family to respond in quite different ways to a sense of scarcity, with one of them grabbing or acting out as a way to get noticed and another counting on the ability to please and charm. Frequently, such scarcity reactions are an outgrowth of one of the children having been the favorite of one or more caregivers and / or the recipient of more of the available positive interaction exchanges and care from an overstretched or inadequate parent.

Whatever the cause, the children come to believe that there is a preferred "good" child who will be "treated" and indulged and another who is "bad" or a disappointment who will be picked on or deprived. If there is a subsequent loss of or separation from a caregiver, the children are left stuck with the misunderstanding that there will never be enough emotional energy to meet their needs, which is likely to become a self-fulfilling prophecy. As they struggle with their grief reactions, quite often one child becomes "too good to be true," wary of rocking the boat for fear of driving the current caregiver away, while the other becomes locked into the provocative "bad" child role and does the grief work and grief behavior for both.

When siblings play out a good/bad split, the initial intervention frequently takes place with the provocative youngster, because of concern about the child's difficult behavior. It is important, however, not to ignore the vulnerability of the closed-down sibling, who is unduly anxious about looking good, being right, not making mistakes. Sometimes helpers are reluctant to work with "good" children, for fear of rocking the boat or upsetting the children. This is unfortunate, since it is likely that these youngsters will continue to feel guilty and anxious, locked into unresolved sadness and anger. They may become quick to tattle, relishing the discomfort and embarrassment of others, yet afraid of trying new experiences themselves. This makes them feel inferior to other children, despite their apparent assumption of superiority.

Interestingly enough, when a "bad" sibling begins to discover ways to get positive energy, the "good" sibling is likely to experiment with negative interactions. Sometimes this involves using whispered taunts or secret pokes to make the provocative child blow up; caregivers should not assume that the loud, provocative child is always at fault. More often, the "good" child, particularly if helped to own his or her feelings about the loss, will take up where the provocative child left off, having seen that the caregiver remained available to the "bad" sibling even when he or she was acting up.

When six-year-old fraternal twins arrived for their first session several months after their adoption, the good/bad split was clearly evident. Sherri (the "good" twin), an attractive feminine little girl whose long blond hair was tied back with a ribbon that matched her frilly dress, marched in her patent leather shoes to the doorway of the playroom, where she informed the helper that Shelley was bad because she "peed her bed." Shelley, a female version of Huck Finn, with wild, curly, uncombed red hair and large freckles, then appeared, wearing bib overalls and untied sneakers. She immediately responded by starting a loud argument with her sister that ended with her punching Sherri.

Shelley explored, first with her mom and then with her dad, what she might experiment with that would please them about her. She picked one thing from each parent's list, taking her wet sheets off her bed willingly and coming in from swimming when called. Within three weeks, both parents were able to see that Shelley's problem had been an outgrowth of never having lived in a family where she and her sister were equally appreciated. When they responded to her beginning attempts to please them, they were delighted with the increasing positive interactions with this previously difficult child.

As the helper worked with Shelley and her parents to try to enhance their "good" connections, both helper and parents worked with Sherri on owning and expressing her feelings about her past losses, reassuring her that she was entitled to have her own feelings about what had happened.

As Shelley became more and more of a delight, the helper warned the parents that they would know if they were truly on the right track for both girls if Sherri tried to keep the good/bad balance that had played itself out both in the birth family and in two other foster families by assuming the opposite role. Sure enough, the following week the parents reported with some pride that Sherri had begun to wet her bed, and they were hopeful that she would be able to loosen up and become a less compulsively perfect youngster. The final piece of rebalancing involved asking both girls directly in each other's presence if they thought they were now living in a family were there was room for two "good" kids or whether one or the other of them was going to need to take on the "bad" kid role. "Was it possible that they both now had the chance to be loved and wanted, both when they were good and when they made mistakes? Could that be?" In response, one of the children looked at the floor; the other shrugged her shoulders. Turning to the parents, the helper put the same questions to them, confident that they would be convincingly adamant that there was plenty of room in their family for two well-behaved children who would, like all youngsters, make mistakes, but which they would work out within the family without anybody having to leave. In time, each of these sisters was able to establish her own place in the family.

UNDERSTANDING SHAME ISSUES

The strong sense that they have somehow failed may cause children who have experienced loss to feel deep shame. Feeling publicly exposed, mortified, and humiliated, they seem to think that everyone is waiting for them to fail again. Because they feel so unworthy and unlovable, these children have a great need to appear perfect, above reproach. This can cause them to avoid asking for help or expressing confusion and to overreact even to mild criticisms or suggestions that they could or should do better. When asked to do something they find difficult, they respond by avoiding the task, procrastinating, or constantly criticizing their performance, unlike children who accept themselves, who are likely to voice their more evenly balanced views of themselves with nondefensive statements such as "I'm not so good at drawing people, but I'm really good at drawing rockets." When children who feel compelled to be flawless are challenged by a situation, they may explode, perhaps destroying the paper or project that makes them feel inadequate. They may apologize excessively, as if to say, "Please love me in spite of my shortcomings, and don't leave me! Don't stop liking/loving me!" It is as though their buckets have sprung leaks that prevent them from recovering their previous levels of self-esteem. Even if positive energy is available, they may discount their need for it or their ability to get it and shrug off positive strokes. Some children become unable to respond trustingly to caring or affection ("How could anyone possibly love or want me when my own father [or mother] . . ."); some seem unable to accept praise or validation because it threatens their life view, which, however unpleasant, is all they feel they have ("What do you know?" "If you like me/my work, you must be stupid." "You have to say that, you're my mother."). Like Groucho Marx they have no interest in belonging to the kind of club that would accept them as members. Their good feelings about themselves and others slowly drain away, and they may become highly anxious or avoidant, weeping, seeming dazed, collapsing into themselves, becoming immobilized.

Mitigating Shame and Restoring Self-Esteem

Children who suffer from shame must relearn how to see themselves clearly, rather than as perfect or perfectly bad. They need to recognize that some of their behavior may be a result of not knowing how else to get their needs met or to defend themselves and that, if what they are doing isn't working well or makes them feel bad, they deserve to take care of themselves and to end up feeling good.

One ten-year-old expressed teary concern about how slow she was at learning to write in cursive and obsessed about how everyone else in her class was having no trouble. A check with her teacher indicated that this was not the case, that Benita's writing, while not the very best, was well within the range of what others were producing. The teacher met with Benita, spread out twenty-two unsigned writing worksheets done by the class, and asked Benita to pick out hers, which she was unable to do because there was no noticeable difference. Then the teacher had Benita line the papers up in three groups from best to worst and asked her which group she thought her paper was in. Only then was Benita able to let herself realize that she was not in what she considered to be the bottom group, although she was still unclear about which paper was hers. Finally, her teacher pointed out her paper, making it concretely clear that she was doing average to above-average work.

Additional conversations with Benita made it clear that she spent every day looking at every single variable, including her academic performance in each subject, her apparel, who wanted to sit with her at lunch, and who did best at recess, and comparing her performance with her classmates', keeping track of each instance where she felt she was not the very best. She was finally challenged to choose a day and make a list of who was the very best at each item she considered important. When she presented her list, she was encouraged to notice that no single person in her class was the very best at everything and invited to consider whether it was fair of her to expect herself to be so perfect.

It is wise to tell children again and again that it is OK for people not to know something: "Everyone makes mistakes; that's how we learn. You will have other chances to try again. Meanwhile, let's see how you can fix this problem now." "You spilled some milk; here's the sponge." "So you forgot your homework and got a bad grade. What can you want to learn from that and do differently next time." Lying and tantrums are often shame-based defenses in which children revert to all or nothing, good/bad thinking when they do something wrong. Unable to maintain their self-esteem when they fall short, they deny their mistakes, blow up, or bolt to defend themselves. The harder adults try to get them to own up, the more their lying, anger, or other attempts to save face escalate. Rather than trying to nail them down, it can be much more productive to help them focus on how they can fix the error, wipe the slate clean, and start over: "Martin, no matter whether you knocked Jenny down by mistake or on purpose, she still got hurt. What do you think you might do now to make things better?" "Tenisha, I do not like it when you take money from my purse. You owe me five dollars, and you can pay me back by doing the dishes and cleaning up the kitchen after supper this week."

These children also need help understanding that owning up to mistakes and taking responsibility for shortcomings instead of working fruitlessly to deny them will give them a lot more time and energy to figure out different and better ways to behave and things to do. Because they are so outer-focused and inwardly critical, they often can benefit when their dilemmas are couched impersonally: "If a good friend had this problem, what would your advice be?" This strokes their senses of competence while confirming that other people sometimes have problems, too.

To be able to acknowledge their flaws, these children must be able to recognize their accomplishments. The more they can do this for themselves, the less they will need to rely on outside validation and constant reinforcement and encouragement. But if they have grown up hearing "Don't brag" or "Don't be conceited," they may have trouble saying positive things to themselves. Likewise, children from families where adults withhold positive attention or say primarily negative things to and about them have no model as to how they might nurture and encourage themselves. They have little idea how to go about filling their own buckets with positive feelings. A good first step toward helping children value themselves again is to take advantage of genuine opportunities to praise them: "What a beautiful picture you've drawn. You should feel really proud of yourself." "You did a good job of cleaning up. You should feel good about yourself." After a time, caregivers and helpers can begin to check to see if children are incorporating these messages so that they can begin to reinforce and congratulate themselves:

HELPER/CAREGIVER: What a beautiful picture you've drawn. What should you say to yourself?
CHILD: I dunno.
HELPER/CAREGIVER: What do I say to you?
CHILD: You say, "You should feel good about it."
HELPER/CAREGIVER: Well, do you?
CHILD: Yeah.
HELPER/CAREGIVER: So can you say that out loud? Terrific! Good taking care of yourself.

Praising the child's developing competence is particularly beneficial: "You did a good job." "You made a good choice." "You are really getting better at that." So is attribution, which involves sharing the good things said about the child by another adult: "The doctor said that you were a really strong baby." "Your dad told me that you were good at figuring things out, and I agree with him." A particularly strong kind of attribution happens when one adult says something complimentary about the child to another adult in the child's presence: "Randy did a really good job of figuring out a tricky situation today without lying about it. He's trying harder and harder to be an honest person." Praise in the form of attribution seems to be hard for children to discount, in part because most children are under the impression that adults don't lie to one another and in part because if it was important enough for the adults to talk to each other about it must really be important.

When praise is brushed off, verbally or with a shrug or a shake of the head, it helps to address the child directly about the problem: "I said something nice to you, and you didn't believe it. How can I say it so you will?" Both eye contact and physical contact may help, as may giving some forewarning of what is to come: "Duke, look at me for a minute [perhaps cupping the child's chin gently or touching him on the shoulder]. I have something nice to say to you. Are you ready to listen?"

UNDERSTANDING SELF-BLAME

Whether children actually experience a loss during the ages of magical thinking or whether grief causes them to regress to this earlier kind of reasoning, a great majority of children assume that they are somehow at least partially, if not solely, responsible for their loss. Quick to edit out of their minds the parts that others play, they ask themselves, "What's wrong with me?" or "What did I do to be punished like this?" Many children decide, "I was so bad [in some particular way]" or "I was so unlovable that even my own mother [or father or significant other] didn't want to be around me." Once labels such as "bad" and "unlovable" have been self-imposed, they can deal long-lasting, sometimes permanent blows to children's self-esteem and may also contribute to behavioral patterns in which children act out how they believe they were bad or unlovable or seem determined to prove just how bad and unlovable they are. Even years later, it is not unusual for them to be stuck in a particular behavior or thinking pattern that seemed to them to be a pivotal issue at the time of the loss, either continuing that behavior unduly or avoiding it to the extreme. Caregivers are likely to respond by becoming annoyed and angry, or by withdrawing, or perhaps by sending the child to live somewhere else, which further erodes children's feelings of self-worth and reinforces their conviction that previous losses are their own fault.

If the loss or separation also involved an element of relief—the death of a loved one after a long and painful illness, a separation from an alcoholic or abusive caregiver, a divorce where peace replaces the fighting, the death or placement of a sibling whose needs have sapped the family's ability to cope—children may experience intense guilt if they believe that their own impatience or jealousy brought about the loss, especially if it is noticeably painful to others involved. Often children find it a great relief if a helping adult shares that such wishes are normal and understandable, that the children may not have been the only ones who felt that way some of the time, and that wanting or wishing to have something happen does not automatically make it happen. As Viorst points out, "We have guilt about our bad feelings and we also may have great guilt for what we have done and what we didn't do. Guilty feelings too—irrational guilt and justified guilt—are very often a part of the mourning process" (1986, 241).

Assessing for Self-Blame Issues

Although children do not necessarily complete their developmental tasks on a particular time schedule, they master such tasks sequentially, and when a child does not move on, it can suggest a source of difficulty. For example, when children experience a loss at the age of two and a half, they are likely to connect the loss to one of the developmental tasks that plague children of that age and their caregivers. If they decide that the loss occurred because of the oppositional and independent behavior common in two-year-olds (such as incessant statements of "No" or "Me do it"), they may become stuck in either negative, controlling behavior or over-compliant behavior. Should they decide that toileting mistakes were the primary source of loss, they might continue wetting and/or soiling long beyond the time when most children have mastered toileting or show marked anxiety when they wet or soil. If children experience loss at age three, however, their guesses about the cause of the loss might be different, because they are working on different developmental tasks. The phenomenon can be so striking that a helper may be able to judge from behavior alone how old a child was at the time of a major loss. A book such as *Child Behavior* (1955), by Frances L. Ilg and Louise Bates Ames, can aid helpers in determining what types of behavior are typical to various ages and stages in child development and which ongoing behaviors may be connected to self-blame.

Although self-blame seems most often developmentally connected, occasionally children make coincidental connections, putting together two unrelated situations that they transform into a source of self-blame through magical thinking.

A child orphaned in a tragic accident, when asked why her parents hadn't come home as they had promised, whispered very softly, "It's because I kept spilling my milk. I'm really very messy."

Tony was a five-year-old who was very little trouble. He did get angry with his two-year-old sister, Yolanda, sometimes, especially when she intruded on his play. One day as he was making roads in the dirt for his truck, Yolanda insisted on sitting on his nearly completed project. Tony yelled at her to move and when she didn't, he hit her on the head with his truck, making a small cut that bled profusely. Yolanda screamed frantically; his mother came running in great alarm and scolded Tony soundly. Months later, when his father left to seek work in another state, Tony thought that his dad left because Tony had been too aggressive. Without being helped to understand what was really happening, Tony might have developed into a child who hit other children more frequently than most or one who was unable to fight back but provoked abuse from other children by his behavior.

It helps to observe or find out how well children respond to praise and criticism or whether they have trouble making or keeping friends. Do they seem overly defensive, assuming that others don't like or approve of them? Are they prone to name calling? Often what bereaved children feel about themselves is evident from what they say about themselves: "I'm no good." "I'm dumb!" Conversely, though, they may say to others what they really feel about themselves: "You're so clueless." "Get a life." Children who attribute their loss to "wrong feelings" may decide no longer to allow themselves those particular feelings or perhaps any feelings at all. The degree to which they believe their survival depends on not feeling can be heard in the force with which they say "I don't care, and you can't make me!" Children who attribute their loss to "wrong thinking" often become anxious about their ability to think correctly, which may cause them to have difficulty learning in school, making decisions, setting goals, or trusting their experience. Many of them seem to give up, as evidenced in their constant reiterations of "I can't," "I'm confused," "It's too hard," or "I don't know." They may feel completely blocked or blank inside, especially when stressed, which can make them feel or be less sensitive or insightful than others. Children who attribute their loss to "wrong behavior" may become stuck in that behavior or at the point in the developmental process when the loss occurred.

There are a number of ways to determine whether or how children might be blaming themselves. Helpers can also simply ask children why they think the loss occurred. One way is to use an embedded question, beginning with a personal statement, "I'm wondering . . ." (or some variation), followed by the question ". . . what do you think might make a mother do something like that?" Other openings are: "I was thinking about what we talked about, and I was trying to guess what you would say if I asked you why . . . , " or "I'd like to hear what you think about. . . ." Point-blank questions are also an option: "So your dad decided he was not going to live with you anymore. What would make a dad do that?" "There you were, a little kid only this tall, and your parents just disappeared. Why would a mom and dad do something like that?" Because children themselves are often so frank and direct, frequently they will respond quite matter-of-factly, without seeming to become offended or defensive. Some children will blurt out their theories about how they brought the calamity upon themselves, greatly relieved finally to have someone with whom to share their burden.

Helpers might also try asking questions symbolically. In *Getting to Know the Troubled Child* (1976), Looff describes an exercise for exploring how children see themselves that can be used by people who are not trained to do standard projective tests. First, he asks the youngster to draw a person. Then he leads the child into conversation by saying that behind the good drawing there must be a good story: "Would you say that this person is a boy or a girl? A man or a woman?" "How old would you say he is?" "I guess he should have some kind of name; what shall we call him?" "He's probably like all boys. I wonder what he likes to do especially?" "Is there anything in particular he's proud about?" "Like all boys, he probably has some tough times. What might worry this Jimmy?"

Using art activities and then asking children to tell stories about their drawings can be a rich source of information so long as helpers remember that the symbolism in children's art merely provides clues as to what might be going on. Helpers should check all their guesses with the child before drawing conclusions; until the child confirms the validity of an assumption, it is not necessarily significant information.

Asked to draw a picture of a house, Marcy, age six, chose a bright orange piece of paper and used a green crayon to draw a typical house, with a peaked roof, chimney, two windows, and a front door. Sneaking a glance at the helper, she picked up an orange crayon and colored in a pane in one of the windows. The color showed, but only slightly.

HELPER: Looks like part of your window is different. Can you tell me about it?
MARCY: Yeah, it's broken.
HELPER: How did it get broken?
MARCY: The mother threw the doll out the window.
HELPER: Why would a mother want to do something like that?
MARCY: Because the baby was yucky.

Marcy, in her fourth foster home, had "broken" down the three previous placements by what could easily be described as "yucky" behavior. This conversation provided a good opening for talking about her separation from her birth mother as well as subsequent losses, starting Marcy on her way to relieving her stored-up guilt and self-blame.

Helpers can also ask questions about how children see themselves: "I'm wondering how you have been feeling about yourself lately. If you were giving yourself a number, with 10 being the best kind of eleven-year-old you could be and 1 being the worst, where would you put yourself?" (With children too young to understand this kind of numerical scale, helpers can ask them to show how they feel by holding their hands a tiny bit apart to indicate "bad" and farther and farther apart to show "okay," "good," "great," "fantastic.") "Other kids have told me that after their parents separated they felt embarrassed and didn't want anyone to know. Was it like that for you, or was it different?" You may not even need to ask; the child may allude to, or claim directly, feelings of inferiority, separateness, and embarrassment about the loss.

Working on Self-Blame Issues

Those who work with children of separation or loss should not underestimate how strong the need is in many children to blame themselves rather than to think that life can hurt them randomly and with no warning, which makes them feel too overwhelmingly vulnerable and helpless. It is important to provide children with accurate information, understandably presented, so that they can answer "how" and "why" questions to their own satisfaction (see chapter 2). Children seem to be most likely to assign detrimental self-blame when no one talks with them in a way that makes sense to them about what led to the loss, reassuring them that it was not their fault (if it was not), or when they are given only partial information and sense that there is more to the story than they are being told.

Thirteen-year-old Crystal came into foster care when she was four and a half. After she was adopted at seven by her foster parents, her family continued to keep in touch with her birth grandparents, who had been a positive, consistent part of her life. Crystal was referred for therapy by her family doctor because both the physician and Crystal's adoptive mother were concerned that if she continued to display markedly low self-esteem and excessive passivity and to avoid taking responsibility for herself or setting goals, she might get into serious difficulty or get pregnant, because of her tendency to go along with whatever her peer group suggested. As the helper got to know Crystal, it seemed increasingly clear that some of her passivity was connected to her misunderstanding about why she had not stayed with her family of origin.

It appeared that Crystal, who had been in the middle of the very controlling, out-of-bounds behavior frequently seen in children who are four to four and a half when she left her birth family, decided that she was being punished for having refused to do what she was told and for having taken charge of her life. She seemed to have decided that never asserting herself in those ways again would keep her safe from additional losses. To complicate matters, Crystal had picked up, as many children do, that neither her adoptive mother nor her grandparents were open to discussing the events leading up to her placement, and so she had avoided initiating conversations that might have clarified her misunderstanding.

The actual story was that Crystal's mother's life-style was so rejecting and hurtful that talking about her was extremely painful to Crystal's grandparents. During Crystal's early years, while she still lived with her birth mother, her grandparents had grown increasingly concerned about their ability to keep her safe from their daughter's behavior; eventually they called protective services to report neglect and abuse, and their call led to Crystal's placement into foster care. The deepest family secret was that Crystal's mother killed herself after her parental rights were terminated, and all the adults involved, both the adoptive parents and the grandparents, felt partially responsible for the death.

In order for Crystal to take better care of herself and assume more self-control and self-determination, she needed to know what had happened, to be allowed to grieve and respond, and to redecide how to see herself and live her life in light of a fuller understanding about what had led to her adoption.

HELPING CHILDREN UNDERSTAND THEIR PERSONAL HISTORIES

Because information about the past is emotionally laden and quite complicated, children frequently need additional help in taking it in and keeping it straight. They are often fully convinced that they have caused their own losses and so are understandably reluctant to discuss their failures. If they have skipped over parts of the grief process, discussion may reawaken old pain and confusion as well. So, although many children are eager to find out the "truth" about their pasts, others want to avoid it at all cost. Consequently, how to bring up the subject and get children talking are usually the first two obstacles helpers face. There are a number of ways to help them do this.

As is usual with children, a good place to begin is wherever they seem to have the most energy invested. Crystal, for example, needed to understand why she had been separated from her birth parents and placed for adoption.

Crystal's helper decided to use representative puppets as a way to help engage Crystal in a discussion of her family history. Taking out a handful of wooden tongue depressors, she began the conversation by saying, "Today I want to sort out a few things about you and your family. I know that you have a dad named Larry. How shall we draw him for this puppet? Let's see, he's got black hair—do you want to draw him, or shall I?" Crystal picked up a black marker and drew an obviously balding man with a beard and a mustache. When asked to label the puppet, she wrote "Dad" across the bottom.

"OK. Now who else do we need in this family?" On a second tongue depressor, Crystal drew a face with blue eyes and curly brown hair that she labeled "Mom." She made another puppet with straight blond hair and blue eyes and glasses that she labeled "Crystal" and one with black hair and brown eyes labeled "Dan" for her older brother. "Good work. I'd know pretty well what these folks looked like, even if I'd never met them."

Laying out the appropriate puppets on the table, the helper then began, "So, how this story starts is with a mom and dad who had a little boy named Dan. Then, when Dan was eight, your mom and dad, who had been wanting a little girl, heard about you from their social worker, and you moved in to be part of this family. [Crystal's puppet joins the others.] Now, I think I know the answer to this question, but where had you been living before that? With your gram and gramp, huh? How about making a puppet for each of them? [Crystal draws two more puppets, labels them, and puts them on the table.] You know what your mom and dad told me? They told me that, in the beginning, although your gram and gramp were around and took care of you sometimes, the way grandparents do, you lived with your birth mother, Shirley. I heard that she had blond hair like you and greeny-blue eyes. Have you ever seen a picture of her? No? Well then, for now we'll have to guess. Do you want to draw a puppet for her, or shall I?" Crystal slumps in her chair; her helper draws a puppet for Shirley and lays it on the table.

"So, there you were [the helper moves Crystal's puppet alongside Shirley's], living with Shirley. How come you went to live [moving Crystal's puppet back into her adoptive family] with your mom and dad and Dan?"

Using such step-by-step reenactments of the past allows helpers to check out what children know and what they think they know, want to know, or find difficult to talk about.

As you bring up the subject of loss, particularly if it involves difficult or painful information or stirs up old feelings and memories, children may feign indifference ("Who cares?" "I know all that stuff") or divert you to another subject ("Do you know what my teacher did? It was really unfair . . ."). If children have not broached the subject of past losses or want to talk only about the present, you may want to give them the chance to take turns doing something else. Try to gauge how much of the story to tell at a time by watching children's ability to pay attention. When they begin to look spacy or to yawn, enough has been said, and it's time to change activities and do something fun, leaving the remainder of the information to be covered on another day. Eventually, however, it will be important to return to the history work so that children do not come to feel that what happened or their part in it is too terrible to be addressed openly.

Some children may try to distract you by getting silly, falling out of their chairs, inappropriately coloring on you or themselves, or becoming very active either physically or verbally. Even if you are comfortable with such children and committed to helping them toward resolution, this resistance can be a challenge. Children often will take any tack to avoid dealing with the frightening and painful feelings connected with past events. The helper should adopt a compassionate but firm attitude in response to children's attempts to push this information away. You might confront the reaction directly: "This is hard for you to hear. It makes you want to change the subject." Or you could say, "I'm really glad someone helped you get everything straight. It makes what I need to do much easier. Can you tell me what happened so I can understand it? Then we won't have to talk about it anymore."

Using Puppets to Make Sense of Multiple Losses

We know that the most difficult losses to master are untimely losses, those where there is no experience of the finality of an actual corpse, those where there has been a highly ambivalent relationship. But loss comes in all shapes and sizes. It is not unusual for children to have several different caregivers. Following divorce, children may be taken care of by grandparents or one parent until the second parent is able to make other living arrangements, or the custodial parent may have a series of live-in adult friends. Children with overburdened or immature parents may spend years moving from one relative to another. Or children may enter the public welfare system and experience a number of moves from one family to another before a permanent arrangement is made. Children may also reexperience a sense of loss when the finalization of an adoption terminates the possibility of being reunited with their birth parents; or when divorced parents remarry, thereby making the divorce seem irreversible; or when a child is born of a new union. If a noncustodial parent remarries someone who has custody of children from a previous marriage, a child who is only allowed to visit may suffer from a deepened sense of loss. Similarly, children who acquire stepbrothers and stepsisters may lose their familiar positions in the family—no longer the oldest, the youngest, or the only boy, for example—which precipitates yet another loss.

Puppets are an excellent way to help young children sort out multiple losses or complicated family relationships.

"First there were Pat and Allen. They met each other in high school and decided to get married. Your records say that Pat had brown eyes and dark hair. Can you draw me a puppet of what you think Pat looked like? OK, now let's make one for Allen. He has eyes like yours and curly hair. OK. After they had been married for a while they found out that there was a tiny baby growing inside Pat [the helper places a blank tongue depressor across the Pat puppet's body]. By and by, that baby was born, and that was you! Your parents named you Tim after your grandfather. [The helper draws a face on the child's puppet and labels it.] You were healthy and strong. You did all the things that babies do: you ate, and you slept; you played, and you cried; you needed to have your diaper changed; you learned to roll over and to sit up and to crawl. When you were about this tall [indicating with hand] and just big enough to be walking and getting into things the way all kids do, Sally was born. Do you want to make a puppet for her, or shall I? [Sally's puppet joins the others.] But things were not going too well for Pat and Allen. Allen wanted to be out with friends much of the time [the helper moves Allen's puppet away from the rest of the family], and Pat thought he should come home and help with the house and the children. They fought a lot [the helper makes the puppets fight, inviting the child to give them words to say]. One day Allen just didn't come home at all. Pat was very angry. She was probably sad and scared, too. She waited for several days wondering if something terrible had happened. Then Allen called and said that he had decided to live with his parents and that he was not going to come home ever again to Pat and you and Sally. So Allen moved away [the helper removes his puppet]. Pat was so confused. She didn't know what to do. Then she decided that the best way to work things out was for her to find a way for someone else to help take care of you and Sally. So the three of you went to live with your auntie Vi and your uncle Bill and their twins Allie and Angie. Let's make puppets for them, too." The helper lays out the new puppets on a different part of the table and moves the puppets for Pat, Tim, and his sister alongside the new family constellation.

Using this technique, a helper can make successive moves quite concrete, talking about the reasons for them and incorporating a good deal of information in a way that the child can grasp.

The "feeling faces" cards discussed in chapter 4 can be used to

---

6/21/9-	★ 4/30	7/8	★ 4/30	12/17
Pat & Allen get married	Tim born	Move Walnut St. apartment	First birthday	Sally born

8/25	9/16	★ 4/30	6/28	7/1
Mom starts work	Start day care at Gail's	Fourth birthday	Pat & Allen get divorced	Move to Genessee Road

add details to the story. After going through the history, a helper might go back to the beginning and do the story again, this time asking the child, "How do you think they [or you] felt?"

"In the beginning, there were Pat and Allen. They met in high school and fell in love and decided to get married. How do you think they felt? [Happy.] Probably. They may also have felt a little scared, because they had never been married or had their own apartment before and so that was new to them. Then they found out they were going to have a little baby. How do you think they felt? [Happy.] I bet you're right. Maybe excited, too. And they might have felt a little scared or nervous because they had never had a baby to take care of before and they may have wondered what it would be like and whether they would know how to do all the things that babies need. Then you came along, a handsome, healthy, smart baby. Now how do you think they felt? [Happy.l Yes, I think they may have felt excited and proud just like lots of new parents. They may also have been a little scared because they were not used to being parents, and they wanted to do a good job. Allen wanted to work extra hard to make enough money to take care of you and your mom. But when he finished a day at work, sometimes he felt like going out and having fun with his friends."

Another way to go about working with a child on history is for the helper to cut out shapes while talking to the child, as a way of keeping him or her involved and interested. Picking up a pair of scissors, the helper could begin to cut the outline of a person or a house:

"Today I'm going to tell you a story. I may need you to help me

★ 4/30	★ 4/30	7/15	8/10
Second birthday	Third birthday	Allen leaves	Move to Bill & Vi's

★ 4/30	5/9	9/4	12/5
Fifth birthday	Ted moves in	Start preschool	Mom & Ted get married

out. This is a story about a woman named Pat [the helper cuts out a figure to represent Pat] and a man named Allen [cuts out a figure for Allen], who lived in a tall apartment house [cuts it out and put Pat and Allen shapes or puppets on it]. After a while they had a tiny baby named Tim [cuts out a baby's shape], and about the time he was learning to walk they had another baby [cuts out her picture and place it with the family], whom they named Sally."

Helpers could use different colors of construction paper for different birth families to keep straight which children are biological children of which parents, something that can become confusing in remarriage and foster or adoptive families. Helpers might also want to include the schools and best friends that have changed with the various moves. Again, important friends and neighbors, schools attended, and remarriages can be included, and the exercise can be completed by discussing the feelings associated with the story.

Using a Time Line to Make Sense of Multiple Losses

Helpers might help older children explore and understand their histories by using time lines and graphs similar to those they may have used in school. On a large sheet of newsprint, draw out a time line and fill in the years from the child's birth to the present. You can use dates (1989, 1990, and so on), or you can use ages (infant, one, two, and so on). Then go through the child's history, using a contrasting color to mark changes in caregiver or moves. A section of the finished time line might look something like the one across the top of these two pages.

179

You might finish by talking about the feelings that accompanied the various changes in the family situation.

After you have introduced these techniques of recording history, let a week or so pass and then ask the child to tell you the story. This allows you to find out what has been understood and retained and what is still confusing or misunderstood. It is also helpful to ask both the child and caregiver to watch for patterns that might indicate remaining points of self-blame or other concerns about the child's role and responsibility in what has happened or is happening, so that these issues, too, can be addressed.

Because children can often show or work on their issues through play, using figures and props such as play people, a vehicle the people can fit in, and miniature household possessions (stove, sink, refrigerator, table and chairs, beds, toilet, and whatever else seems called for) often can provide clues and opportunities to initiate discussion. Helpers must be careful, however, not to direct play but simply to observe it for patterns. If the same pattern occurs repeatedly and its meaning is not clear, the helper can ask questions to establish its significance: "I see that the mom is leaving again. How do you think [some character in the drama] feels? How do you think Mom feels? [Some character] is watching the mom leave. What do you think he [she] feels? Is there some way he [she] could make things change?"

Despart developed a technique in 1946, described in the *American Journal of Orthopsychiatry*, which uses fables to explore children's conceptions of the cause of losses. For example:

- *The Funeral Fable* (to investigate hostility, death wishes, guilt feelings, self-punishment): "A funeral is going down a street, and people ask, 'Who died?' Somebody answers, 'It's somebody in the family that lives in this house.' Who is it?" For the child who has no conception of death, tell the fable this way: "Somebody in the family took a train and went way, way far away and will never come back. Who is it? [List the members of a family.]"
- *The Anxiety Fable* (regarding anxiety and self-punishment): "A child says softly to himself, 'Oh, I am afraid!' What do you suppose the child is afraid of?"

- *The News Fable* (to test the wishes and fears of a child): "A child comes back from school [or from playing], and the mommy says, 'Sit here for a minute, I have something to tell you.' What do you suppose the mommy is going to say?"
- *The Bad Dream Fable* (for a check on the preceding fables): "A child wakes up one morning all tired, and says, 'Oh, what a bad dream I had!' What do you suppose the dream was about?"

You can successfully use variations on the Despart fables, such as, "The mom packs a suitcase. She is very angry. A child asks what is happening. The mom says that someone is going away and not coming back unless something changes. Who is going and what has to change?" Or, "A child hears parents fighting. They are yelling loudly. What do you think the parents are fighting about?" Or, "Someone dies [or goes away]. Everybody thinks they know why it happened. But a child knows a secret reason. What do you think the secret is?"

Eight-year-old Cody was showing signs of being increasingly troubled and depressed as he tried to sort out how to please his parents who were getting a divorce. As power struggles broke out between his parents about visitation and custody issues, each caregiver would persuasively argue with Cody that he should spend more time with them. He would agree with one and then change his mind later to please the other, whose arguments sounded equally fair and reasonable to him. As it became obvious that he was a main source of conflict between his parents, he became agitated and weepy. His helper sat down with him and cut the following props out of construction paper: A house, three people in graduated sizes, a dozen red hearts, and a dozen blue clouds. Putting the three figures on a table, the helper began, "In the olden days, when moms and dads got divorced, people said that the children were from a 'broken home.'" The helper then picked up the house and tore it in half. "Do you think your house is broken?" Cody laughed, "Of course not!" The helper moved the two pieces of house aside. "When moms and dads get divorced, sometimes they are so upset that they seem to be coming apart. Do you think your mom is broken? What about your dad?" "No? I think you're right. I think they are very upset, but I think they are not broken and they will figure out a way in time to make themselves feel better again." The helper then placed the smallest cutout figure between the two larger figures and said, "What about you? With all this pulling and pushing and tug-of-war, are you likely to get broken?" When the child did not respond, the helper brought out the pile of red hearts and blue clouds and said, "Often when a family is going through a divorce, they can feel as if their hearts are being broken and their dreams are being broken. I think some of that is happening in your family. Can you show me who has a broken heart and who has broken dreams?" The child tore one heart in half and laid it on the father figure. Then he said, "Mine used to be like that, but I'm feeling a little better about knowing that my parents are not going to get back together." He covered himself with three intact hearts. His helper gently prodded, "That leaves your dad with a broken heart. Whose job is it to help him feel better?" Cody answered, "I don't know," to which the helper responded, "I think it is his job, and I think he is smart enough to figure out grown-up ways to help himself feel better. It could take him some time. You need to know that your job is to work on fixing your own feelings, and he needs to know that it is his job to work on fixing his. While he is figuring things out, he needs to know that you love him. . . . What about broken dreams? Who in this family has broken dreams?" Cody tore up cloud after cloud after cloud and covered himself and his father with them, to which the helper responded, "I think you are absolutely right. And sometimes broken dreams hurt even more than broken hearts. Can you tell me about the broken dreams?" As the child shared his thoughts, it became evident that he was aware that his mother was in a new relationship and had new love feelings and new dreams while he and his dad both wished that things could be as they had been. He was able to draw some pictures of what kinds of new dreams he might want to make in this new situation and then could talk with his helper about how he and his mom and his dad would all be able to find new things to love and look forward to, new dreams to dream and to make come true.

Throughout the activity, Cody was reassured that it was his job to figure out what he needed to do to take care of himself and that unless he was being unreasonably mean he could tell his parents what he thought and wanted and needed. He was also told that if there was something he needed to talk to either or both of his parents about that was too hard or too scary he and his helper could do it together. The following week Cody was much more energetic. He asked his helper to write a letter with him that said, among other things, "Cody wants his mom and dad to know that he loves them very much and that he is not part of their fight and does not like being in the middle. He would like his mom and dad to remember that they both love him and want to take good care of him. He would like his mom not to ask him what happened when he was visiting with his dad and his dad to not ask him what had been going on at his mom's. He wants to work on figuring out how he can enjoy himself and feel comfortable with his dad when he is at his house and with his mom when he is at his mom's. And he would like them each to try to figure out how to be happy and make new dreams for themselves when he is with them and when he is not."

When you feel that children are sharing symbolic confusion or misunderstanding about events in their own lives, you can comment, "Do you sometimes feel like that is what happened to you?" Another way to respond is to say, "It looked [or sounded or seemed] to me just then as if that was a little like what happened to you." Again, such guesses are just guesses and should be checked out with the child. If the child disagrees, the helper can either let the conversation drop or say, "We have a difference of opinion about that, I guess."

Making a Record for the Child

Puppets, cutouts, and time lines are excellent ways to clarify children's past and remove self-blame, and if the helper is the child's caregiver and will continue to be available for information and clarification, it is often enough in the near term. But if the helper is not the child's usual caregiver, some permanent record should be made of the child's history and either given to the child or the child's caregivers, so that the child can review it at any time, either as a reminder or as a means of incorporating new information. Such a record can also help a child's caregivers respond to questions or comments about parts of the child's life that they did not share.

The two most common ways to make these records are the life story and the life book. In the life story, the helper writes out what he or she and the child have discussed together, including the reasons for various changes and the feelings that have accompanied these changes. In the life book, the helper brings together in a scrapbook or notebook pictures of the child at a young age, pictures of important people such as birth parents and other caregivers, and memorabilia such as might be found in a baby book. Each picture should have a caption identifying who or what is portrayed, how the person or thing is important, and why the picture is in the book. If no photographs are available, the child can draw pictures of important people and places, using whatever information is known or can be deduced. (Caution: Do not have the child cut out pictures from a magazine as a substitute for photographs. Magical thinking tends to turn those people into "my real parents," which only confuses the issue.) I describe how to prepare a life book more fully in my book *Adopting the Older Child*.

If you are working with a child in foster care, a good way of keeping records is to supply each foster parent with a large manila envelope on an annual visit that might coincide with the child's birthday or the beginning of the school year. The child's name and the date are printed on the envelope, and the foster parent is asked to save in it schoolwork, snapshots, awards, or anything else that records the child's growth, so that when the child returns home or moves on, the history and mementoes can move, too. In part because they wish to remain part of the child's memories themselves, most foster parents are very cooperative about this, and it makes the task of record keeping much easier.

It takes time to gather the information necessary to help a child piece together past life experiences and make sense of the reasons behind them. But there are immeasurable rewards for doing so. Whatever energy you expend to complete this work will be well worth your time and trouble.

UNDERSTANDING AND WORKING WITH CONTROL ISSUES

As children try to ward off the feelings of helplessness engendered by loss and the changes it entails, to hold on to their self-esteem, and to handle their anger, they often try to control life by becoming overly competent and self-reliant, oppositional, overly passive and compliant, or anxiously avoidant. Each of these responses is a potential problem and may continue into adulthood. It is not unusual to see more than one kind of control reaction in a child, and suggestions made for dealing with one type of controlling behavior may very well be appropriate for another. For this reason, all such suggestions are collected together at the end of the section.

Overly Competent and Overly Self-Reliant Children

Some children become prematurely competent or self-reliant as a way of keeping themselves safe. Perhaps their attempts to make and maintain satisfying, positive relationships or to reestablish connections have been unsuccessful, and they have come to believe that reaching out, getting close to, or depending on others is too hurtful and disappointing to risk. Perhaps they have become convinced that they cannot count on adults to keep them safe. Overly self-reliant children also often have caregivers who deny their own needs and feelings and encourage their children to do the same. Sometimes caregivers encourage and support premature mastery and competence in their children because they find it easier to deal with children as if they were adult companions or partners rather than ordinary children with all the normal demands of immaturity.

Such children are likely to refuse help and make it clear that they are able to handle things independently and would rather do things themselves, their way. Though they may not pose problems for those who deal with them, children who control through mastery are likely to become isolated and lonely over time because they shut others out. As adults, they may not know what they need, or, if they do, they may be unable to ask for it or to turn to other people for help, support, or comforting for fear that they will be

185

chastised or rejected because of their neediness—which they feel will be seen as unnecessary, unacceptable, and intolerable. Overly competent and self-reliant children are also likely to have difficulty making commitments or delegating or sharing responsibility as they grow up. They may be driven to keep very busy and to overextend themselves as a way to ignore their inner needs, dependencies, and loneliness. They are likely to play hard, to make everything a contest, and to overachieve, taking on more and more challenges out of a need to reassure themselves and prove to others that they truly are worthwhile, competent people. As children and as adults, they may believe that they are loved for what they do, what they have, and how often they win, rather than for who they authentically are.

Parentified Children: Some children try to grow up very quickly in order to replace an absent caregiver or older sibling. Many experts believe that this reaction is a way both to keep the lost person around and to comfort and reassure themselves during active grief. Children may use the same words and gestures and take on the same interests, responsibilities, and habits as the absent loved one. This response may be encouraged by caregivers who send the message directly or indirectly that they need someone to fill the place that is empty and to assume the role of the one who is gone. These children come to believe that they are most lovable when they concentrate on being someone other than themselves, which greatly constricts their own development and sense of identity and frequently leads to deep resentment as the child matures.

A classic example of a parentified child can be seen in the Shirley Temple version of *Rebecca of Sunnybrook Farm.* Rebecca is a bright, talented youngster who is taken by her stepfather to a radio audition, where he hopes to exploit her talent. His abrasive manner causes difficulty, but Rebecca charms the receptionist, "You'll have to excuse him, I've told him not to act that way. I've been taking care of him ever since my mother died." When the receptionist responds, "You poor child!" Rebecca replies, "I'm not a poor child, I'm very self-reliant. My mother told me to always be that way." The phrase "I'm very self-reliant" is used six times in the two opening scenes. When Rebecca's stepfather subsequently drives her to the country and dumps her on her Aunt Miranda whom she has never met, Rebecca responds, "Maybe it's all for the best, he's been an awful trial to me."

In real life, parentified children are often confused and conflicted about the role they have assumed and the needs they deny. Apparently able to deal with major challenges and changes resiliently and easily, underneath they long for someone to look out for them.

One preteen who appeared to be a calm, self-sufficient, and loving big sister, much to the relief of her overburdened family, which had suffered a traumatic loss, was haunted by a recurrent nightmare in which she found herself in a strange house where she was pursued by giants. Over and over she tried to get away, all the while lugging her younger brother on her back as she struggled to get them both to safety. When she was caught by the giants, they laid a curse on her, causing her face to freeze into a grotesque mask. The only cure, she was told, was to go to a nearby diner and find someone who would give her the money to buy a soft drink. When she had consumed it, she would return to normal. In her dream, she approached the people sitting at the counter, frightened to ask for help for fear they would shrug her off and turn her down and yet equally frightened that if she did not approach them for help, she was doomed to remain a monster. At that point, she would wake up trembling and wanting to call someone to comfort her yet terrified to wake anyone up, thinking that they might be angry and not come to her, and also afraid to call out, because although she questioned their existence, if the giants that were so real in her dream should be under her bed, they might hurt her if they knew she was awake. Night after night she would lie awake in the dark weighing which path was more fraught with danger.

Parentified children not only take care of others, particularly those in their families, but also begin to discipline and correct others, driving them away because they are intrusive and bossy, full of unwanted advice and criticism. They are likely to boast, overstating or flaunting their abilities as a way to compensate when they need to reassure themselves, especially when they feel unwelcome, unsure, or inadequate, which only puts others off further. One wonders how other children would have responded to Shirley Temple's Rebecca and how well she would have been able to make any friends in a peer group.

Caretaking Children: Some children attempt to master life by making themselves indispensable to others so that they will never be abandoned again. They become caretakers, often subjugating their own needs, trying to please other people at all costs. This response may be supported by caregivers who appreciate and are most likely to notice them when they are being thoughtful, generous, and self-effacing. Because these children strain themselves trying to maintain a pleasant self-image, they may have little energy left over for authentic self-awareness. They may become so outwardly focused that they grow increasingly unsure as to who they really are. They may become unable to figure out or say what they truly think or feel because they have not been encouraged to develop or express their own thoughts or feelings or to think for themselves. This is exacerbated if, when they have shared their observations and reactions, they have been dissuaded, rebuffed for "being so sensitive," or pressured into agreeing with what others around them think and feel.

Caretaking children may try to buy friends with excessive flattery or with gifts. They often feel inadequate and depressed and anxious when others are uncomfortable or when they can't fix things for others because they feel that it is their job to keep everyone happy. They are likely to project their needs onto others, looking for someone or something to rescue and love as they wish to be rescued and loved; hoping subconsciously that the recipients of their caretaking will be so charmed and grateful that they will repay in kind. Many of them identify strongly with animals and have very important, perhaps their most significant, relationships with pets, by whom they feel needed, understood, and appreciated. Many of them want to be vets or social workers when they grow up.

Caretakers often continue to suffer loss and deprivation as adults because they tend to enter into relationships with people who need them so desperately that they will never be able to reject or leave them but who are too needy or immature to be able to enter into a reciprocal relationship. In the end, they are likely to feel used, abused, and victimized by those they have set out to rescue.

Oppositional Children

Children who feel particularly buffeted by life often try to control everything in their environment because they are afraid that they will suffer if they relinquish control. In their struggle to stay safe, their lives become one battle after another. They often become extremely oppositional, refusing to accept limits, fighting and arguing about rules and routines and ignoring or refusing to comply with reasonable requests and demands. No matter what limits are set for these children, they repeatedly overstep the boundaries, sending messages that say clearly, "I don't need you to tell me what to do," "I don't care what you think," "You can't make me," all of which communicate that they feel people are out to hurt them again. They are often difficult patients for the person who has to administer a shot, examine their ears, or work on their teeth, for they are likely to fight back, terrified of being under the control of a powerful, hurtful adult. They box themselves in with the hostility and the wish to retaliate that they create in others, and yet they feel unable to give up the oppositional behavior that they believe keeps them safe. In time, their fight for control becomes increasingly senseless and desperate as they respond to the attempts to make them obey and curb their outrageous behavior. They often feel trapped and refuse to let themselves try or care because they feel there is nothing to gain and nothing more to lose.

Underneath their aggressively controlling behavior, oppositional children are often significantly depressed and hopeless. They may begin to sleep more than usual, to have problems in school with adults and peers, to exhibit poor academic performance, suffer from physical complaints, and become involved in delinquency, fighting, and vandalism.

Overly Passive and Compliant Children

Some children respond to their feelings of helplessness by giving in to them, becoming overly compliant and passive. They begin to think of themselves as hopeless victims. Feeling powerless, incompetent, and inefficient, they tend to discount their abilities to take charge or to tackle problems and work them out and to disregard cues that they are in trouble. They may not let themselves know, for example, that they are failing a subject until a warning slip or the failing grade comes, regardless of how often they have been warned by the teacher or how many quizzes and tests they have failed. They do not ask for help or share their problems, perhaps because they have denied them too strongly to be able to acknowledge them or perhaps because if others knew they were in trouble, they would have to start dealing with it themselves. They are likely to become passive and fatalistic about life, so much so that they often fail to make plans, to carry out responsibilities, and seem just to live from moment to moment. As a result, they underachieve, convincing themselves that they never wanted success anyway. When they do succeed, they often discount it and credit it to luck, which is extremely damaging to their self-esteem. They may show little emotion except for silliness, flippancy, or contempt. No matter how serious a situation, they laugh it off.

Bowlby points out that such learned helplessness would likely be diagnosed in an adult as a depressive disorder because so many of the symptoms of depression often accompany it. Overly passive and compliant children admit to feeling low, sad, discouraged, and hopeless, and they often show other classic symptoms of depression, including failure to grow, difficulty sleeping, fatigue or lethargy, loss of interest in things, difficulty concentrating, and wishes or thoughts about dying or killing themselves.

If these children fight their feelings of helplessness, they often do so in passive-aggressive ways. They may dump their feelings on the helper, for example, by asking for help but discounting any suggestions with a "yes, but . . .," often so successfully that would-be helpers feel helpless too. Sometimes they not only externalize and project their helplessness but then verbally attack the helper, whom they accuse of being ineffective or unconcerned.

Overly Anxious Children

Some children spend so much time reliving and analyzing the past that they are unable to participate fully in the present. They try to control things by paring down what they allow in, increasingly constricting their worlds with suspicion and hostility. Overly anxious children may begin to view life as full of threatening surprises with painful consequences that they are powerless to remedy and to fear that all their relationships will end in failure. They may sit life out, anxiously wondering what will happen next. Sometimes they are so preoccupied with when a treat will be over that they focus on how much time is still left instead of taking in the experience. They tend to hate change, to be afraid of the unknown, and to avoid new things, situations, and strange places. They lack spontaneity because they believe that it is too dangerous. They feel like cowards and misfits, especially when peers discount and taunt them as they fall further and further out of the mainstream.

One overly anxious child with no history of being abused, when asked, "If you could be any kind of animal at all, what would you be," answered, "Well, I wouldn't want to be a bull because they put you in bullfights and stick you with swords. And I certainly wouldn't want to be a pig because I'd end up pork chops in someone's freezer. And I wouldn't want to be a bug because someone would smash me. And I wouldn't want to be a bird because someone might shoot me. How about lizards, do they live a long time? I guess I might be a lizard like the kind that changes, a chameleon, because then I could hide wherever I was and no one could hurt me."

These children often exhibit anxiety about personal safety, but usually only when they feel they are in someone else's power. Fearless while pumping themselves high on a swing, they panic on a merry-go-round or a roller coaster, where they are not in control. Similarly, although they may be somewhat predisposed to car sickness, once they are the ones behind the wheel, the problem often subsides.

Working with Children Who Have Control Issues

Children with control issues—whether they give away their control or are overly controlling—need help recognizing that, though they may not be able to control others, they do have some power to control themselves and their own responses. When they are given

191

chances to make decisions and to control ever-increasing parts of their lives, such children often begin to find it much easier to accept authority in other areas. Even when there can be no choice, caregivers can set firm limits in ways that continue to allow freedom. Many oppositional children will thrive when given fair control of choices that don't involve a power struggle. Giving children choices with logical consequences is one way:

"You must do your homework. I can't say yes to your going to the game tomorrow unless all your homework is finished. You may decide whether you want to do it now and have time for the game tomorrow, or whether you will decide to do it tomorrow instead of going to the game."

Giving the child two or more good choices is another way:

"I know you would like to stay. That is not your choice; it is time to go. Your choice is to decide how you'd like to go to the car. Do you want to walk to the car, hop, or have me carry you?"

Either of these methods sets the stage for the caregiver or helper to encourage the child's self-esteem: "I like the way you took care of that homework so that you could go to the game. Good choice." "It was fun watching how well you skipped to the car. Good work."

Children will sometimes make what seem to others to be bad choices; then the consequences must follow, or further negotiation must occur. Often caregivers or helpers can simply point out, without controlling, that such choice may not work out well, asking, "Is that a good choice or a bad one? Will it work out for you or not?" When youngsters who have been given acceptable choices try to add an unacceptable option, a reminder is in order, "That is not one of your choices; your choices are [name them]. Which would you like to choose?" Remember that the goal is not to control children but to help them make choices that work out well for them. Oppositional children do not respond well to losing more and more privileges until their lives get so curtailed that there is no reason for them not to continue to escalate their out-of-control behavior.

Caregivers sometimes overlook the positive aspects of children's demands for self-determination. They may need help seeing that it sometimes takes more self-esteem to say no than to be compliant. Helpers should point out the strengths involved:

The helper observes, "Wow, Mr. Goulet, after listening to what you told me last week and hearing from the two of you today, it certainly sounds as if Kelly is really good at saying no. Kelly, I've heard you say 'no' or 'no way' to every suggestion your dad has made." Kelly flashes her dad a smug look, while he seems relieved that at least the helper isn't being conned into believing he has overstated the problems he runs into when he tries to parent his daughter. Turning the tables on both of them, the helper continues, "You know, Kelly's got a good thing going. Imagine how concerned you'd be, Mr. Goulet, if she got to be thirteen or fourteen and couldn't say no! It's what she says no to and how she says it that need some fine-tuning. The thing we have to work on now is helping her understand how to use the power of her no in a way that works better."

Helpers need to understand what kinds of self-expression and self-determination are allowed in a child's family. Is the child allowed to do his or her own thinking? To make choices? Is the child allowed to disagree? Which rules of the family are negotiable and which are not? Have things gotten bad because the caregiver is also feeling helpless and worn down from dealing with the child? Does the caregiver now see the child's every attempt to assert autonomy, appropriate or not, as a challenge, a war to be won?

Some children have trouble accepting adult limits yet are easily led by other children. They can be shown that they are choosing to give up control of their power to figure things out and take care of themselves by turning it over to their friends:

Tyrell, who seemed determined to do whatever he wanted regardless of his caregiver's rules, was confronted about his repeated transgressions, which usually involved getting into trouble with the boys he hung out with after school.

HELPER: So even though your mother told you not to play in that empty building, you and Leon went anyway. I'm wondering why you made that choice when you knew your mom would be really mad.

TYRELL: Well, Leon made me.

HELPER: He did? How did he do that? Did he pick you up and carry you there?

TYRELL: No, but he called me chicken.

HELPER: He called you chicken, and then you had to go?

TYRELL: Yeah!

HELPER: Does that always work for you? Anybody can get you to do what they want by calling you a chicken? Your head is saying yes, and your shoulders are saying you're not sure. Let me check it out. What if Lacey [his older sister] decided that she didn't want to do the dishes when it was her turn. Maybe she could just point her finger at you and say, "Tyrell, I bet you are too chicken to do these dishes. Chicken, chicken, chicken!" Then would you have to do the dishes?

TYRELL: No way!

HELPER: I guess that chicken power is something you know how to say no to. Let's see what you know about saying no to Lacey when she uses it and what you don't know about saying no to Leon when he does.

Children, adolescents in particular, may need to be helped to see that there can be power in saying yes as well as in saying no:

"Jan, I hear you saying 'no way' to 'most everything in your life right now. You don't want to follow the rules at home, you don't want to be in school, you don't want to get a job. I know what you don't want; now I'm interested in what you do want. If you could make a plan for yourself, what would you decide to say yes to?"

Working with overly controlling youngsters can be confusing because underneath their hostile, oppositional, reactive exteriors, they often feel as though they are unable to win and are deeply depressed. Many of these youngsters and adolescents have become trapped by their own behavior and reactions. They are like abused animals backed into a corner who strike out without thought in their pain and desperation, only to find that they are caged more and more tightly and goaded and jabbed as a consequence. They respond well to helpers who approach them with understanding and respect, who are sensitive to their dilemma and willing to hear them out but who make it clear that they expect youngsters to be aware of and accountable for the choices they make. They benefit from being asked respectfully how their current behavior seems valuable to them and where they believe it is working and also from being confronted with the truth if their behavior contributes to their difficulty. Their automatic response, "I don't care!" helps adults remember that part of what is wounded is the youngsters' self-esteem and that supporting them often involves making it clear that they are worth caring about and taking care of and that they can make good choices and take good or better care of themselves. Children like this are often helped by being praised for their efforts in their own behalf and helped to feel competent about doing so: "It's good to see you taking care of yourself in a way that doesn't get you in such a hassle." "Seems to me that you made a good choice about that."

Being in charge, being included in decision making, and exercising control over some areas of their lives seem to work well with both overly controlling or overly passive children. There are many ways to promote self-esteem and help children take and relinquish responsibility more effectively, both on their own and under the direction of the adult. One thing that children can control easily, for example, is their own breathing. A good game is to ask them to close their eyes and concentrate on their own breathing until they can feel and hear it. They can experiment with holding and releasing their breath, with breathing at different rates, and with raising and lowering some part of the body in time to their breathing. Other useful activities include start-stop games such as "Captain [or Mother], May I," in which children take turns giving and receiving directions as to what steps are allowed, or the statue-making game, where child and adult take turns spinning and then releasing the other, who then drops into a position and holds it. Children might be asked to lean as far forward as possible before they fall to the ground or put their foot out to regain their balance. All these, as well as more formalized exercises, such as kung fu, tai kwan do, tai chi, and yoga, can help children learn that they can make choices regarding their own physical behavior in other arenas as well, such as choosing to stop doing something particularly disruptive.

Controlling children also can benefit from learning how to take care of themselves (though not by pushing them to take on responsibility before they are ready). For instance, because there is such a close connection between nurturing and feeding, when children know how to cook, they often feel that, if the chips were down, at least they wouldn't starve to death. Even very young children can be taught to make a sandwich or fix a bowl of cereal. Slightly older children can learn to cook eggs, pancakes, hot dogs, or other simple dishes as soon as they are tall enough to use a stove safely.

Overly self-reliant children benefit from being encouraged to recognize that everyone has needs and that such needs can be acceptable and reasonable. This can mean helping them accept that they are worth taking care of, too. They often respond well to having requests for help noted and rewarded in a way that takes into account their need to be independent. This might mean saying things like, "Here's the pencil you wanted. Good asking for what you need." Or, "I'm happy to help you close that sticky window, good job of taking care of yourself by asking." In order to heal, they need relationships with people who send them clear messages that they are loved because they are who they are; that their true authentic selves are valuable; that they are not loved or respected just for what they have, what they win, and what they do. In much the same way, parentified children respond well to being told and shown that they are responsible people but that they are not responsible for others' problems or happiness or for making others look good.

Overly anxious children, on the other hand, need help believing that they are competent, functional people. When they express a fear or concern, adults should listen thoughtfully and give concrete information, if it is available, to counteract the fear, rather than just brushing it aside. Caregivers and helpers are wise, however, to watch their tendencies to hover, to jump in with help too fast. Such rescuing tells children that they are right to doubt their ability to figure things out. Adults would do better to say and show such youngsters that they can take their time and try to figure things out at their own pace.

Brandy fluctuated between weeping about how difficult her

math was and then attacking the caregivers who tried to help her, accusing them of helping her "wrong." Her depressed self-confidence appeared to cause her to be swamped by feelings of helplessness when she felt confused or confounded, leaving her unable to break the task at hand into manageable steps but resentful of the superior mastery of anyone who tried to help her. When her befuddled caregivers asked her how to help her "right," Brandy responded, "You should let me show you what I know and then just tell me what to do when I get stuck."

Children like Brandy work best when they are left to themselves, confident that an adult is nearby to help if necessary. Such children also respond positively when helpers offer assistance by asking, "Where are you stuck?" If they don't know, helpers can ask, "Show me what you've tried."

These children, more than others, need to feel that they know what to do in an emergency—how to call the operator, how to report an emergency, how to respond in case of fire. Adults can initiate conversations that make children feel secure about their ability to get help if a caregiver is not present.

ADULT: What would you do if we lost each other at the grocery store?

CHILD: I'd ask someone at the service desk or the cash register to help me find you.

ADULT: What would you do if you got home from school and I was late?

CHILD: I'd go to [place] or call [person] [rehearsing whatever has been arranged].

Obviously, adults should avoid worrying these children by talking excessively about complex problems—such as environmental or political issues—that will only make them more anxious. Instead, they should try to pick up on clues as to specific concerns and address those. If discussions at school or in scouts or reports on the news or in the paper lead children to seek more information, they should be given accurate information about what is going on, whether they themselves are in danger, and, if so, what steps are being taken to protect them, and they need to be told, "I like how you are figuring out how to take good care of yourself."

When bereaved children come to believe that they do not have to be perfect (or helpless or take control or be in trouble) to receive attention and when they no longer fear being close, they tend to be more able to assume appropriate control of their lives and make and maintain positive connections with others. The loss remains, but they are less likely to complicate the healing process with behavior that makes it difficult for them and those around them to let go and move on.

LOOKING BACK, LETTING
GO, AND MOVING ON

❦

6 One response to bereavement in both children and adults is a driving need to make sense of what has happened and to understand the hows and whys that led to the loss. This comes partially from the need to restore order and meaning and partially from the hope that understanding why the loss occurred may help prevent losses in the future. Sometimes, however, understanding takes years. Children, in particular, often need to revisit and readdress grief experiences and their feelings about them as they grow and develop, and sometimes their behavior or recurring concerns will signal that they need help. Perhaps they were very young at the time of the loss. Perhaps caregivers were too stunned to help their children through what was happening or demanded too much comfort and nurturing themselves, leaving their children with no energy to work out their own sadness, anger, anxiety, and ambivalence. Perhaps children moved as the result of a crisis. Or perhaps they have simply reached a developmental stage where questions about personal history are common, as often happens around ages six or seven and ten to twelve and during adolescence.

UNDERSTANDING RECYCLING AND REACTIVATION

Most adults can remember times of reactivation and recycling from their own lives. As we mature, passing through one life transition to another, it is common to want to reconnect with parts of our pasts, to check out elusive memories, to sort out fact from fantasy. Adults revisit old homes and schools. They attend reunions. They revel in family memories and stories about their parents and about themselves. They take their spouses to see childhood neighborhoods and often enjoy sharing childhood pictures. Many adults can still remember their first visit back to their elementary school after they moved on to junior high or high school and the sense of wonder at how familiar it looked and smelled and how small the gym suddenly seemed or how low the drinking fountains were.

Writing about attachment, Bowlby observed, "When the effort to restore the bond is not successful, sooner or later the effort wanes. But usually it does not cease. On the contrary, evidence shows that, at perhaps increasingly long intervals, the effort to restore the bond is renewed; the pangs of grief and perhaps an urge to search are then experienced afresh. The person's attachment behavior appears to remain and under various conditions may be reactivated anew" (1980, 42). It is no wonder, then, that so many adopted and foster children have times of preoccupation about their birth parents and cling to the memories they have or the stories they have been told about them. It is even less surprising that children often wish or actively try to find those parents to reclaim the pasts that only they know. Similarly, children whose parents died or divorced go through periods of wanting to get more details about their loss(es). Children whose parents divorced may want to check with them and other family members to clarify why the marriage didn't last.

Whatever the loss, feelings of yearning and pining are likely to recur throughout life for children and adults who have suffered important losses. Children will most likely have times when they wonder how their lives might have turned out differently and question what might have been if the loss had not occurred. They may have very strong reactions to situations that bring back memories of the helpless or desperate feelings that accompanied the loss or reawaken wishes that a person or family structure could be restored to take part in an important occasion such as graduation, marriage, or the birth of a new baby. For children who have parents who are physically present but emotionally unavailable, important life events may intensify the old yearnings that the parent would somehow become more involved and supportive.

Grief can often be cyclical; anniversaries, holidays, changes in season and the day length, a return to old places or familiar situations, and the recombining of families may all reawaken bereaved feelings. Grief and loss recyclings also occur connected to developmental rite-of-passages, such as significant birthdays (the thirteenth, sixteenth, eighteenth, and twenty-first, for example), graduating from high school or college, entering or finishing basic training in the service, getting a good job or a promotion, getting married, and giving birth. As previously discussed, children may also reexperience a sense of loss when the finalization of an adoption terminates the possibility of being reunited with their birth parents; or when divorced parents remarry, thereby making the divorce seem irreversible; or when a child is born of a new union. If a noncustodial parent remarries someone who has custody of children from a previous marriage, a child who is only allowed to visit may suffer from a deepened sense of loss. Similarly, children who acquire stepbrothers and stepsisters may lose their familiar positions in the family—no longer the oldest, the youngest, or the only boy, for example—which precipitates yet another loss.

As Bowlby (1980, 158) points out, a number of situations also may cause recycled or delayed grief:

- an anniversary of a death that has not been completely mourned or a separation that has not been resolved. This is often seen in older children who begin to grieve after they have been in their new step- or adoptive families about a year.
- a new loss, even one that is apparently minor. Recycling sparked by this type of catalyst is evident, though often unrecognized, in two common situations: the temper tantrum or sense of hopeless despair often triggered by the loss or breakage of an object and that period of adolescence when the growing youngster experiences one loss after another—loss of friends as they outgrow one another, loss of elementary school and teachers, loss of boyfriend or girlfriend, loss of innocence, loss of comfort with dependency at just the time when life is making extra demands.

201

- reaching the same age as the parent at the time of death.
- a loss suffered by someone with whom the individual strongly identifies and for whom he or she provides encompassing care.

Children may be vulnerable to recycled or delayed grief when something triggers a misunderstanding or strong feeling left over from the original experience.

One youngster whose father was fatally injured in an accident at work when she was four and a half seemed to have made a good adjustment with no apparent difficulty. At age eight, however, she went on a visit with her Brownie troop to the fire station, where an invitation to climb inside the ambulance set off such a strong phobic response that she fainted. Somewhere along the line, she had linked her father's death to his ride in the ambulance, knowing that he was dead by the time he got to the hospital. As she related, "There was nothing anyone could do. They just put him in there, and he died."

School personnel are wise to be sensitive to activities that trigger grief confusion and relapse. When children are asked to draw pictures of their families, for example, they must decide whether departed parents or siblings are still a part of the family and whether or not to include them in the picture. Inclusion may precipitate questions and challenges from classmates, while omission revives the emptiness and loneliness of the initial loss. Even the simple question "How many children are there in your family?" poses great difficulty for siblings of a child who has died.

Recycling may include particular forms of behavior displayed at the time of loss, such as an increase or decrease in appetite, activity, aggression, or self-control, as well as sadness, discouragement, and yearning. Although sometimes frustrating to caregivers and children (and helpers as well), these times of reemerging trouble or preoccupation with what has happened in the past can be ideal times to help children realize that they need to understand better what has happened to them, and to make peace with their strong feelings about it. It is important for helpers to check out whether unsettled issues from past losses are resurfacing and/or whether there are factors within the existing life-style that might be complicating a child's expression of concern or confusion. Because every major loss disrupts the development of self-esteem, the smooth progression of life, and the sense that events are predictable and meaningful, recovery requires that damaged self-esteem be repaired, continuity reestablished, and a sense of meaning restored. To recover as fully as possible from a loss, children should receive satisfactory answers to the following questions:

1. Why did loss or separation occur?
2. What could I have done to make it work out differently?
3. What can I do now to return or reconnect?
4. What have I said to myself about myself and my ability to maintain relationships and achieve success in the future?

Answering these questions may require some degree of continuing attention throughout bereaved individuals' lives. Ideally, answers should come as soon and as fully as possible at the time of each loss and separation. Even if this happened, however, it is likely that the same questions will require periodic reexamination at later developmental stages or as significant life events raise new questions or offer new ways of more complete understanding. The variables influencing which questions surface, when and how they present themselves, and how they might need to be addressed appear to be a child's age at the time of the loss, the nature of the loss, the amount of denial or other defense mechanisms at play in the grief, and the kind and amount of separation work performed by the child and the family.

Understandably, many helpers and caregivers feel overwhelmed and confused as to where and how to begin to sort out the myriad elements involved. A good start is to review notes taken from interviews with the child and other caregivers, to read through all available records, and to make a chart with columns noting the dates of significant losses, moves, or changes and whether each event involved someone leaving or joining the child's family, what is known about the atmosphere surrounding the change and the manner in which the child was separated from previous caregivers, whether a separation was sudden or rejecting, and whether it involved a permanent loss (i.e., has the child had no contact with the caregivers since the move?).

Such material often provides valuable clues about sources of difficulty and alerts caregivers and helpers as to when sensitive times and situations are likely to occur. For example, it is not at all unusual for a child who has changed families several times before at a particular time of year to begin to deteriorate into old patterns of interaction or emotional upset when that time of year rolls around again. Or for children who have been settled in one or more living situations for a similar number of months or years to deteriorate when the same amount of time has elapsed in a new setting. It seems that such echoes from the past reactivate separation anxiety or the expectation of another loss. It is almost uncanny how often children repeat old patterns and resume or escalate old behaviors as a reaction to conscious or unconscious memories. Many of them appear bound and determined to force a change of caregiver at "dangerous" times of year in order to avoid having another terrible, out-of-control move take them by devastating surprise again.

Merely being helped to understand that their reactions make sense and are predictable can help older children recognize that past hurts are seeping into their present circumstances and making them vulnerable. Once that becomes clear, they are free to disconnect themselves over time from the power the past has been exerting.

One fourteen-year-old began school well each year but deteriorated by about the end of the fifth week of school. When asked why by a new helper, the boy repeated the things he had been told: "I just don't stick to things." "I have poor study habits." "The work just gets harder by then, and I can't keep up." The helper said, "Maybe so, but I find it really interesting, looking over your past school records, that the comments about your getting into trouble all start within two days of the date you moved into your adopted family—*every single year*. Seems to me that the little kid inside you says, 'Well, this is when I blow it and mess everything up," so you do. I'll be interested to see if you can reassure that two-and-a-half-year-old inside you that you will try to take better care of him by starting a new habit. Want to try it?"

Sometimes the trigger for the reactivated grief behavior will be connected to something that is not clearly represented in the chart. The caregivers and helpers are wise to suspect some kind of recycling grief reaction, which is causing a return to past difficulties. Repeating the record-keeping questions suggested in chapter 5 may uncover some previously unidentified source of difficulty.

Scott was a fifteen-year-old boy who had been in his adoptive family for almost six years and whose behavior had never stopped being a problem. Ultimately, he was referred for therapy to see if he might be in need of residential treatment. His parents felt they had tried everything with him and that they were living in a state of siege at home that was becoming intolerable. After opening interviews, it was clear that Scott was missing large components of what he needed to know to be able to understand why he and his beloved younger sister had originally come into foster care and why they had subsequently been separated into two different residential programs. His deep grief and confusion were compounded because he knew that after the first three years his mother had taken his sister back home to live, but he had been left in residential care for another two years. When he did move, it was not to go back home but into a new family.

Through life history work, Scott was helped to come to significantly better terms with what had happened to him, enough so that his behavior, both at school and at home, improved remarkably. He felt proud of his progress and his increasing control of himself. Parents and school personnel were delighted. This adjustment remained stable for some months, but in the late fall his parents placed an emergency call to his helper. All the old behaviors—lying, being provocative, sullen passive aggression—had returned almost overnight. His parents were totally discouraged and disillusioned and wanted him seen immediately.

The helper began the work by reviewing Scott's recently compiled life history to see whether the sudden deterioration was an anniversary reaction. Had Scott moved before around this time? Had anything occurred recently that replicated something that had precipitated previous moves or difficulties? The only new variable appeared to be an upcoming sixteenth birthday. During the subsequent appointment with Scott a variety of possible connections were explored:

HELPER: Scott, one thing I know for sure is that when someone has been doing so well and feeling so good about himself, it takes something important to bump him back into stuff that used to get him into a hassle or into trouble. I've been thinking about it, and I'm wondering if maybe you just don't feel comfortable doing so well. Do you think that you may just need a break and a chance to let things slide for a while?

SCOTT: No way! I'm going to be grounded over my birthday and have no party. Do you think I'd decide to slide now and do that to myself?

HELPER: Sounds like you're pretty sure that you want things to be going on differently. I'm wondering what might have gotten you stuck in this old place. I've got some guesses I'd like to check out with you, would that be OK?

SCOTT: Yeah.

HELPER: OK. I heard you mention your birthday, and I was wondering about that, too. Here are some things that I was thinking. First, sometimes kids get upset because there is something they really want for their birthday, and they don't think they will get it. Is this being a problem? [Scott shook his head no.] OK. That's not it. What are you hoping for?

SCOTT: A mountain bike. And I know my parents think I've been trying really hard, and they'll do the best they can about it unless I blew it this weekend.

HELPER: OK. Another thing that happens sometimes in families where one kid has been the one to get into the most trouble for a while is that the kid thinks he doesn't deserve a good birthday or that he won't get as good a birthday as other kids in the family. Any of that going on for you?

SCOTT: I don't think so. My folks are pretty fair. They always get me good stuff and try to make it a good day.

HELPER: OK. One more thing I was wondering. You know how we've talked about the little kid inside you and how he still has feelings and stuff left over from what happened before? Tell me a little a bit about what you remember about birthdays before you came into this family, if you can.

SCOTT: Ohhh, I remember my birthdays, all right! Especially the ones at the home. The staff would get things all ready for my cottage to celebrate. And some time before my birthday my ma would call and tell me she was coming to visit for the day and to bring a present for my party. So after school, I'd get all dressed up, and I'd sit on the front steps, and I'd wait. And I'd watch for the social worker's car, and I'd wait, and I'd watch. And after a while I'd try not to cry. And other kids would say, "Where's your mother? Where's your mother?" but I never knew what to say. After a while, I'd get called for dinner, and I'd have cake. But she never, ever came. I was the only kid there whose mother never, ever came. . . . [There are tears, wiped away angrily.]

HELPER: Ohhh. I see. That must have been really hard. Inside what did you tell yourself?

SCOTT: The obvious. My ma was sorry I was even born.

HELPER: [After a long pause] Is that what it still feels like?

SCOTT: I don't know. Let's just drop it, OK?

HELPER: OK, if that's what you want to do. I have a wish, though. And that is that you let yourself know that you are not that little boy waiting on those steps anymore, feeling he has no family to be glad he was born. You've got a mom out there in the waiting room who wants to give you a good birthday. I wonder what you would need to do or say to yourself so you could help that little kid inside you not have to wait through one more bad, disappointing birthday?

SCOTT: Wait a minute—you think I'm part of the problem?

HELPER: I don't know for sure. What do you think?

The following week, Scott asked to have his mother participate in his session. He told her he had figured out that he had gotten used to having a messed-up birthday and that he wasn't going to do the things that made that happen anymore. If he forgot and started screwing up, he wanted her to remind him to take better care of himself. And he had also been thinking about it, and he thought that, since his birthday came so close to Christmas, he'd probably been messing up Christmas as well, and he had decided that he wanted to stop that, too. Would she help him if he forgot?

There was no feedback from Scott or his parents about behavioral difficulties following this meeting in November. Christmas evening, the helper got a call from Scott's mother. "We just had the first, all-day, wonderful Christmas," she said in tears, "Thank you." Obviously, the real credit here goes to a family willing to hang in with their son and to a young man who was willing to learn to take better care of himself.

Unfortunately, when grief and recycling are connected to physical reactions instead of behavioral reactions they may be much harder to change.

Charles, who had multiple caregivers before being adopted at two, had such strong avoidant attachment that there was concern that he might be unable to form attachment bonds at all. He did eventually attach strongly to his adoptive mother, but, although he was able to be away from her and to go to camp with a sibling, he developed a pattern of becoming ill whenever she went away from him. Even in college, he continued to develop bronchitis or pneumonia whenever his mother needed to travel for business or chose to take a trip for pleasure. He understood the reasons for his anxieties, but he felt that, as he approached adulthood, he should be able to work through this problem. That he was not able to was immensely frustrating for him.

Charles's helper knew that choked-back feelings that force themselves to the surface in the guise of bronchial constrictions and other physical symptoms may recur for years, but that, remarkably, however late there arises an opportunity to rage or sob about a childhood loss, the experience may cause even long-term physical problems quickly to decrease or even disappear. Consequently, arrangements were made for Charles to participate in a group workshop that specialized in reworking core emotional issues in conjunction with ongoing therapy. Charles found the workshop profoundly moving and felt that it delivered on its promise to help him resolve unfinished business. He discovered that, for him, not only did his physical reactions to separation subside, but he also felt more confident about his ability to embrace his life more fully and that he felt more whole than ever before.

Another major area of recycled difficulties has to do with changes in relationships (or comings and goings) at times of separations. For example, preparation for or ending a visit with a noncustodial parent often restimulates the grief process:

Max, who is nearly twelve, waits at the airport with his dad for a flight back to his mom's. He has really enjoyed his summer visit with his dad and his dad's family. His stepmom is fun, and the two little kids like him a lot. It has been a wonderful vacation: camping and backpacking, being old enough to have some really good talks with his dad about growing up yet still feeling comfortable roughhousing or sitting with his dad by the campfire with their arms around one another's shoulders. He has missed his mom and his friends and is looking forward to getting home, but the leaving is so hard. To top it off, his flight has been delayed, and he and his dad are just trying to kill time. There is the usual small talk: "Did you remember to pack your retainer?" "Do you want some gum or a magazine?" Max can feel distance returning between them. He wants just to go and get it over with or to be able to stay. Shoot, now he is starting to sniffle like a little kid. He absolutely is not going to cry this time, please God. They're calling his flight, he and his dad exchange one last long hug until Christmas, and he is following an attendant down the ramp. Max decides he hates airports.

From what we know, even though visiting and parting from noncustodial parents can be difficult, such arrangements allow, perhaps even encourage, children to work toward accepting their new situations in their own way, at their own pace. Upsetting though it can be in the beginning, ongoing visiting ensures a degree of continuity in these children's lives, avoiding total and complete loss, and discourages them from building overly negative or positive fantasies about the absent parent, helping them gradually accept that things are unlikely to change back to how they were and diminishing their feelings of personal responsibility for the loss. Through the repeated experience of reconnecting and then letting go, children can often find a balance between the need to relinquish what has been lost and the wish to hold on to it and instead concentrate on figuring out how to use visits to help make the best of the situation.

For children who are unable to have visits, even for good reasons, recovery work is likely to be significantly prolonged. Children who never become aware of the conflicting needs to hold on and to let go or who are unable to admit these needs to themselves or to others may seem to avoid the pain that follows loss. But the conflict that they bury is unlikely to be worked through. It may impinge on other areas of life, making it difficult to begin anew, or it may fester, breaking forth later when more losses or yearnings are experienced. For children for whom visiting is possible, it plays a useful part in helping them work out their grief, let go of wishes and fantasies, and then move on.

Yearning for the comfort and support of an absent parent also increases in adolescents at the approach of high school or college graduation. It is at those times that the ghosts of other parents can pose special difficulties for adopted individuals. Some have trouble accepting that they will have no chance to let these parents know that things have worked out well and that no grudges are held, understanding has been gained, forgiveness granted. Others actively seek these other parents out. Many young people who had minimal contact with a parent following a divorce or marital separation may request or force a change in their custody arrangements in their teens or twenties. It is becoming so common for children whose parents divorced when they were young to request or force a change of custody when they reach early adolescence that the courts might be wise to build into custody agreements the details of how arrangements might be renegotiated later at the request of an adolescent. Too often, a change in custody arrangements leaves the previous caregiver or the adolescent feeling rejected because of misunderstandings and events that could have been avoided if everyone involved understood this kind of active recycling behavior.

As the years move children of loss closer and closer to adulthood, the last lingering wishes to experience a relationship with missing parents while still a dependent child must be put to rest.

They may express the wish to check out how their lives might have been different, to learn those things about life, about themselves, and about the estranged parent that they would have come to know if the family had remained intact.

Checking for Gaps and Misunderstandings

When good-byes have been sudden and final, it is highly likely that the intensity of the loss and whatever led to it will have left misunderstandings that complicate the recovery process:

Marcus, at age eight, had already lived in several different families. During his first visit, he was asked to draw a picture of his current adoptive family, with whom he had been living for eighteen months. As he drew his picture, he spontaneously volunteered, "This is my best mommy except maybe for Chris," leading the helper, as children often do, to what might need to be the next focus.

The helper asked Marcus what he liked about Chris:

MARCUS: She was the first mommy who loved me.
HELPER: How could you tell?
MARCUS: She let me play my own way, and she cried when I left.
HELPER: Why did you leave there, Marcus?
MARCUS: [Tearfully] I guess she just couldn't take care of me anymore.
HELPER: Do you know why?
MARCUS: No.
HELPER: What did people tell you about it?
MARCUS: No one told me anything, I just got in the car and left.

This exchange established which particular loss was most important to Marcus and what kind of unfinished business might be interfering with his progress. After all, if you finally get a mom who loves you but for unknown reasons can't care for you, is it worth it to trust that life will give you anything different?

Particularly interesting was that Marcus's perception of his good-bye from this particular mom was so different from how his caseworker had described it. She explained that the adoption disruption had occurred following a sudden marital separation, that the adoptive mother had loved this child truly and had held on to him as long as possible. That the morning before Marcus was moved, the mother had telephoned the caseworker within Marcus's hearing to tell her that she had been thinking about suicide and was checking into a hospital. The caseworker had gone to the house immediately to support both child and parent, and all three had talked about what needed to happen and why. This conversation was repeated the next day. When Marcus's helper shared the caseworker's memories with him, his response was, "Oh, that's right. Now I remember."

Some children exaggerate their inadequacies, confessing to one and all how bad and unlovable they are; others go to extremes to hide either themselves or the information about their loss. Often such children have a good deal of the information stored away, but usually there are pieces missing, particularly regarding the hows and whys of the loss, which may not have been explained in a manner understandable to the child or which the child may not have been ready to hear or believe. A giveaway to this difficulty is often a telltale singsong that replaces the child's normal conversational tone and sounds as if the child is reciting a lesson learned by rote: "Well, you see, what happened was my father didn't love my mother anymore, and they fought a lot. He left. Now he lives with Marla and Tommy and Larissa, and they are his family." The kinds of questions about feelings and magical thinking discussed in earlier chapters may uncover whether and where the child needs help.

Adolescents who have been in constantly reorganizing family settings or in foster care are often very hostile when the subject of the past comes up, refusing to rehash their history one more time with one more person. Helpers can often arouse their interest by asking them to tell their own histories. Usually they will relate in a bored fashion things like, "When I left my first family, I went to live with the Thompsons. Then I left there, and I lived with some lady and her son. Then. . . ." "Wait a minute," a helper can interrupt. "Let's go back to the very beginning. First, you were born. When was that? OK, where? You don't know, huh? What time of day were you born? Do you know how much you weighed?" For children with a somewhat chaotic background, there is almost always some part of their history of which they are ignorant and about which they are curious. Given the usual preoccupations with self common to teens, such an interest in the nonpainful parts of their personal history can help them reconnect to their curiosity and forge a tie with the helper who says, "Hey, I bet this stuff is written down somewhere. You want me to see if I can find it out for you?" The helper must make it plain that the adolescent is entitled to whatever information is available and that he or she can count on the helper's assistance getting it if that's what's wanted: "You know, Randy, this stuff is *your* history, and you have every right to know everything we can find out about it. What do you think?" Adolescents are particularly interested in learning what others have said (or written) about them and in having a chance to agree or set the record straight. Often their reluctance becomes real eagerness as they begin to understand background information better.

Recycling and Reworking Good-byes

Ideally, when children separate from their caregivers and move on, they should receive their permission to be happy, loved, successful, and loving. Often, however, they are moved so quickly that there is no time for a shared, thoughtful good-bye. Or they are victims of a sudden, unexpected loss or a separation that proves to be permanent and final. In such cases, children become anxious about their ability to maintain relationships. They may become afraid to let themselves grow close to caregivers again, even in small ways. If they do let their defenses down, their mixed feelings about the dangers of being close and being loved may cause them to get into trouble in order to retreat to a more comfortable distance.

Amalia, who acquired a stepmother at seven, insisted on holding herself aloof. She seemed to go out of her way to reject any invitation to play or interact with her new mother. After a while, she would occasionally relax a bit and share a confidence or allow herself to be cuddled and read to. Inevitably, however, she was likely to express her mixed feelings about growing close: Her hug would turn into a stranglehold; her kiss would end in a nip.

This kind of behavior can be very confusing to caregivers until they begin to recognize the pattern. Once they understand the reasons behind the behavior, they can let such children know that they are lovable, worthwhile, capable, and responsible at this particular moment and then back off physically and emotionally to give the children space so that they do not need to act up or become obnoxious in order to get distance. As children come to believe that intimacy need not lead to separation or vulnerability, the moments of closeness are likely to increase, and a cycle of positive interaction can begin.

A history of sudden and/or final losses can also trigger strong grief recycling when adolescents are leaving home. As they get ready to go away to college or to move into their own homes, they are likely to become extremely touchy and difficult to live with. During the period leading up to the move, it is not at all unusual for them to anger easily and to strike out verbally at caregivers and siblings. I often refer to this stage as the "puff adder ending," as caregivers relate their bewilderment over their youngster's unpredictable hostility, observing that it is much like living with a venomous reptile that slithers around the kitchen and sinks its fangs into parental ankles for no apparent reason.

Often this behavior stems from past separations or losses that were sudden, ugly, and/or angry and felt rejecting and out of control; the adolescent feels compelled to reenact the situations and recapture those feelings. Often if a caregiver says, "I know that when you have left families in the past mostly there has been a whole lot of anger going on. If that is what you need to do again, we can do it that way. Frankly, though, I'd much rather enjoy our time together instead of fighting and hurting each other's feelings. The choice is up to you, however, and I'll follow your lead," the youngster is able to leave in a different way, and the attacks and provocative behavior diminish or cease altogether.

When previous losses have not only been heated and hurtful but final as well, adolescents may orchestrate the move to match the old pattern and outcome. Some act as if they are being unfairly evicted, even when it has been their choice to move. Others arrive in their new setting with a great deal of supportive parental involvement only to report months or years later that they were appalled at how their caregivers just dumped them off and abandoned them. Some cut their caregivers off and maintain only minimal contact for a time, while others accuse their caregivers of not showing enough interest in them.

Children who did not have the chance to share healthy good-byes find accepting their loss and their feelings about it much more difficult. They need a chance to say their good-byes in whatever way is possible. Perhaps they can say good-bye during a funeral or memorial service or a visit to the grave. Older children may want to read newspaper accounts of the death or the obituary or review the funeral register again and again, to make more real what happened and to reassure themselves that the person who died was important to many people and that others were affected by the death. In the case of a divorce or separation, perhaps the child can visit with the noncustodial caregiver and talk the situation over, saying good-bye to what has been but gaining reassurance that caring will continue even if there is to be no visiting. Perhaps the absent caregiver can be encouraged to write a letter or make a tape for the child, explaining that he or she will no longer provide daily nurturing, wishing the child well, and saying good-bye. When children have had multiple caregivers, perhaps each of them can be asked to write or tape messages of good-bye and good wishes or to visit so that good-byes can be shared in person. Any of these experiences can help children complete their understanding of the changes in their lives so that they can move on to new relationships with their self-esteem intact while continuing to care deeply about the lost family member.

When a caregiver has disappeared or is unwilling to communicate with a child about the events leading up to the separation, the child must say good-bye symbolically. One way to unload wishes and feelings is to write letters to be sent to the caregiver or to share with others. If the caregiver is dead, the letter can be read aloud at the grave site or to other important people in a child's life. A child could also call the absent caregiver on a play phone to express feelings and say good-bye. The child could be asked to visualize the absent caregiver and to have a conversation with him or her. Play figures might be used to act out a meeting, a good-bye conversation, and a parting. The helper can initiate one of these activities by saying something like, "When you stopped living with your dad, you never really had a chance to say good-bye to him. You've been thinking about him a lot, and it seems to me as if you are ready to say good-bye to him as the parent you live with. That doesn't mean you'll ever stop loving him; it just means you'll say good-bye to living with him while you are growing up. If you could call him up [or write him a letter or talk to him] today, what kinds of things would you like to say to him?" After the child has responded, the helper can ask what the child would have liked the father to say in return and whether the child is afraid something bad might happen if good-byes were exchanged.

The helper must be certain, of course, that the process of grieving has been completed except for this final step. It would appear that most adults take two to three years to integrate a major loss into their lives, whereas children who have lost a parent appear to need at least seven. "Regardless of how effectively grieving is done, it cannot be collapsed in time," Simos tells us. "Events such as birthdays, anniversaries, and other important dates are associated with that which has been lost and these calendar events must be experienced at least once after the loss before the bereaved can feel the pain of living through the event without that which he has lost. It takes, therefore, at least a year before each of these calendar-related events can be lived through" (1979, 411). Surely, then, symbolic good-byes should be delayed until this year is over to be certain that the child is ready for them. (Actual good-byes to the departing caregiver should be said before and at the time of loss, if possible, and any time thereafter, without waiting for the year to pass.)

Drawings of how the child remembers a good-bye scene from a particular family and/or discussions about those scenes and what led up to them can reveal much about what has been denied, misunderstood, or repressed and how it might now be showing up in behavior. To check out what they remember or fantasize about past families and how they feel about them, children who have lived in more than one family can be asked to draw a picture of each family or to write their names on index cards and then rank the families by arranging the pictures or cards according to which the child feels was the best and which the worst (this is possible even if partings took place in infancy). School-age youngsters often will readily assign "grades" to different families or caregivers, showing the helper where they had strongly positive or negative experiences that might need to be explored. Adolescents particularly seem to relish being asked to judge those whom they feel have judged them, although here helpers must be particularly careful not to join adolescents in a one-sided diagnosis of where the difficulties originated. Additional information can be obtained by asking children to rate their families on a scale from one to ten on how comfortable they felt (or think they would have felt) or on how difficult it was to leave. All of this information can then be used to identify what kinds of good-byes still need to be said if children are to experience some sense of closure.

Lifting Curses

Some children and adolescents (and some adults) grieve for years because of a curse, either self-pronounced or unintentionally inflicted by a caregiver or by repeated moves or situations that have led to attachment difficulties. These persons may act out their curse over and over. Most self-pronounced curses result from the magical thinking described in chapter 1. Other curses are said in anger by one or more caregivers: "You'll be the death of me yet." "You'll drive me crazy." "You'll never make it." "Who could love a kid like you?" Obviously, the best way to lift these curses is to get the person or persons who made them to take them back: Self-cursed children are helped to understand the adult reasons behind the loss or separation; former caregivers can modify or take back accusations. Sometimes, however, curses must be lifted in other ways, perhaps by helping children or adolescents rework their thinking (as was done with Scott about his birthday), by helping them work on their fears regarding the possibility of future losses or rejections if they let down their guard and trust again, or by helping them undo a curse through symbolic play. The helper may need to say clearly and repeatedly, "I'll be glad when you can stop thinking that there is something wrong about you."

217

Raoul, who left a foster home suddenly after four years, struggled for some time to overcome his sadness and anger at his foster mother. He was able to release enough of his feelings that he began to progress again in school and enjoy his new foster parents. But his previous foster mother's anger haunted him. He continued to see himself as a burden. During a play session, he was asked if he would like to pretend to call her up and apologize for the crisis that had precipitated his move.

RAOUL: [Using play telephone] Hello, Ma?
HELPER: Yeah, this is me.
RAOUL: I wanted to say I'm sorry about what happened. I wanted to say I have another family, and I am doing OK.
HELPER: That's good. I wondered about you and how you were doing. I know you're gonna do just fine 'cause you're a good kid a lot of the time, just not when you get so mad. I hope you'll do good there 'cause I think you can. I hope you'll like it, too.
RAOUL: Yeah, well, it's OK here.
HELPER: That's real good.
RAOUL: That's all I got to say.
HELPER: OK, good-bye.
RAOUL: Good-bye.

With Ronnie, another technique was used. During one play session, Ronnie set up blocks as a house and put a mother doll and three girl dolls inside. This reflected Ronnie's personal history: Born prematurely, he later came into protective service for abuse and neglect, at which time his mother seemed relieved to sign his relinquishment papers, although she kept his three sisters, whom she parented adequately. Four years after his placement into a very supportive, sensitive family, Ronnie still struggled with his feelings that his mother thought he was worthless and threw him away but kept his sisters. During the play session, Ronnie walked a small boy doll to the door of the house he had built. He made the boy doll knock on the door, and the mother doll answer. "Hello," said the boy. "I'm your tiny baby boy, Ronnie." "Ronnie who?" asked the mother doll, slamming the door in his face. The helper said, "It might go like that. Let me show you another way it might be." She walked the boy doll up to the door and repeated Ronnie's greeting: "Hello, I'm your tiny baby boy, Ronnie." "Oh, Ronnie," said the mother doll, "Look how you've grown! I must have made a good plan to help you find a family with a mom that knows how to take care of boys. It was really hard for me. I'm glad you got what you needed. Good-bye." Ronnie's face grew thoughtful. Within the next two weeks, his posture improved, his behavior became less provocative, and his displays of tension became less frequent.

Coming to Grips with Impotency: Wishes and Fantasies

Many children remain bound to an absent caregiver by their wishes for what might have been. These powerful wishes, which follow many people well into their adult years, are found not only in people who lost caregivers as children but also in those who yearned to get something from their caregivers that they were unable or unwilling to give. Having made an identification with a particular story, children may reactivate it off and on throughout their lives, especially when they feel lonely or life seems hard and unfair. They may hold on to the promise of a happy ending, keeping their hopes primed unduly, acting out the fantasy first in play and later in real life, endlessly seeking a "happily ever after" resolution that can never be.

It is not always easy to figure out what fantasies children have or have had as to how their lives might have been different or how they might have been different if a loss had not happened or had occurred differently. Themes that recur in play, a favorite story, an admired TV character—any of these may provide clues about children's wished-for attributes or outcomes. The following exercise is useful for clarifying unfulfilled wishes while at the same time encouraging acceptance of the impossibility of making such wishes come true and suggesting that there are other ways to satisfy longings:

"Katie, for your homework assignment this week, I want you to write me a story. I'm giving you an outline, and I want you to fill in the rest of the story and bring it when you come next time. OK?"

The outline read: "Once upon a time, there was a little girl who really wished her mom/dad/both would [fill in]. That would have been good for her because [fill in]. Instead she got a mom/dad/both who [fill in]. That was bad for her because [fill in]. She/he tried everything she/he knew. [If an older child, adolescent, or adult were doing the exercise, he or she would list what was tried]. But nothing worked. Now she is deciding to get what she wants by [fill in]."

Twelve-year-old Katie's response went like this: "Once upon a time there was a little girl who really wished her mom and dad could get along and that they both liked children. She wished her dad would listen to what she thought and that her mom would teach her how to try new things without being afraid. That would have been good for her because she would have known how to be sure of herself like other people. Instead she got a dad who was much too busy and important to listen to anybody and a mom who was shy and afraid of new things and never wanted to do anything but try to make her dad happy and had no time to teach Katie anything. That was bad for Katie because she thought that her ideas were no good and that she would never be able to know how to make friends and be good at things like other children. Finally, her mom and dad got a divorce and things got really bad so Katie tried to hurt herself and ended up in the hospital. She talked with her mom and with her dad about how she thought things were, and they each promised that things would be better, but nothing seemed to change much. Now Katie is deciding that her mom and dad are just how they are but that she can find other people to listen to her ideas. Katie is deciding that she can find other grown-ups to help her learn what her parents don't know how to teach her. She is getting much better at making friends and sharing her ideas, and she learned to do that by trying new things and finding out that people could be nice to her while she was still learning. Katie is deciding that she can be who she is and that she has her own power to give herself a happy life."

It is also useful to determine whether children believe there is something else they could do or could have done to prevent the loss or separation: "Do you sometimes think maybe if you could do it over, you could fix it?" "Is there anything that you think you could have done to make it work out differently?" Children have to come to grips with the fact that there are areas in their lives where they have no choices and no influence: Decisions about which adults will care for them are out of their control; so is the possibility of reunion with a caregiver following death or, often, separation. They may need help maintaining their self-esteem and sense of self-determination when facing up to their helplessness in certain areas. Part of the necessary support comes from caregivers who appreciate their children's developing capabilities to think, feel, solve problems, do good work, and make good choices. Helpers, too, can gently encourage children to let go of fantasies about how they might make things work out differently, respecting their desires for a different ending but pointing out the limitations on effecting it.

Ricky had come into the foster-care system at age four as a result of severe neglect by alcoholic parents. Seen at nine, Ricky was still wrestling with his wishes to return to his parents. "I'm older now," he argued. "I can take care of myself." "That's partly true," his helper said. "But what would you do if no one was working to earn money for your food and electricity?" "I'd just get a job." At this point, Ricky could have been told forcefully that he needed to be in school, that it was his job to work at growing up and not to worry about taking care of his parents, that nine-year-olds can't get jobs, that the law says kids his age have to be in school. But this approach would only have driven his fantasies underground. The helper chose instead to follow Ricky's line of thought:

HELPER: You know, that's an interesting idea. Maybe if you had gotten a job in the first place, you would still be at home—what do you think?

RICKY: Yeah.

HELPER: Let's see. Imagine it with me: There you are a fine little boy about this tall. You wake up in the morning, and you're hungry, but you can't find anything to eat. Your parents are both sound asleep. You are tired of being hungry, and you decide that what you will do is get a job. You look for your clothes; what do you think you might wear?

RICKY: I know, my red corduroy overalls!

HELPER: Sounds good to me. Gee, Ricky, do you think you knew how to button when you were four? [This question gently begins to establish some reality.] OK, now your shoes. What about it, could you tie your shoes when you were four? Well, never mind, they'll probably give you a job even if you just tuck the shoelaces into your shoes. OK, now let's go down the stairs and out the door. You live on a pretty busy street; we'd better cross at the light up there at the corner. While we're waiting for the light to turn green (do you think you know about not crossing when the light's red?), let's see what kind of a job you're looking for.

Ricky, who was either a smart nine-year-old or had been giving this some thought, volunteered that he thought he could get work in a filling station or else bagging groceries.

HELPER: OK, there's the green light, and there's a filling station just across the street. Why don't you ask the man for a job?

RICKY: Hey, Mister, I need a job.

HELPER: "Well, that's swell, because I need someone to work for me." [Ricky's eyes grew bigger.] Looking good, Ricky. But, wait. Here comes another grown-up, and he's asking for a job too. [Ricky's face fell.] "I'm sorry, son, but I think maybe you are too short to wash the windshields."

RICKY: I'd just get on the hood of the car and show him.

HELPER: You know, I bet you could do a good job of that, too. The trouble is that even if he wanted to hire you, he couldn't. There is a law that says that kids your age have to be in school and they can't get jobs like that.

RICKY: Well, I hate that dumb law.

HELPER: I can see that. But what can you do about it? Maybe when you are a grown-up you will want to try to get them to change it. But right now I think you are stuck.

By entering into Ricky's fantasy and gently and supportively leading to the question "But what can you do about it?" the helper was able to show Ricky that his wish was unrealistic while at the

222

same time helping him retain his self-esteem, despite the recognition of his helplessness in the here and now. Adding that he might one day have the power to fix what prevented his hoped-for ending also helped him to accept the current situation without relinquishing all hope.

ENDING THE WORK

As children rework their leftover misunderstandings and remaining confusions, often the child who has been labeled hyperactive will reduce or discontinue hyperactive behavior as the need to run away from bad feelings or self-blame disappears. There is often a marked decrease in separation anxiety, and it is not unusual for bed-wetting to diminish or cease. Because of their increased ability to concentrate, children often demonstrate significant gains in their academic ability and performance. Their understanding of themselves grows, and their relationships with others improve markedly as they stop discounting their own abilities. They are no longer afraid that their behavior or personalities will cause others to abandon them, and so they are more able to make emotional commitments.

Ending Grief Work as a Caregiver

If you are a caregiver who has been helping a child through the grieving period, there will probably be no clear ending to signify the child's passage from active grief into integrated grief. You may notice particular milestones in the recovery process or there may be no outstanding changes, simply a steady progress to the point where you recognize that your child is again functioning well. The task that seemed so overwhelming and confusing in the beginning has unfolded in logical and understandable ways. Even if some grieving remains to be done, you feel more confident in helping the child through it, using the skills and information you have learned. You may also feel that you and your child are more in tune with one another, more tolerant of each other's differences, and more secure in your ability to reach out to each other and meet with understanding. By sharing a loss and working through it together, your ties have been strengthened, your wounds healed. You, too, can now move on to other concerns and interests with a sense of a job well done and pride in having helped your child through a difficult time.

Terminating Treatment

Like any other loss, separation from the helper should be expected and gradual. The child should feel strong and confident about his or her ability to cope without regular support from a helper. Termination should not leave the child (or the child's caregiver) feeling helpless or worried that he or she has done something wrong. Because of their histories of repeated loss, the termination of a therapeutic alliance with an adopted child needs to be handled especially carefully, in a manner that does not replicate old negative losses and that takes into thoughtful consideration the major issues to which adopted children have particular sensitivity.

When you feel that the child is ready, you can propose less frequent meetings as a kind of reward: "You have been working really hard for quite a time. You have earned a vacation, some time off to do what you want to do, just to have fun. I think what we should do for a while is see each other one week and then give you a vacation the next. How does that sound to you?" With a younger child whose sense of time is incompletely developed, you might say something like, "I think you should have more time between our meetings for being with your mom and playing, instead of having to make this long trip so often." This message should convey your confidence that the child will find other useful and interesting things to do and that nothing bad will happen if the child misses a meeting. You should allow the child to resist or object. If the child objects strongly, you may want to ask how many more times he or she feels you need to meet weekly before the frequency of your meetings is reduced. Usually, if the child has resolved most of his or her conflicting feelings over the loss, the idea of meeting less often will be readily—sometimes eagerly—accepted.

During the final sessions, it is a good idea to review for the child, and often for the child's caregiver, just what you have accomplished together. By reviewing what the child originally shared and what each party—caregiver, child, helper—has come to understand, the helper has a chance to double-check that the work is truly as completed as it can be at this time. This process also allows the child to take credit for the tasks completed and the growing that has taken place. It is a pleasant way of making sense of what has been done and a further reinforcement of the child's sense of mastery and self-esteem. You should commend the good choice of seeking help and working hard to remove any lingering feelings of inadequacy because help was needed in the first place. With an adolescent or a child capable of hypothetical reasoning, you might also explore the question "What do you want to leave behind you here and what do you want to take with you as you leave?"

After a month or six weeks, old disputes or misbehavior may recur, signaling that the child's problems may not be as close to resolution as you have judged them to be. More likely, however, child and caregivers will recognize that things are running smoothly despite fewer meetings and feel proud of how well they are managing; this feeling should be encouraged. At this point, you may want to space meetings a month apart after completing whatever schedule was agreed to initially.

Often, the first meeting after a month's interval is the good-bye meeting. Or you may want to give the child more say in scheduling the termination date: "We've been meeting every other week for a while now, and I think you're doing swell on your own. It looks like it's almost time to say good-bye to your coming here for a while. How many turns do you think you'll need to get ready to say good-bye?" Frequently, children answer realistically that they will need one, two, or three more turns. Sometimes they ask for forty more turns or some other large number; the helper must then explore their needs further. Often children try to avoid the difficulty of saying an official good-bye by replying, "I don't need any more turns. I'll just stop today." This is not a good plan because it does not allow the child to prepare for the impending separation by dealing with the feelings it arouses and turning to alternative means of support. Children often return for help twelve to twenty months after the original work has been completed, when one of life's stresses triggers a new problem. Such problems are often resolved in only two or three sessions; the child and the helper know each other so well that they are able to get things sorted out quickly.

Helper and child frequently come together for their final meeting with feelings of pride and joy combined with sadness at the parting. Often it is helpful to the child if the adult expresses these mixed feelings: "When I thought about seeing you for the last time, I wanted to shout how fantastic it was that you've done such great work that you won't need to be coming anymore, but at the same time I was feeling how much I'm going to miss you, too." Often both helper and child will want to reserve the possibility of future meetings or an ongoing relationship, even if only in memory: "You know that if you ever get mixed up about something that you and your dad can't figure out, I'll hope that we can work on it—all three of us?" "You have my phone number [or address], and if you ever want to check in, I'll be glad to hear from you." "I'll never forget you."

You may want to give the child a parting gift or a written message of good wishes as something tangible to take away from the final session. The child may also wish to leave a note or present behind to ensure that he or she will be remembered. Some helpers treat the final session as a party and serve refreshments. As the meeting closes, you may want to ask the child, "How do you want to say good-bye for now?" Whether or not they have had much physical contact with the helper, children may want a good, strong hug, even though they may have difficulty asking for it. This often feels like a good way of parting to the adult, too. Finally, the helper should tell the child, "Thank you for being my friend. I've learned a lot from you. Take care of yourself." And the shared work comes to an end.

BIBLIOGRAPHY

Bandler, Richard, John Grinder, and Virginia Satir. 1976. *Changing with families*. Palo Alto, Calif.: Science and Behavior.

Bettelheim, Bruno. 1950. *Love is not enough*. New York: Macmillan.

Bowlby, John. 1969. *Attachment*. Vol. 1 of *Attachment and loss*. New York: Basic.

———. 1973. *Separation: Anxiety and anger*. Vol. 2 of *Attachment and loss*. New York: Basic.

———. 1980. *Loss: Sadness and depression*. Vol. 3 of *Attachment and loss*. New York: Basic.

Brenner, Avis. 1984. *Helping children cope with stress*. Lexington, Mass.: Lexington Books.

Clarke, Jean Illsley. 1978. *Self-esteem: A family affair*. Minneapolis: Winston Press.

Colgrove, Melba, Harold Bloomfield, and Peter McWilliams. 1977. *How to survive the loss of a love*. New York: Bantam.

Despart, Louise. 1946. Desperate Fables. *American Journal of Orthopsychiatry* (January 16): 100–113.

Dreikurs, Rudolf. 1974. *Family council*. Chicago: Henry Regnery.

Fahlberg, Vera I. 1991. *A child's journey through placement*. Indianapolis: Perspectives Press.

Garmezy, N. 1983. Stressors of childhood. In *Stress, coping, and development in children*, ed. N. Garmezy and M. Rutter. New York: McGraw-Hill.

Grollman, Earl A. 1967. *Explaining death to children*. Boston: Beacon Press.

———. 1975. *Talking about divorce*. Boston: Beacon Press.

Ilg, Frances L., and Louise Bates Ames. 1955. *Child behavior*. New York: Harper and Brothers.

Jewett, Claudia L. 1978. *Adopting the older child*. Harvard, Mass.: Harvard Common Press.

LaTour, Kathy. 1987. *For those who live*. Rev. ed. Omaha, Nebr.: Centering Corporation.

Levin, Pam. 1974. *Becoming the way we are*. Deerfield Branch, Fla.: Health Communications.

Linn, Erin. 1990. *One hundred fifty facts about grieving children*. Incline Village, Nev.: The Publisher's Mark.

Lonetto, R. 1980. *Children's conceptions of death*. New York: Springer.

Looff, David H. 1976. *Getting to know the troubled child*. Knoxville: University of Tennessee Press.

McNamara, Joan. 1992. *Resources for families adopting sexually abused children*. Greensboro: Family Resources (1521 Foxhollow Road, Greensboro, NC 27410).

Moody, Richard A., and Carol P. Moody. 1991. A family perspective: Helping children acknowledge and express grief following the death of a parent. *Death Studies* 15:587–602.

Oaklander, Violet. 1978. *Windows to our children*. Moab, Utah: Real People.

Pothier, Patricia. 1976. *Mental health couseling with children*. Boston: Little, Brown.

Rawlings, Steven W. 1993. *Marital Status and Living Arrangements March 1992*. U.S. Bureau of Census, Current Population Reports P20-467. Washington, D.C.: U. S. Government Printing Office.

Samalin, Nancy. 1987. *Loving your child is not enough*. New York: Viking.

———. 1991. *Love and anger: The parental dilemma*. New York: Viking Penguin.

Simos, Bertha G. 1979. *A time to grieve*. New York: Family Service Association of America.

Stuart, Irving R., and Lawrence Edwin Abt. 1981. *Children of separation and divorce: Management and treatment*. New York: Van Nostrand and Reinhold.

Trieschman, Albert, James Whittaker, and Larry Brendtro. 1969. *The other twenty-three hours*. Chicago: Aldine.

Viorst, Judith. 1986. *Necessary losses*. New York: Simon and Schuster.

INDEX